G000272739

# IT WILL YET
# BE HEARD

# IT WILL YET BE HEARD

*A Polish Rabbi's Witness of
the Shoah and Survival*

LEON THORNE

EDITED BY DANIEL H. MAGILOW AND
EMANUEL THORNE

FOREWORD BY ISAAC BASHEVIS SINGER

RUTGERS UNIVERSITY PRESS
NEW BRUNSWICK, CAMDEN, AND NEWARK,
NEW JERSEY, AND LONDON

Library of Congress Cataloging-in-Publication Data
Names: Thorne, Leon, 1907–1978, author. | Magilow, Daniel H., 1973–, editor.
Title: It will yet be heard : a Polish rabbi's witness of the Shoah and survival / Leon
    Thorne ; edited by Daniel H. Magilow.
Other titles: Out of the ashes
Description: New Brunswick, New Jersey ; London : Rutgers University Press, 2018. |
    Includes bibliographical references and index.
Identifiers: LCCN 2018003441 (print) | LCCN 2018022576 (ebook) | ISBN 9781978801660
    (epub) | ISBN 9781978801684 (web pdf) | ISBN 9781978801653 (hardback)
Subjects: LCSH: Thorne, Leon, 1907–1978. | World War, 1939–1945—Personal narra-
    tives, Jewish. | BISAC: HISTORY / Holocaust. | BIOGRAPHY & AUTOBIOGRAPHY /
    Religious. | RELIGION / Judaism / History. | POLITICAL SCIENCE / Political Free-
    dom & Security / Human Rights. | SOCIAL SCIENCE / Jewish Studies.
Classification: LCC D811.5 (ebook) | LCC D811.5 .T48 2018 (print) | DDC
    940.53/18092 [B]—dc23
LC record available at https://lccn.loc.gov/2018003441

A British Cataloging-in-Publication record for this book is available from the British
    Library.

Copyright © 2019 by Rutgers, the State University of New Jersey
All rights reserved
No part of this book may be reproduced or utilized in any form or by any means,
electronic or mechanical, or by any information storage and retrieval system, without
written permission from the publisher. Please contact Rutgers University Press, 106
Somerset Street, New Brunswick, NJ 08901. The only exception to this prohibition is
"fair use" as defined by U.S. copyright law.

∞ The paper used in this publication meets the requirements of the American
National Standard for Information Sciences—Permanence of Paper for Printed Library
Materials, ANSI Z39.48-1992.

www.rutgersuniversitypress.org

Manufactured in the United States of America

*This book is dedicated, in deep humility, to those heroic martyrs who perished in the European ghettos and concentration camps because they were Jews and because they lived Jewish lives. They died as the world looked passively on. May this book serve to remind mankind of what happened to them—and may they know, in heaven, that they are remembered, their stories told, their experiences recalled, and their heroism extolled.*

עוֹד יִשָּׁמַע בְּעָרֵי יְהוּדָה וּבְחוּצוֹת יְרוּשָׁלַיִם
קוֹל שָׂשׂוֹן וְקוֹל שִׂמְחָה קוֹל חָתָן וְקוֹל כַּלָּה

*It will yet be heard in the cities of Judah, and in the streets of Jerusalem.*
*The voice of joy and the voice of gladness, the voice of the bridegroom and*
*the voice of the bride.*

—Jeremiah 33:10–11

# CONTENTS

# IT WILL YET
# BE HEARD

# INTRODUCTION

In the 1961 preface to the first edition of his memoir, Rabbi Leon Thorne (1907–1978) justified publishing this remarkable autobiographical account of his life during the Holocaust and its immediate aftermath with a curiously defensive tone. Thorne noted that by the early 1960s, there were already "thousands of magazine articles and hundreds of books and plays and poems and true-life accounts" of Jews' wartime experiences. Nevertheless, he added, "No life is like another and no man has lived another man's life. I feel that what happened to me was different in spirit if not in detail from what others lived through."

Both before and after the Holocaust, Thorne's life was one steeped in Jewish learning and tradition. Born in 1907 in the oil boomtown of Schodnica in Eastern Galicia, then part of the Hapsburg Empire, he studied philosophy and theology at universities in Lemberg (Lwów), Vienna, Würzburg, and Breslau. He was ordained when only nineteen, and between 1945 and 1948, he served as a rabbi to surviving Jewish communities in Rzeszów, Poland, and Frankfurt am Main, Germany, before immigrating to the United States in 1948. Thorne's wartime memoir indeed stands apart—even among the scores of accounts that have appeared since 1961. His Holocaust experiences were not those of a secular Jew who suffered in the larger and better-documented ghettos and camps like Warsaw, Łódź, Auschwitz, and Dachau. Leon Thorne was a religious man who instead confronted death in places with relatively unfamiliar names like

Schodnica, Sambor, Drohobycz, Lemberg, and Janowska. Memoirs of this sort are comparatively rare among firsthand accounts of the Holocaust.

The New York–based Yiddish newspaper *Der Tog* first serialized Thorne's story. It was originally written in German and later translated—sometimes awkwardly—into a heavily edited English version that appeared under the title *Out of the Ashes* in 1961. Further editions appeared in 1976, yet the memoir never found a wide readership—not only because the Holocaust had yet to become the household word it is today but also because the book appeared quietly through Rosebern Press, a small publisher in New York. Thorne himself felt that the translation did not entirely represent his experiences accurately, so in the mid-1970s, he began to revise and expand a text that he had first written in German while hiding in a bunker, per-haps fearing that no readers of Yiddish would survive the war. To this first part, which conveys the desperation and immediacy of a memoir com-posed in the middle of a genocide, Thorne later added a second part with additional stories of the Holocaust and its immediate aftermath. This sub-sequent historical treatment, written decades after the fact, is a memoir as well but also a witness account and a work of history by a trained scholar.

Unfortunately, Leon Thorne died in 1978 before he could publish the expanded text, thereby depriving posterity of a rich and deeply moving account of the Holocaust and its aftermath. His view of his experiences as "unoriginal" might technically be true but only because the single-minded determination of Germans and their auxiliaries to murder every Jew has standardized the sorts of horrors that readers encounter in Holo-caust memoirs. Many of the episodes Thorne recounts resonate closely with classic texts by Anne Frank, Elie Wiesel, Primo Levi, Art Spiegelman, and others that have found broad audiences. But Thorne's work provides insights into the Holocaust that few other books can. We see the events through the perspective of a religious man who not only served as a Jewish chaplain in the Polish Army but also witnessed antisemitic violence during and after the Holocaust and who helped smuggle Jews out of the ruins of postwar Europe. Beyond these unique experiences, his work adds nuance to commonplace understandings of moral behavior in the Holocaust not only of perpetrators but also of victims.

Part I begins and ends in a claustrophobic hidden bunker underneath a Polish peasant's stable. It depicts familiar scenes and characters of the survivor memoir genre, as it documents Thorne's time in the ghettos of Sambor and Drohobycz and in the Janowska (or "Janover") forced labor camp in Lemberg (Lwów). In part I, we read troubling reports of sadistic and capricious camp guards, heart-wrenching accounts of the murders of entire families, and passages that emphasize that those who did not experience the Holocaust personally can never truly grasp it. Part II begins in the immediate hours after liberation when Thorne and his companions emerge like the living dead from their underground hideout. Their initial joy of liberation soon collides with the reality of the mass destruction that surrounds them. In words that capture the conflicting emotions of survival, Thorne writes, "We envied our dead loved ones who no longer had to cope with a world left cold and barren by war. I recalled the words uttered by the prophet Ezekiel when he found himself in the midst of the valley of dry bones: 'And He said to me: "Son of Man, can these bones live?" And I answered: "O Lord, Thou knowest."'"

Part II then details Thorne's experiences as a Jewish chaplain in the Polish Army and as a member of the *she'erit ha-pletah* ("the surviving remnant" in Hebrew), the Jewish displaced persons whose struggles and victimization persisted in the ruins of Poland and occupied Germany. He shows vividly how the war's end in no way ended Jewish persecution. In the two parts of *It Will Yet Be Heard*, the Holocaust is not so much a break with history as it is the logical consequence of prewar antisemitism fueled by centuries of religious hatred that continued after 1945. One particularly illustrative episode is his firsthand description of the infamous Rzeszów pogrom on June 12, 1945, scarcely five weeks after hostilities ended in Europe. Although the riot claimed no lives, it was a clear and early sign that Jews were still not welcome in Poland and that Polish authorities would do little to protect them. The violence began when a Polish mob claimed that the tiny postwar Jewish community in Rzeszów, where Thorne had become the rabbi, had ritually murdered a Christian child. In actuality, the blood cited as evidence was chicken blood left by the *shochet* (kosher butcher) who lived and worked in Thorne's kitchen. Sadly, this occurrence was not unique in the postwar period, as similar anti-Jewish riots in Kraków, and most infamously, in Kielce on July 4, 1946, claimed dozens of casualties. The topic of postwar antisemitic violence and the difficult questions it raises about Poles' behavior and responsibilities remain a divisive topic in Poland and a major focus of Holocaust research. Experiences with such violence and the disturbing casualness with which Poles still circulated antisemitic slanders made it clear to many other Jews that their future lay elsewhere. Some of these survivors, including Thorne, worked for the clandestine underground network known as Bricha (Hebrew for "escape") to smuggle Jews from Soviet-occupied Eastern and Central Europe to the American Occupation Zone or Palestine.

Beyond its importance as a lucidly written primary source about the wartime ghettos in Eastern Galicia, the Janowska camp, and the continuation of violence in Poland after the war, Thorne's accessible text is valuable for other reasons. *It Will Yet Be Heard* exposes common misconceptions about the Holocaust that scholars have thoroughly debunked but that might still be unclear to popular audiences. One of its most important interventions is to challenge the idea of the Holocaust as a morality tale of good versus evil. Thorne certainly gives due credit to those who risked their lives to save others, including his cousin Naftali Backenroth, who saved Jews by making them indispensable to the German war effort, and the Jesuit priest Father Bronislovas Paukštys, who hid Lithuanian Jews in his church, including Thorne's future wife.

But elsewhere, Thorne pulls no punches in his criticisms. Even as he condemns many Poles and Ukrainians for their antisemitism before, during, and after the war, he, like many Holocaust memoirists, reserves some of his harshest censure for members of the Jewish Councils (*Judenräte*) and the Jewish Police for their self-serving behavior and readiness to betray other Jews. "By the middle of 1942," he writes, "the Jewish Council in Drohobycz and other communities had lost what little leverage it possessed with the Germans and lent itself as an instrument of Jewish liquidation.[ . . . ]With rare exceptions[ . . . ]the people who sat on the Jewish Councils were corrupt men who represented themselves only and served their own interests, doing the bidding of the Germans and hoping that they and their families would survive." But leadership positions were not prerequisites for such treachery. "In every town," Thorne notes, referring to Jews and Gentiles alike, "there were extortionists who took the last money from Jews, assuring them that they would help them escape and delivering them instead to the Gestapo. They earned money from two sources and became rich in the process."

By emphasizing in 1961 that even though all Jews were potential targets, many were far from paragons of virtue, Thorne was already breaking the same taboo that the philosopher Hannah Arendt would two years later in her famous 1963 book *Eichmann in Jerusalem*. As a reporter for the *New Yorker* covering the trial of Adolf Eichmann, a key planner of the Holocaust whom Israeli Security Service agents had captured as a fugitive in Argentina, Arendt wrote about how the trial became an opportunity for Jews to tell the world the story of the Holocaust, even aspects not directly relevant to Eichmann's case. Arendt was widely accused of blaming victims for their own victimization in her reporting because she dared to suggest that the Jewish Councils helped grease the gears of genocide when they collaborated and acted as willing mediators between Germans and local Jewish populations and as executors of German deportation plans.

*It Will Yet Be Heard* likewise criticizes non-Jewish figures who are typically only idealized for their actions. Thorne's explanation of how he and four other Jews hid in a Polish peasant's tiny underground bunker blurs the popular image of Holocaust rescuers as saintlike "righteous Gentiles" who, motivated by idealism or religious convictions, selflessly risked their lives to save Jews. The memoir makes abundantly clear in its opening pages that, like many Gentiles who assisted Jews during the war, Thorne's rescuers, Stanisław Nendza and Franz Janiewski, could not claim the moral high ground, at least not entirely. "We are grateful to them, naturally," Thorne writes, "but it should be pointed out that they are not placing themselves in danger for idealistic reasons alone. They are hiding us from the Gestapo for material reasons as well." These material reasons included not only substantial upfront payments but also Thorne's written promise to surrender half of his fortune from the oil wells in Schodnica (today Skhidnytsia in Ukraine). This represented no small sum, as the area around Schodnica and Drohobycz was rich in oil and the site of a massive petroleum boom that began in the mid-nineteenth century.

As it adds nuance to our understandings of moral behavior during the Holocaust, It Will Yet Be Heard is also important as a source for a key episode in literary history. The literary critic Leon Wieseltier, whose mother Esther (Stella) Backenroth was Thorne's cousin and cellar-mate, has written that the description in part I of the shooting of Bruno Schulz might be one of the first written accounts of the tragic murder of this enormously gifted writer and artist.* Schulz, whom Thorne calls the "Pride of the Jews of Drohobycz and all of Galicia," has been justifiably compared by literary scholars to Marcel Proust, Jorge Luis Borges, and particularly Franz Kafka, whose works Schulz helped translate into Polish. On November 19, 1942, however, a Gestapo officer in Drohobycz shot Schulz. He did so to avenge the murder of his own "personal Jew" by an SS officer who had previously spared Schulz's life because he liked his drawings and had him paint murals on his villa. His literary oeuvre is small, but "if Schulz had been allowed to live out his life," the Nobel literature laureate Isaac Bashevis Singer once wrote, "he might have given us untold treasures," adding that "what he did in his short life was enough to make him one of the most remarkable writers who ever lived."

It is regrettable that Leon Thorne's story has heretofore failed to attract a broader audience because his lucid, economical prose style vividly captures the terror as it unfolded. He was a gifted narrator who painted lucid images with just a few strokes of the pen. Yet during the author's lifetime,

---

* Esther (Stella) Backenroth's Holocaust experiences are recounted briefly in Yaffa Eliach's Hasidic Tales of the Holocaust (New York: Oxford University Press, 1982), 219–226.

only one review of the book *Out of the Ashes* appeared, also by Isaac Bashe-vis Singer. Singer recognized the memoir's importance as a product of its brutal eloquence. Writing in the August 20, 1961, issue of the Yiddish daily *Forverts*, he asked rhetorically, "Who needs the great literary works, to what purpose the writings of Tolstoy, Dostoevsky, or Proust, when Dr. Thorne can, in simple language, without exaggeration or embellishment, give us the entire bitter truth." Singer added, "Those who still harbor illusions about the human species would be easily cured if they would read each day a chapter of Dr. Thorne's book." By including the illusion-shattering chapters from the bunker that Singer read, the previously unpublished ones written after the war that form part II, and a translation of Singer's review, this new edition makes Rabbi Leon Thorne's experiences available to new generations of readers.

Daniel H. Magilow

# FOREWORD

## "OUT OF THE ASHES"

*Yitzhok Varshavski (Isaac Bashevis Singer),*
*Forverts, August 20, 1961*

*Translated by Marc Caplan*

Those who still harbor illusions regarding humankind and who continue to use the usual phrases would be easily cured of their optimism if every day they would read a chapter from Dr. Leon Thorne's book *Out of the Ashes*. The content of the story does not differ from the thousands of other works about the Holocaust. It's actually the same story with the same moral. The same type of person who eats the meat of animals and murders animals to tear off their fur or for the simple pleasure of going on a hunt is also capable of doing the same to his own species—and what's more, when it comes to his own species, he's even crueler. What Dr. Thorne tells about the Germans, the Ukrainians, and the Poles could also be said about all other peoples. Even among Jews, many have been found who have bartered over human lives.

What need is there for great works of art, what need is there for the oeuvres of Tolstoy, Dostoevsky, or Proust, when Dr. Thorne is able to give us with simple words, without ornament or eloquence, the whole, bitter truth? Even an artwork of the highest quality couldn't offer a thousandth as much.

Dr. Thorne, a scholar and an intellectual, wrote his work in a cellar in the village Schodnica (Skhidnytsia),* not far from Sambor (Sambir) and Drohobycz, Galicia. He is from a Galician family that had owned oil wells. The cellar belonged to former employees of the Polish oil industry, Stanisław Nendza and Franz Janiewski. The two employees were well paid by the Jews and were also offered contracts so that when Poland was liberated, they, the employees, would be made partners with the Jews.

Dr. Thorne's experiences deal with the years leading up to that cellar from which he was liberated by the arrival of the Russians. To have survived everything that Dr. Thorne went through, one would have to have extraordinary health, limitless vitality and willpower, and a lot of money and connections. How exactly he managed to have any money after what he underwent—that remains unexplained in this work. He descends from a rich lineage; his family had money. Money was used in the concentration camps, in prison, even at the gates of hell itself. The beaten and burdened Jews in Europe tried to save themselves with the two famous Jewish means: money and hiding. Neither was of use to the six million, but a very few Jews here and there managed to save themselves, and Dr. Thorne is one of them.

His family was murdered. Now in America, he has a new wife, new children. The new wife made her own way through the Kovno ghetto. I met both of them, husband and wife, at the home of Rabbi Kreitman last Simchat Torah: two models of the Jewish will to survive and of the Jewish power to believe. This latter power is in the eyes of the author more wonderful than the will to survive. Just from reading this work, the author of these lines was thrown into doubt and not for the first time.

Dr. Leon Thorne went through the notorious Janowska concentration camp, a sort of slaughterhouse for Jews. Previously, the Germans had systematically extracted the last drop of energy from the Jews, each portion

---

* Place names are listed first in the form that Singer uses and thereafter, when necessary, in their contemporary form. —Translator

of labor that one can obtain from hungry and lost souls. Thereafter, they were told to dig their own graves, and they were done away with. When they were led to their deaths—so the author tells us—a crowd of Gentiles stood by and called, "Hey, Moishe, give me your coat! Where you're going, you won't need it!" "Hey, Malke, give me your shoes! You can walk just as well barefoot when you're dead!" The Gentiles mocked and laughed.

Dr. Thorne escaped from the camp in a wagon filled with corpses. Later, he dug his own grave. There is no limit to the pain, the indignities, and the evil that this learned Jew was forced to endure. But when millions are murdered, there must be someone who remains. No matter how meticulously the German worked, he couldn't outsmart everyone.

Darwin's theory of natural selection worked there with an uncanny precision. The weak—those who are quickly overcome by doubt and are lost—they were the first to go under. The physically strong and those born with a stubborn and strong will to live struggled longer. Everything could be used as a means to prolong life: a little money, acquaintance with a peasant, a profession that the Germans needed for their own purposes, a pit or a hole in which to hide in this or that moment. Some Jews sought protection by becoming policemen and leading others to the slaughter.

People behaved like chickens. One group was slaughtered; the other pecked out grain from the trash. An animal optimism and senselessness kept the sacrificial victims alive until it was their turn. The courage not only to fight back but even to take one's life was missing. But suicides were nonetheless not uncommon.

This is what Thorne describes in chapter 13, "The Poor Cannot Afford Suicide": "On occasion an incident came to one's attention that stunned and shocked. One such incident concerned two families occupying one room. The Hausmanns were old and childless; the Birnbaums, who I'd known back home, had two children. One day, I heard loud weeping in the room adjacent to ours, where the two families lived. I ran to find out what had happened. Entering, I saw Mrs. Birnbaum and her eleven-year-old son, Janek, lying dead on the sofa. The two Hausmanns, husband and wife, stood near the sofa looking down at the two corpses, wailing loudly. I tried consoling them—after all, suicides were such a commonplace occurrence. Perhaps they were better off, I said. But the two mourners paid no attention to me, raising the pitch of their wails. Then Hausmann turned his tear-stained face to me and said in a sepulchral tone, 'They used the cyanide we bought for ourselves! It was *our* poison!'"

When I read this book, I realize that the human tragedy is far, far from over. First of all, not all of the murderers have been brought to justice. They go on with their lives, the Germans, drinking beer, benefiting from the colossal economic upswing, and boasting in the taverns of their murderousness. We in America have sent them billions of dollars. We are now prepared to go to war for their Berlin. Second, I know that neither the Gentiles nor even the Jews have learned anything from all that has happened. The beast within men has not yet been stilled. It wants to do further evil.

Dr. Thorne received his rabbinical ordination when he was nineteen. He studied in the rabbinical seminary in Vienna and in Breslau (Wrocław) and received a PhD from Würzburg. After the war, he became a military chaplain in the Free Polish Army. He was one of the first members of the Central Committee of Jews in Poland* in Lublin. Between 1946 and 1948, he served as rabbi in Frankfurt am Main and as editor of the journal Yeshuran. Since 1948, Dr. Thorne has lived in the United States.

*Out of the Ashes* was written in German and translated into English. It is published by Rosebern Press in New York. Those interested in purchasing the book should contact the Jewish Center in Brooklyn on Eastern Parkway. One can probably also receive the work—or receive a referral—at other bookstores.

It is painful to read such a book, but it also possesses a power of catharsis. Such books allow us to experience the truth without theories, without easy solutions. Dr. Thorne describes for us how Jews prayed while awaiting their deaths, how Jews fell into the pits that they themselves had

---

* Established on November 12, 1944, the *Centralny Komitet Żydów w Polsce* (Central Committee of Jews in Poland) was the official political representative of Jews in Poland between 1944 and 1950. See also part II, chapter 3, note 7.

dug—with the "Shema Yisrael" on their lips. He tells us about groups of Jewish children who hid themselves in forests.

Over and over again, the book mentions God. Every Jew has asked the same question: Why did God allow this? And the answer is always the same: What do we know of the ways of God?

*Out of the Ashes* is a tremendous document of the Jewish Holocaust, written from someone who experienced the worst but came out intact not only physically but also spiritually. It requires a great deal of faith in the highest powers to begin a new life, to become a parent, to remain a Jew—a rabbi—to spread Torah and Jewish learning, even to write a book.

Dr. Thorne and many others like him have had the illusion that their stories would change the world. But who is the world? At the very least, Jews should not forget.

# AUTHOR'S PREFACE

Sixteen long and eventful years have now passed since the writer emerged from the shadow of death with a lifetime of experiences etched in his mind and a battered manuscript written under enormous handicaps, describing in detail the years of the Hitler terror.

Since that time, there have been other survivors who have told their stories; there have been thousands of magazine articles and hundreds of books and plays and poems and true-life accounts.

The story of Anne Frank has captured the imagination of the world. *The Wall* by John Hersey was a Book of the Month Club selection, and it, like the *Diary of Anne Frank*, has appeared in millions of paperback editions everywhere. Meyer Levin, in his autobiography *In Search* and in his best-selling novel *Eva*, has told, graphically, the stories of survivors.[*]

Why, then, another book by yet another writer?

No life is like another, and no man has lived another man's life. I feel that what happened to me was different in spirit if not in detail from what others lived through.

I owe a special word of gratitude to my good friend, Dr. Benjamin Z. Kreitman, executive vice president of the United Synagogue of America,

---

[*] *The Wall* (1950) was the writer and journalist John Hersey's fictionalized account of the Warsaw Ghetto. The novelist Meyer Levin was known for his gushing review of *The Diary of a Young Girl* for the *New York Times*, which played a key role in making Anne Frank's diary into a signature text of the Holocaust. Levin's *In Search: An Autobiography* appeared in 1950 and his Holocaust novel *Eva* was published in 1959.

who has taken an affectionate interest in my welfare and has been my faithful guide for many years. Without his friendship and support, my life in this country would have been more difficult. He has made it easier, and I shall always be grateful to him.

I cannot conclude my expressions of appreciation without paying special tribute to my dear wife, Rachel, who is intimately acquainted with the events described in these pages and whose love and encouragement have meant much to me during the relatively peaceful years of adjustment in the United States.

If the reader gains some insight into the period, some realization of the hell and terror of the Hitler years, I shall consider my work well done.

Leon Thorne
New York, 1961

# PART I

# CHAPTER 1

# THE CELLAR

The circumstances under which I am compelled to write these lines are enough to discourage the hardiest of chroniclers. But I am driven by so strong a compulsion and commitment to put down everything I've experienced, witnessed, and been told about the Nazi crimes against my people that nothing short of death will deter me. The despairing cries of my fellow Jews in the ghettos and death camps never leave my consciousness. Their cries must not go unheard. I dare not hope to come out alive when this nightmare is over, but I labor at my memoirs believing they will survive me and be published.

Five of us are hiding out in the cellar, under a stable situated on the premises of an oil well in Schodnica, a Galician town in the Carpathian Mountains. In the stable overhead, there are a pig, a goat, twenty rabbits, and some poultry. The clucking and grunting go on all day long. The cellar is six feet long, four feet wide, and five feet high. We cannot stand upright, although we can stretch out when lying down.

I am here with my younger brother, David, who was a robust, happy youth before the war, very much at home in the Talmud,[1] but who is now a troubled twenty-three-year-old, his health undermined by the Hitler years. Dr. Isidor Friedman, a successful lawyer before the German *Stukas*[2] appeared over our Polish cities and towns with their message of death and

1. The Talmud is the major body of Jewish law and tradition.
2. The Junkers Ju 87 airplane was commonly called a *Stuka*, an abbreviation of *Sturzkampfflugzeug* ("dive bomber").

destruction, is the third male member of our small group. Most affected by our sedentary life, Dr. Friedman insists that we "exercise" at least five minutes a day, even though it is impossible to stand up straight without bumping one's head. We do deep breathing when it is not unbearably hot and knee bending. We play a little chess, Friedman and I. He plays an aggressive game but not a very good one; to keep the peace, I let him win on occasion. He has prevailed on us to learn English, which he volunteered to teach. One of the two women here, Louisa Mahler, demurred. "What use can I have for English?" she said. "At the rate the Gestapo is flushing out our people from the hideouts, I doubt if I'll ever have any use for my own language, Yiddish!" But Dr. Friedman, one of Poland's best trial lawyers before the war, was not easily put off. "The mind must be occupied!" he declared. The Mahler woman, recently made a widow by the Nazis, keeps busy playing cards with Esther (Stella) Backenroth, a cousin of mine who is David's age.

Every now and then, one of our landlords raises a plank of the stable floor and throws down a Polish newspaper published in Lemberg[3] and a German one from Berlin, in which, along with the propaganda, war news is given in great detail. This we read avidly, between the lines, hoping to find there what we are all fervently praying for—a turning of the tide.

Considering how little there is at our disposal, how little privacy there is, we are a harmonious group. The two women make use of the bed sheets, which they hang up whenever they find a need for them—to wash up or for other reasons. Lately, the Mahler woman has been bleeding, a little more than she customarily does, and she finds it necessary to use the sheet more frequently. Her indisposition is of some concern to all of us. I hope—we all do—she will soon improve.

There isn't very much furniture here, but we manage. We have two spring mattresses, a wooden bench, a little narrow table capable of holding

3. The city known in German and Yiddish as Lemberg (Lwów in Polish and L'viv in Ukrainian) was the capital of the province of Galicia. More than 140,000 Jews, a third of the city's total population, lived there at the start of World War II. Thorne refers to it variously as Lemberg and Lwów.

no more than two saucepans at most, and a small shelf. The spring mattresses are spaced a half meter apart, one above the other, with my brother and I sleeping on one and the two women on the other, above us. Dr. Friedman uses the wooden bench for a bed. The floor and walls of the cellar are constructed out of wooden planks.

Our only source of light is a candle, which burns day and night. Someday it may be possible for us to have electric lights installed by means of camouflaged wiring, but not yet. An air shaft built into the double wall of the stable provides us with our breathing air, but when it is hot outside, we get very little fresh air. At night, the outside air is cooler and helps us breathe.

We have a makeshift toilet. In a corner of the cellar, there is a niche, one yard wide, built in for toilet purposes, with a bucket in a box. This is what we all use, men and women alike.

Once every day, in the evening, of course, the well-camouflaged entrance to our hideout is opened up for food for the next day and a pail of water. Each day, there are potatoes, soup, some bread, and on Sunday, a little butter and a bit of sugar. We also receive tobacco, cigarette paper, matches, and candles. In return, we pass out the pots and pans used the previous day as well as the toilet bucket.

Thanks to our landlords, two families, we live as we do. Both Stanisław Nendza and Franz Janiewski are oil workmen who formerly worked for us. Although Poles are forbidden by the German authorities, on penalty of death, to aid Jews, these two Polish families have dared to help us.

We are grateful to them, naturally, but it should be pointed out that they are not placing themselves in danger for idealistic reasons alone. They are hiding us from the Gestapo for material reasons as well. First, we pay them very well for their cooperation, and in addition, we have promised them, in writing, that half our fortune in the Schodnica oil wells— which we are confident will be restored to us after the war—will belong to them. The papers have been signed by us and are here in the cellar.

I write while lying on my cot, leaning on the bucket of water, which is covered by a thick piece of cardboard. This is my desk.

It is difficult here, but we know what the alternatives are. Our people have been massacred in the cities and deported to death camps; none are left in the towns. Even in the labor camps, according to my latest information, only a few thousand are left. In 1939, three and one quarter million Jews lived in Poland.

It is questionable whether we five can survive in the cellar until the end of the war. We are too vulnerable. Hideouts are being uncovered all the time. A word spoken too loudly, a cough, or sneeze can be heard by a passerby in the street above.

Time is short. I must get on with my work. I will write with objectivity, without embellishment. I'll make my notes in copybooks and send them, along with my notes from the camps and ghettos, by way of my landlords, to an "Aryan" friend of mine. Should I survive the war, I plan to arrange for publication. Should I perish, I have arranged to have the notes sent to Jewish organizations in the United States or Palestine with the intent of having them published.

And now, in the name of God, I begin to write.

# CHAPTER 2

# SCHODNICA

Schodnica is so small, it is not even on the map. Buried in the Carpathian Mountains of Galicia, fifteen kilometers from the closest railway station, it had a population, at the outbreak of the war, of five thousand, one-fifth of whom were Jews.

Years ago, there occurred what some Jews in town called a "revolution." It was a trivial event, really, too trivial for any historian to record. As a matter of fact, it is altogether doubtful that the event even happened. As the story goes, an Austrian policeman (Galicia then belonged to Austria) stabbed a man in a café owned by a Jew, causing a near riot by a crowd of rowdies who threatened to burn down Jewish homes and kill their inhabitants. Fortunately, a heavy rain came pouring down, drenching the crowd and dispersing it.

Because the incident was one of the few turbulent and threatening moments in our placid town, I heard it alluded to as a "revolution" during my childhood.

Although a quiet town, Schodnica was not an insubstantial one. It was the first locality in Eastern Galicia where oil was discovered, more than one hundred years ago. A Jew played a major role in its discovery.[1]

---

1. The discovery of oil in Eastern Galicia in the mid-nineteenth century led to the rapid modernization of what was previously a provincial backwater of the Hapsburg Empire. Particularly after the discovery of a massive gusher in 1895, Schodnica attracted international attention, and like other population centers such as Borysław and Drohobycz, it became an oil boomtown. The Backenroth family played a central role in developing the oil industry in the region. For more on this history, see Valerie Schatzker's *The Jewish Oil Magnates: A History, 1853–1945* (Montreal: McGill-Queens University Press, 2015) and Alison Fleig Frank's *Oil Empire: Visions of Prosperity in Austrian Galicia* (Cambridge, Mass.: Harvard University Press, 2005).

His name was Meilich Backenroth; he was the grandfather of my grand-father. He found the oil by accident. Digging in his garden, he was sur-prised by a sudden spurt of dark-brown liquid shooting out of the ground. It was crude oil—of which he had not the slightest idea—used in those days as cart grease and for lighting purposes, in a rather crude fashion. The full significance of Meilich's discovery was realized only some time later by his youngest son, Itzik. The young man, wearing sidelocks and the fringe garment of a pious Jew, took his life in his hands and started for Lemberg and then for the distant capital, Vienna, carrying with him a bottle of the liquid for analysis. Soon after his return, hundreds of engineers descended on our once-peaceful town to drill for brown "liquid gold." Oil brought wealth to Schodnica, and the Backenroth family prospered. The Jewish community, comparatively small, was tolerated by the Christians and per-mitted to lead its own life.

In September 1939, Germany invaded Poland, and the good life, the peaceful life, came to an abrupt end. Moving from the east, Soviet troops occupied Lemberg and Schodnica. All property was expropriated, and the now ex-owners of the oil wells were reduced to the status of beggars. Two years later, on Friday, July 4, 1941, a pogrom broke out in the area. The Rus-sian troops had evacuated the sector five days earlier, and the natives—the Ukrainians, practiced in the art of pogroms—assaulted Schodnica before the Nazi armies approached the town.[2]

Several days later, the Wehrmacht stormed into town with Slovakian troops and issued the following order:

1. All Jewish men between the ages of twelve and sixty and women between the ages of eighteen and forty must register for forced labor.
2. All Jews ten years old and over must wear a white badge ten centimeters wide, embroidered with the Star of David, eight centimeters wide.

---

2. As recounted in a 1959 *yizkor* (memorial) book, Germans occupied Schodnica on July 1, 1941, and "actively assisted the local gangs" of Poles and Ukrainians in the ensuing three-day pogrom (an anti-Jewish riot). Two hundred Jews were murdered, most in a nearby forest.

Thus it began. Jews were put to cleaning sewers and gutters. Although not physically demanding, the work was intended to humiliate and degrade. Receiving no pay, Jews were allotted a daily bread ration of seventy grams; non-Jews received four hundred grams.

Soon after the Germans arrived, Gestapo agents entered the nearby village of Urycz, drove all the Jews to a forest, and murdered them. The sole survivor was a six-year-old boy named Leichtman, whose father had immigrated to America several years before and had earlier sent papers and money for the family to join him. The Germans invaded Poland a week before the family was to leave for America. The Gestapo officer in charge of the massacre, a murderer named Monta, had sworn he would not let even one solitary Jew in town escape with his life. But the Leichtman boy marred the German's plan, managing to make his way—more dead than alive—to Schodnica, where his uncle lived.

Monta, an ethnic German who had lived in our region for several years, was not appeased by the Urycz massacre. He made arrangements to massacre the Jews of Podhorodce as well. This murderer, who many years earlier had lost a lawsuit to a Jew named Pyrnitzer, was having his revenge. He spared only the lives of two Jews, Katz and Weiss, who had testified on his behalf at the trial.

It was in this fashion that the Jews in the nearby villages perished.

News of the murder rampage, when it reached us in Schodnica, caused wild panic. Rumors flew that the Gestapo intended to kill all of us in the region. Abandoning our homes, carrying with us what we could, we fled to nearby cities, some to Borysław, some to Drohobycz, some to Stryj. My family ran to Sambor.

꧁

# CHAPTER 3

# SAMBOR

Before the war, Sambor, a town in eastern Galicia, had a population of twenty-one thousand, one-third of them Jewish, many of them earning their livelihood as grain dealers and craftsmen. The town was famed as the home of Rabbi Uri Yolles, the founder of the Sambor rabbinic dynasty, who attracted hundreds of followers and admirers from neighboring towns and distant places.[1] They came in large numbers to Sambor, seeking advice from the Rabbi and paying homage. During the time of the Baal Shem Tov, a great Talmudist made his home in Sambor, Rabbi Yitzhak Charif. Understandably, the Jews of the town took great pride in the two spiritual leaders and in Sambor, where they once lived.

Soon after the invasion, the Gestapo gave the Jews of Sambor four hours to pay thirty-five thousand złotys, threatening to execute all the members of the newly established Jewish Council unless the order was carried out.

I must digress for a moment and state my views about the Jewish Council, which was a German creation.[2] We Jews had nothing to do with

1. Uri Ha-Kohen Yolles (1833–1910) was a descendant of Rabbi Yisroel ben Eliezer (1698–1760), often called the Baal Shem Tov, the founder of the eighteenth-century Jewish revivalist movement known as Hasidism. Yolles founded a rabbinic dynasty in Sambor in 1878.
2. A Jewish Council or *Judenrat* (plural *Judenräte*) was a governing body that Germans established in occupied Europe and in Jewish ghettos. They remain controversial, as some critics, including Thorne, accuse them of collaborating in self-serving ways that facilitated the Holocaust. Jewish Councils were constantly forced to choose the lesser of evils in no-win situations, which Holocaust scholar Lawrence Langer has aptly termed "choiceless choices."

its formation or functions; the members had not been democratically elected but were appointed by the German military authorities. The newly elected Polish mayor of a locality would propose to the military a Jew of his acquaintance as *Obmann* (chairman). This person would then select his colleagues to work with him.

Why a Jewish Council? Whom did it serve? It did not represent the Jews or heed their petitions. Its function, at the start, was to supply Jewish workers for the most difficult and dirtiest jobs in the area. All Jewish males, as already told, between the ages of twelve and sixty and females, eighteen to forty, were ordered to register.

If the Germans ordered the appearance of fifteen hundred workers, the council summoned two hundred more in the event the masters changed their minds and desired a larger contingent. The additional hundreds would sit around all day long in the expectation of an emergency call. If an assigned worker failed to appear on time, he had to be reported or handed over to the German police.

The council, which was headed by Dr. Samson Schneidscher and among whose members were Dr. Zausner, Dr. Frey, Dr. Halpern, Schnor, Lehrer, and Becker, offered some small measure of relief to the Jews, doing away with sadistic German and Ukrainian soldiers who in the past were in charge of the work details.[3] However, the difference was not that marked, as the German and Ukrainian overseers tortured and humiliated many Jews, the old and the women in particular, during working hours.

Soon the council was given another responsibility by the Gestapo: to distribute bread among the Jews, a task too ordinary for members of the "master race." The bread ration came to four ounces daily per person. The council opened centers for distribution.

With each passing day, the Germans made new claims on the council, and in time, a soup kitchen was opened and an ambulance station,

3. Throughout his memoir, Thorne's use of "Dr." accords with the European convention of using the title to indicate that a person had earned an advanced university degree, not that the person was necessarily a physician. The chairman of the Sambor *Judenrat* (Jewish Council), Dr. Shimson (Samson) Schneidscher, was by profession a lawyer.

where Jewish doctors contributed their services. To settle disputes, a law court was established by the council, and it included Jewish former judges and lawyers, who rendered legal and fair verdicts accepted by the people. Merely by threatening to hand over difficult cases to the Germans, the Jewish Council was able to enforce its sentences and thus give itself a definite authority. The council even established a prison, which was used occasionally. All these institutions were housed in the Jewish Council building.

With all of its tasks, the council required money, making it necessary to impose a tax on all under its authority. A special tax office, with executives, was created. At the beginning of each month, each person received his assessment from the tax office, based on his ability to pay. If in one's opinion the assessment was too high, he was permitted to challenge it. If he lost, he had to accede or receive a warrant of distress and an order to sell his possessions. This, however, happened rarely.

As the council's activities expanded, it was found necessary to create a Jewish militia, headed by a Jewish commander. This militia was accorded recognition by the district prefect, and the militiamen were limited in proportion to the number of persons in a given area. A member wore no uniform except a blue cap with the Star of David and a number. Sambor had forty such militiamen.[4]

In the beginning, decent men belonged to the militia, but as it became plain that the Germans planned to use the group against the Jews themselves, the better men quit, leaving behind only the disreputable ones who were insensitive to the sufferings of their fellows. Some of them were sufficiently depraved to take advantage of their victims, enriching themselves at their expense. In due time, the Jewish militia became the object of derision and hate.

The Germans continued issuing anti-Jewish ordinances, all of which were aimed at demoralizing and humiliating the Jews as well as robbing them. Homes and real estate were expropriated, although this was

4. Through the Jewish Councils, German occupiers across occupied Eastern Europe established units of Jewish Police auxiliaries known as the *Jüdischer Ordnungsdienst* (Jewish Police Service). They often recruited known criminals as members.

less sweeping than it sounds, for the Soviet government previously had nationalized most of the Jewish houses and properties. Radios; precious stones; gold, silver, and copper; and foreign currency had to be yielded up to the Nazis on pain of death. All dray horses, bicycles, and other equipment used for moving about had to be surrendered. Domestic animals and poultry were also taken away, as were sporting goods and uniforms. There were other orders involving limitations on moving about, a 7 p.m. curfew, and the impounding of goods such as furniture and clothing. The Germans were very thorough.

There were so many orders issued, and so much confusion about them, that the Germans themselves were not always sure what the laws were. First, there was an edict banning the Jews from walking on the sidewalks, then another order keeping them from the roads. Under such conditions, where were Jews to walk? This led to a meeting of the minds of the Security Police and the district prefect, and it was decided that Jews could not walk on the sidewalks or on the roads unless they remained on either extremity of the road—that is to say, not in the middle of the road. That is how ridiculous it became.

On the matter of saluting: if a Jew saluted a German, the Nazi might become enraged because a Jew was being "polite" to a member of the master race, and how dare he salute a Nazi? On the other hand, if a Jew walked past a German without saluting, he might be whipped for failing to honor a German officer.

These conditions prevailed at a time when the Jewish Council was doing all it could to bribe the German authorities to permit the Jews to survive as human beings. Dr. Schneidscher, chairman of the council, was adroit at handling the authorities, bribing the right men at the right time. As a consequence, for a comparatively long spell, Jews were not being killed in town. While the Germans were murdering Jews all over Eastern Galicia, Dr. Schneidscher was helping his people in Sambor to survive.

But in September 1941, his luck seemed to desert him. Gestapo trucks rumbled through the streets of Sambor. The machine guns mounted on the trucks were harbingers of what was soon to come. But Dr. Schneidscher did not hoist the white flag of surrender. He invited the Gestapo chiefs to his office, where they were greeted on entering by a small mound of gold on the chairman's desk: golden rings, necklaces, and earrings. He had amassed the treasure over a period of months, aided by young volunteers who had gone from one Jewish home to the next, prevailing on the people to part with their gold objects to save their lives. The machine guns on the trucks convinced the chairman that he must play his card now. He pointed to the mound on his desk; the Germans stuffed their pockets and withdrew.

The terrified Jews of Sambor, watching the German trucks turn back and leave town, could scarcely believe it. But the Germans, primed for an *Aktion*,[5] detoured into two neighboring towns and massacred the Jewish populations.

During the early months of the occupation, the economic situation of the Jews in Sambor had not been as bad as it was for the Jews in other towns. The Poles in town did not participate in attacks against us with the ferocity displayed by the Ukrainians. However, conditions changed for the worse in the winter of 1941–1942. Starvation decimated Sambor Jews. People died in the streets.

In the east, the war continued unabated. The Germans had not conquered Russia in eight weeks as they had predicted they would, nor did the offensive of October 1941 bring them the successes they had anticipated. We, for our part, were confident that history would repeat itself and that, as in the Napoleonic invasion, the Germans would stumble and break their necks.

When the United States entered the war in December 1941, it meant, so far as we were able to figure it, certain defeat for Hitler. But we also believed that the possibility of a rapid end to the war was now over. We felt pessimistic for another reason too. Now that the Americans had come into the fight, Hitler would no longer feel restrained in his persecution of the Jews, for American public opinion was no longer a factor to the Germans.

---

5. An *Aktion* was a military operation to collect, deport, and murder Jews.

In December 1941, there was another bit of action that few people on the outside knew anything about but that was important to us. The Germans issued their "fur decrees."[6] All furs, or fur coats, were to be yielded up to them. Russian winters were cold. If we gave up our warm coats, we would freeze, while the Nazis, wearing our furs, might survive the Russian frosts. Should we give up our furs and help our deadly foes escape from a cold death in snow, ice, or storm?

The Jews had an answer to this decree, painful though it was. Instead of delivering the furs to the Germans, we burned them. This "fur *Aktion*" was carried out simultaneously in many towns and villages. Not a week went by without a German finding a Jew with furs and shooting him for it. So desperate were the Germans for furs that they became "hotter" properties than gold, diamonds, or dollars.

6. On December 24, 1941, Adam Czerniaków, the head of the Warsaw *Judenrat*, recorded in his diary, "I received a message from Warsaw that—according to an edict—we must surrender all the furs—both men's and women's. I am to be personally responsible. The deadline has been set for December 28, 1941."

—◁—

# CHAPTER 4

# AN ACT OF DEFIANCE

It was the intention of our family, consisting of twenty persons, to remain in Sambor, if we could, until the end of the war. For a small fee, the Jewish Council had us registered as permanent residents, and we were assigned to various tasks, mine being heavy labor. But in time, I was reassigned to a cleaner job, and as it turned out, a better one, the sorting of books. The Soviets, who had intended to make a cultural center of Sambor, had, in the years 1939 to 1941, brought books to town—books in Russian, Ukrainian, German, and Yiddish. When they withdrew in July 1941, the books fell under German control, and the labor office was ordered to assign ten Jews the task of cataloging the volumes.[1]

Work was in full swing when I joined the staff. My colleagues were for the most part teachers and lawyers. I was to be the expert on "Jewish literature." After years of demeaning labor for the Soviets, I was able to read once more, to study several hours daily. It seemed as though it was all a dream from which I did not want to awaken. Thousands of books crowded our office, works on medicine, philosophy, sociology, economics, history, and the science of war. With an unquenchable thirst for knowledge, we became absorbed in many books, often forgetting the bitter reality of our

1. On August 23, 1939, Germany and the Soviet Union signed a nonaggression treaty, the Molotov-Ribbentrop Pact. The treaty included a secret protocol to partition Poland, and as Germany invaded Poland from the west on September 1, 1939, the Soviet Union invaded from the east. The line of demarcation between the USSR and Germany ran through Galicia close to Sambor.

lives. My colleagues, like myself, sat and read. Never once did any of us say, "We are here, deriving pleasure and satisfaction, while our fellows do heavy labor and perform menial and humiliating tasks." It could not last long, and it didn't.

The town commander came by once a week to inspect our work and check on our progress. But his probing caused hardly any anxiety or tension. We had to cope with an enormous number of volumes, which five times as many people could not handle. His once-a-week visit was scarcely enough for him to ascertain our progress. Our regular overseer, a Ukrainian named Wislocki, was a drunkard who had but one major problem: where to obtain enough money for his liquor, coffee, and opium cigarettes. He gave us hardly any trouble at all, as we bribed him with presents, every now and then, and turned over to him our monthly wages, which amounted to eighty złotys. As there were eleven of us, our money kept him comfortably in drink for a brief spell. In return, he more or less ignored us and went so far as to "promote" one of our group, Speiser, a former Austrian officer from Rzeszów, as our "commandant." Not only were we left in peace, but now we had an opportunity to aid the allies.

What we did was really of little significance, when I think of it now in retrospect, sitting in the cellar and writing. But at the time, we believed that we were sabotaging the German war effort by burning military books that the Nazis wanted from us. Apparently, the Russians who had stocked the library had planned to open a military academy nearby and, consequently, filled the place with suitable material. Periodically, we would get requests, which came to us via Wislocki, asking for reference books on special subjects such as pillbox systems, camouflage, the technique of winter fighting, or fortifications. We searched for the desired material and were pleased when it could not be found. But on such occasions as when the reference work was on our shelves, we took it down and destroyed it.

All of us were determined not to yield to the Germans a single title that might be of value to them in prosecuting the war. Never did any of us suggest that we play it safe by occasionally "finding" a desired title to deflect any suspicion of noncooperation. We acted in unison and one day committed the bold act of making a bonfire of all the military reference works marked "confidential." Unfortunately, the bonfire got out of hand, and we feared Wislocki would find us out, but he was drunk, as usual, and we escaped with our lives.

There were, in this work, some light moments as well. I was occupied with the sorting of many volumes written in Yiddish. Most of these were school textbooks, although there were among them novels and even poems. The local commander, a German with a Hitler mustache and polished boots, and his fat deputy who talked with a lisp were most eager to uncover the "dark secrets" of the Jews, which they believed were to be found between the covers of the books crowding the shelves and piled high on the floor. Their minds were crammed full of Hitler propaganda about the evil Jews and their deep dark secrets. Now, they believed, they were in a position to contribute to the Führer's efforts by uncovering a few "secrets" on their own and perhaps earning, in the process, a promotion. Smiling slyly, they would stride into my room and examine some of the books, open them as though expecting some blind revelations but, failing, then turn to me. "What is in this book? Quick, don't lie! What's in it? What does it say?"

"A textbook for children," I replied.

"And this?"

"A Jewish songbook."

"What! Jews sing songs?"

The fat deputy was the more thorough of the two. His eye fastened on Herr Glazer, one of my colleagues. "You'll teach me Hebrew!" the deputy declared. Glazer's father, Rabbi Hirsch Glazer of Przemyśl, had been killed by the Nazis. Now the deputy warned my colleague that he would meet the same fate as his father if he failed to teach him Hebrew in three months.

To this day, I see Glazer's ashen face and trembling lower lip. "How can I possibly do it?" he said to me after the two Nazis had gone. "Three months? One needs years to master the texts."

A few days before Purim[2] in 1942, I was awakened in the middle of the night by loud banging on the door. Hearing Yiddish spoken, I opened. Several men stood in the doorway: Dr. Zausner, the vice-president of the Jewish Council; Becker, a member of the council; and two others. What was happening? Normally, members of the council did not go around ringing doorbells at night.

Dr. Zausner said, "This may sound fantastic to you and absolutely incredible, but there are several Gestapo men from Drohobycz, very drunk, in the *Judenrat* office."

"What for?" I asked.

"To avenge thousands of Persians who were killed by Jews 2,500 years ago, during the period when Purim was first celebrated!"

"They're insane," I blurted out.

Dr. Zausner, paying no attention to my remark, went on, "The Gestapo plans to avenge the dead Persians by killing half the Jewish population of Sambor."

"Have you come to warn me?"

"No, we came to ask for your help," the vice president said urgently.

I was puzzled. What could I do?

They had come to me, Dr. Zausner informed me, because they believed I could supply them with a scientific explanation of Purim and its origins that would, in some fashion, omit the killing of Persians.[3] I had no idea if I could be of help but dressed quickly to go with them. My wife, my father, and my brother bade me good-bye as though they did not expect to see me again.

On the way over, my brain in turmoil, I tried to think of what to tell the Germans. The only "out" that occurred to me was to use the approach of

2. As recounted in the Book of Esther, the Jewish holiday of Purim commemorates the salvation of the Jews in Persia from Haman, the ruler intent on killing them all in a single day. In 1942, Purim fell on March 3.
3. Leon Thorne was ordained as a rabbi at the age of nineteen and continued his seminary education in Vienna and Breslau (Wrocław).

the Jewish historian, Heinrich Graetz,[4] who had written that the story of Purim had no historical basis in fact and the Scroll of Esther, in which the Purim tale is told, originated in the second century BCE in the time of the Maccabeans,[5] so that the Jewish people would be encouraged to maintain their identity. Graetz never persuaded me; I believed he was wrong, that such a piece of fiction could not be made up and that the Jews had believed it for thousands of years. But for the present emergency, unable to think of anything else to say, the Graetz approach was the straw I would seize to keep from drowning.

It was still dark when we reached the Jewish Council headquarters. Although I had been working several months for the German occupation, this was to be my first contact with the Gestapo. I dreaded what was to come.

I was led into a room that was filled with Gestapo officers with faces as malevolent as those of beasts of the forest. My eyes fastened on the swastika they wore on their sleeves and their pistols. In the corner, trying to appear unobtrusive, stood Dr. Schneidscher, the president of the council, and several of the members, all gazing hopefully at me, as though their fate was in my hands.

A Gestapo man, calling for order, flung a question at me. "Why did Jews kill Aryans during Purim?" he demanded.

"According to Heinrich Graetz, a great historian," I said, barely above a whisper, "the entire story is a fabrication." I saw the approving nods of the council members, but the German seemed doubtful and disappointed.

"Tell me, Jew," one of them addressed me, "was this great historian an Aryan or Jew?"

"He was a Jew," I replied slowly, as though eager to postpone our doom, "who taught at the University of Breslau."

---

4. Between 1853 and 1876, the historian Heinrich Graetz (1817–1891) published the eleven volumes of his *History of the Jews*, one of the first comprehensive scholarly accounts of Jewish history.
5. The Maccabeans were Jewish rebels in Judea who revolted against the Seleucid Empire from 167 to 160 BCE.

I felt a sharp blow to my skull; my brain seemed on fire. An instant later, I lost consciousness. When I regained my senses and opened my eyes, I saw a Gestapo man standing over me wooden club in hand, demanding, "You dare bring me proof from a cursed, filthy Jewish historian?!"

Fearing another blow, one that might kill me altogether, I said, "I have further proof. I know of a German historian who has written that statistics in the olden days were different from what they are today, that numbers were counted differently."

The German considered my reply. I did not expect him to believe me. I watched the wooden club in his hand.

"Is this historian Jewish too?" he flung at me.

"No, no," I assured him.

"What was his name?"

"I can't recall," I said, my hand on my skull. "The blow on my head has made me dizzy. But I think it begins with the letter *B*."

He called for a pencil and scribbled something on a piece of paper. Turning to me, he said, "Listen carefully, Jew. We are going to send this information to the Institute for Jewish Research in Berlin.[6] If you lie, we'll return and wipe out all the Jews of Sambor. You and your family will be the first ones to be hanged. You cursed Jew-murderers!"

They left and I rose to my feet, with the aid of the council members, who thanked me, shook my hand, and sent me home with a loaf of bread, a reward for my labors.

6. The institute referenced was very possibly the *Reichsinstitut für Geschichte des neuen Deutschlands* (Reich Institute for the History of the New Germany), a research institute directed by the historian Walter Frank (1905–1945). The institute aimed to eliminate Jewish influences from German history and rewrite that history from a National Socialist perspective.

CHAPTER 5

╼

# THE STORM

That trouble was brewing was evident from the rumors we heard and the new orders that had been issued. Late in July 1942, the district prefect at Sambor had demanded that there be an increase in the Jewish *Ordnungs-dienst* from forty to one hundred men. In itself, this edict could have been useful to us, for it meant that an additional sixty young people would work at light jobs instead of heavy ones. But we all realized that the prefect did not have our benefit in mind. There followed a second order: all villages in the area were to be "cleared" of Jews within three days.[1] I recalled that six months earlier, the prefect had ordered the members of the Jewish Council to appear before him and had told them that, when the time came for transporting the Jews elsewhere, the job would have to be done, in large measure, by the Jews themselves through the council. If any of the German orders were not heeded, he said, the members of the council as well as the *Ordnungsdienst* would be hanged in the center of the town.

The day the first order was issued, the Jewish Council hurriedly called together its staff to draw up a list of all Jews living in the surrounding villages, who numbered almost one hundred. Only those working for the Germans were exempt from the list.

---

1. The *Ordnungsdienst* assisted in the first massive *Aktion* in Sambor that began on August 4, 1942. In the preceding days, Jews from surrounding towns and villages had been concentrated in former Polish army stables near Blich, Sambor's Jewish neighborhood. Roughly 6,000 Jews were deported from Sambor to the Bełżec death camp in this *Aktion*, one of many in the final five months of 1942, when Germans and their local collaborators murdered 250,000 Jews in Eastern Galicia.

The *Evidenzbüro* (Intelligence Office) of the Jewish Council had accurate lists of Jews living both in the town and in the nearby villages. The office of the German Registrar had no lists of the Jews in the area, the files having been destroyed early in the occupation.

The council members feverishly worked through the night; on the morning of the next day, the lists were ready. More than two thousand names were included. The council hired one hundred carts from local farmers to send the entire *Ordnungsdienst* to each village with a list of every Jew in that village.

Two days passed. In the afternoon of the third day, carts loaded with Jews began converging on Sambor from the various villages. On the carts, along with the victims—small children, old women wearing kerchiefs, and white-haired, bearded old men who had not left their villages for decades—were mountains of bedding. A heavy rain fell steadily, drenching the occupants of the carts, the peasants at the stirrups, and the horses. I watched the procession from a distance and wept.

As I sit now in my hiding place, under the stable, I am haunted by the children in those carts, their eyes. I see those eyes in my wakeful hours and in my sleep. That black Friday will remain with me as long as I live.

The Jews of Sambor, moved by what they were witnessing, came forward and offered to take the Jewish families into their own homes. But they were reminded that the German authorities had ordered all the incoming Jews to be placed in military barracks and guarded by Ukrainian militiamen. The town Jews were not permitted to enter this building except for the few who worked in the soup kitchen.

The *Ordnungsdienst*, threatened with the gallows or the Janover extermination camp[2] if they didn't follow the German instructions, took great

---

2. Bełżec, Sobibór, and Treblinka, the so-called Operation Reinhard camps, existed solely for the purpose of extermination. The Janover camp on the northwestern side of Lemberg (Lwów), which Thorne refers to as "Janover" (see part I, chapter 6), was more commonly known as Janowska or the Janowska Street labor camp. Although mass killings and atrocities occurred at Janowska, it was not an extermination camp per se but a hybrid slave labor camp, local prison, and transit camp for Jews being deported to Bełżec.

pains to carry out the orders issued to them. They were to have transported the village Jews to the town, but they found that the Ukrainians—among whom the village Jews lived—were eager to drive them out. The *Ordnungsdienst*, reluctant to carry out its unhappy tasks, discovered that the Ukrainians had already done the job well enough.

The list of tragic tales that unfolded that day is as long as the Jewish exile. One tale remains vivid in my mind. It should be kept in mind that Jews who were employed by the Germans did not move out of their villages. This, however, was not always a "break" for the men and women concerned. There was a Jewish couple with an infant child who, because both mother and father worked for the Germans, were ordered to remain with their employers. Their child, possessing no certificate of occupation, according to orders, had to leave the village. The mother could not accompany the infant, for when any Jew left his or her place of work, the punishment was death.

Her child was taken away from her, but that very night, the mother fled from her village and came to Sambor. With great effort, she was smuggled into the barracks and reunited with her infant. However, the tension made the mother temporarily demented. The Ukrainian guard reported her abnormal behavior to the German police, and that evening, the Germans led the mother out of the barracks and attempted to pry the child out of her arms. She resisted, clawing at the Germans, kicking and biting them. Unable to get the child away from her, they drove the frenzied woman, still clutching her youngster, to the Jewish cemetery. There, two shots united the mother and child forever.

Daily, the situation of the Jews in the barracks grew worse. On Sunday, August 2, 1942, all was quiet, but on Monday, a wild story began to make the rounds that the end was imminent. No one knew how it originated, but everyone was talking about it. It was said that Tuesday, the very next day, all the Jews were to be killed.

Panic-stricken people ran to the headquarters of the Jewish Council in order to learn the truth. But the council officers were tight-lipped. They stood in front of the building, looking grave. Before any questions could be put to them, they shrugged and said they knew nothing, but the expressions on their faces indicated otherwise. We learned that there were fifty boxcars standing on a siding in the railway station, which were to be used to transport the people to another area—to be shot. At least, this is what the Aryan railway workers had told the Jews who had been assigned to the station.

Meanwhile, the hour of the street curfew was approaching, and all Jews had to hurry home. Ignoring the curfew, they waited around, at risk of being shot, hoping for some word from council officials.

Inside the council headquarters, the offices and corridors were mobbed with persons who had come there, notwithstanding the curfew, hoping to take shelter. Council officials themselves had brought their wives and children, hoping to hide them in the attic and cellar.

Council president, Dr. Schneidscher, and his deputy, Dr. Zausner, as well as other officers were summoned to police headquarters. There, they found, along with the police officers, the Gestapo in large numbers, who informed them that an *Aktion* was to be taken against one thousand Sambor Jews. The executions were not to take place in town; the one thousand Jews from Sambor and the two thousand from the villages would be transported to an area selected by the German authorities and disposed of there in the usual manner. The Jewish Council, they were told, would take no part in the *Aktion* but must provide a list of "criminals" and "beggars" to the Gestapo forthwith. They were threatened with collective hanging if they did not cooperate. The council members pleaded for time to plan. The Germans agreed to wait, but not for long, demanding brandy to help them pass the time.

The council members left to return to their headquarters, consulting on the way, arguing about their options, but agreeing on one point. Their choice was limited: they could become either murderers or martyrs. The phone rang periodically, the Gestapo inquiring what action had been taken. Some of the Jewish officials, unable to take a stand, went into hiding themselves to avoid casting a vote.

Eventually, however, the moment of truth had to come. Rationalizing that they could perhaps save other Jews, the council leaders agreed to compile lists, which they knew would send fellow Jews to certain death.

No one seriously believed that the Nazis would limit themselves to the names on lists; it was clear that the council's lists would indicate the houses in which Jews were living. At the time, Jews were dispersed throughout the area and had not yet been driven into a defined ghetto quarter. It seemed that, in yielding to the Germans, the council spokesmen were attempting to save their own lives and those of their families. It was thought by some that the council leaders had received pledges that the Germans would find the Jews no matter what they had decided to do. The council leaders could find excuses to explain their capitulation.

When I learned what the final decision was, I ran back to my home on Kosharava Street, where my family waited impatiently to know what developments had taken place. Would I bring good news, or would I be the bearer of evil tidings? I had to tell them the truth, bitter though it was. I still remember how my young brother cried out in anger and desperation, "The damned criminals! Where can I get a gun? I'd walk to my death without regrets if I could take some of those council members along with me! The dogs!"

My father said, "Something has to be done. If we sit here, they'll come and slaughter us."

My brother said, "Let's resist!"

"Resist with what?" my brother-in-law demanded. "Our bare hands? Or have you a cache of weapons hidden somewhere?"

It was decided to seek a place to hide. We sent my wife upstairs to our landlady, a decent woman, a Pole of Italian extraction, to ask for permission to hide in the cellar. The landlady voiced no objection, provided that we were not discovered by the Ukrainians living in the house. Pledging we would be quiet, the family, all twenty of us, tiptoed down the wooden stairs to the cellar, a dark, damp place filled with empty jars the landlady used for pickling cucumbers and tomatoes. I stood guard at the window upstairs, keeping myself ready in the event it was necessary to run to the Jewish Council headquarters for help.

Suddenly, I became aware that I was being observed by one of the neighbors, a Ukrainian, who smiled slyly and said, "Why are all you people creeping into the cellar?"

My fingers itching to seize him by the throat, I said to the Jew-hater—all the Ukrainians hated us—"No need to conceal anything from you, friend. I need your help; I'm willing to pay for it. If you remain silent, tell nobody what you just saw, not even your wife, I'll pay you well. Right now, I'll give you two new suits, an overcoat, and a gold ring."

He nodded agreement. I trusted him at the time.

Impatient to learn what was happening in town, I started for council headquarters, using a circuitous path. The curfew was on, but people ignored it, arriving in large numbers at the crowded building. Even the sight of corpses in the street, persons killed for defying the curfew, failed to discourage those of us who had no legitimate business to be there. We milled around in the hallways, seeking enlightenment from the council members, who had nothing to tell us. It seemed to me I read guilt on their faces. Jewish militiamen sat in one room, smoking, waiting nervously to be summoned by the Germans to round up fellow Jews and shoot those who resisted. On another floor, a handful of officials worked, compiling lists of persons to be taken away in the *Aktion*. I heard one staff member, then another, mutter, "How are we going to do it? How can we do it?" How were they to find seven thousand Jews to turn over to the Germans for execution? And one thousand criminals? The "criminals" had to be made up of whole cloth. Sambor, in a whole century, could not have produced one thousand Jewish criminals! So they were spreading the net wide. Many of the people now milling around in the council hallways would be among the victims.

At three in the morning, we were startled by the sound of trucks entering the yard. Panic broke out. Officials as well as petitioners tore about in the halls, screaming wildly, "Hide! Quick, hide! The Gestapo is here!"

A long row of military vehicles, trucks, and cars marked with swastikas parked in front of council headquarters, their occupants armed with pistols, rifles, and machine guns. A German officer, his boots glistening in the semidark and pistol in hand, went inside the building, reappearing several minutes later carrying the lists of intended victims and their addresses. He distributed the lists among the men in the cars and trucks, who drove off, disappearing in the dark streets of Sambor, where the Jews slept their uneasy sleep, few of them suspecting they would be taken before daybreak, never to return.

Writing these lines now, I recall thinking at the time, "Is the world aware of the enormity of the crime about to be committed in Sambor?" Since that dreadful night, I've witnessed and lived through such crimes many times over—Sambor a thousand times multiplied, millions of my brethren slain. And my question—Is the world aware of the enormity of the crimes?—remains unanswered.

Sambor is not a large town, and its streets are not many. The Germans, aided by Ukrainians and Jewish militiamen, surrounded the town and posted sentries on street corners to foil escape. They went from house to house, breaking down doors, driving Jews into the streets in their bedclothes, barefoot, into the streets; they searched in attics and cellars. Mothers, in shock, children in their arms, were driven with rifle butts and rubber truncheons to areas where they were herded into groups of fifty and taken to the Jewish Council.

Dr. Schneidscher, the head of the Jewish Council, seeing from his window that the *Aktion* was not proceeding according to the plan outlined earlier by the Germans, began to sob and ran down into the street to reason with the Gestapo. Beaten over the head with a truncheon, he collapsed in the gutter. Council members carried him, unconscious, into the building. Dr. Zausner was then slugged to the ground by the Gestapo for "alerting the Jews" that they were to be taken, with the result that only several hundred were captured. I have it on good authority that Dr. Zausner had done nothing of the sort.

Later in the morning, the Jewish militiamen returned to headquarters blood-spattered, exhausted, and sullen. Their help to the Gestapo notwithstanding, they had been mistreated, roughed up, spat on, and insulted, the Nazis accusing them of not uncovering enough hiding places, of a lack of zeal. As one who watched the bloody spectacle from an attic window in the council headquarters, I can testify that the Nazi complaint was groundless; the Jewish militiamen were not one whit less ferocious than their Aryan masters.

Displeased with taking what they considered a small number of Jews in town, the Nazis, following actions in Turka, Stary Sambor, and Felsztyn, where they rounded up the Jews, returned with their trucks and their machine guns for another try at Sambor.

But now they did not take the trouble to search Jewish dwellings; hand grenades were quicker and more effective. A grenade was thrown inside a house. The police waited until the weapon exploded, then entered. If there was no response, they threw another grenade, then a third. Eventually, the victims emerged from hiding, blood-spattered, in shock from the concussions. Those able to walk were driven to the closest "gathering corner," then taken away in trucks. The sick and infirm, the old and the wounded, were shot on the spot. Several made a futile effort of running away; they too were shot. The murdered, lying in the streets, were eventually dragged away by the Ukrainian militia and thrown in a heap that was growing bigger and bigger.

Agents of the police were not far behind the executioners; they entered the abandoned dwellings and emptied them of all belongings. Senior officers of the Gestapo drove through the streets of the town, checking on the *Aktion*. On occasion, they stopped and emerged from their vehicles to pose for a photograph standing over a mound of dead Jews, like hunters after a safari, smiling proudly over their trophies.

That day, three thousand Jews were herded together and led to their deaths. I saw it. I was a witness. I had been given work to do and was told I would be spared that day. I was safe in the attic for the time being. But what about my family? I could not rest until I learned how they fared. I started down the stairs, intending to make my way home. Outside, I met an acquaintance who told me the dreadful news. They had all been taken, my father, my wife, my brother, and my sister. They had been forced to run at the same pace as the police, who were riding bicycles, urged on by rubber truncheons and whips. Even as I think of it now, sitting here and writing, compiling a record for future generations, my hand trembles, and my eyes film over. I, myself, wonder whether such a thing could happen. Perhaps my mind, affected by what I have seen and experienced, is playing tricks on me.

I say to myself: perhaps you need a doctor. I say to myself: Will people reading my lines believe me? Or will they take me for a madman? Come what may, I must go ahead with my notes.

Returning, momentarily dazed, to council headquarters, I heard Dr. Schneidscher saying something to the effect that all was not lost yet. I stared at him as though he had taken leave of his senses. In my feverish brain, a decision was forming. I would surrender and thus be reunited with my family, even though briefly; we would die together.

It was late in the afternoon as I started toward the sports arena, Korona. I had not gone far before a German policeman stopped me, pointed to two little girls with tear-stained faces and ordered me to take them with me. He would go behind. I addressed the children in Yiddish, held out my hands to them. Their little hands clasped mine as though I were a savior. I could feel in their clasp a trust in me, even as we started toward the arena, where all three of us would die. Suddenly, the blows began to rain down on us and I was running, clutching the hands of the little girls, avoiding their eyes filled with terror and judgment. Near the sports arena, two Ukrainian guards took the children from me, beat them, and carried them off. I never saw them again. The expression in their eyes will remain with me as long as I live.

Driven inside the arena, I stopped to catch my breath and immediately began to look for my family. Several thousand people were herded into the place. The screaming and weeping I had heard in the streets of

Sambor had ceased. I sensed a deep fatigue in the faces of the victims, a resignation. People squatted or stood around, waiting for the inevitable. Only the children wept. A high wooden fence separated us from a large crowd of Ukrainians—men, women, and children who'd been drawn to the arena to watch a new kind of a "spectacle." They seemed to be enjoying themselves immensely, laughing and calling out to us.

"Hey, Moishe, give me your coat! Where you're going, you won't need it!"

"Hey, Malke, give me your shoes! You can walk just as well barefoot when you're dead!"

Suddenly, I caught sight of my family. They stood in a tight little knot on the other side of the arena, as though they would collapse if separated. I started toward them, but police truncheons swung at me, and I was pushed back, reeling. I heard a loud wail, an outcry from a thousand throats, and caught sight of a hearse from the Jewish cemetery entering the sports field. In the next instant, hysteria engulfed the crowd like a tidal wave. My eyes riveted on my family, I called out and gesticulated wildly, trying to attract their attention. My father, finally seeing me, called out weakly, clasped his hands over his head, and pointed in the direction of heaven, as though he meant to convey to me what I well knew, that it was all in the hands of God.

At six in the evening, a new batch of victims, among them members of the Jewish Council and the militia, arrived, driven by the police. So here they were, they who had believed the Gestapo would spare them because of the services they had rendered. I had fully expected this to happen but not so soon.

As dusk fell and heavy clouds marched across the sky and the twenty-first of Av, 5702, on the Jewish calendar was coming to its ignominious end, the Nazis began pushing the throngs to the arena's gates, where they separated us into groups of one hundred and marched us off to the railway station. But I hung back, ignoring the blows until my relatives neared the gate and only ten feet separated me from my wife, who raised her arm and threw some object toward me. A policeman swung at her and at my brother, who tried shielding her. Their faces bleeding, they continued walking toward the exit. It was the last I saw of my wife and my father and sister.

The group to which the police attached me was among the last to leave. We were marched to the last boxcar of an ancient freight train, parked on a siding in a wood. We were shoved into an already crowded car. Inside, pressed tightly together, we heard rain and thunder. Above the cry of the storm, which was like a lamentation, I heard an old man, white-bearded and face emaciated, raise a cry of his own. "Oh, Lord, if it is Your will that we be killed with our wives and children, grant us this wish: kill us old men but not the others. Or let lightning strike us, Lord, and spare us the agony that is in store for us."

The train, pulling fifty boxcars filled with the Jewish population of Sambor and neighboring villages, started for its destination, Janover Camp. It was August 4, 1942.

CHAPTER 6

‒‒‗⟋

# JANOVER CAMP[1]

*All hope abandon*
*Ye who enter here.*

—Dante, *The Divine Comedy*[2]

It was located behind the Lemberg cemeteries, between sand dunes and surrounded by barbed wire, this place of terror and murder. It was near the Kleparów station at the end of Janover Street, and it was there that the bloom of Jewish youth was crushed.

As we approached the camp, the rumors we had heard of it seemed wild indeed. It appeared to be a harmless place, with a handful of houses for the SS officers near the gate, some wooden barracks, and a few small houses and a couple of watchtowers, both inside and outside the gate. Of course, there were guards, but surely this was not the slaughterhouse we had heard it called.

Still, as we came closer, an involuntary shudder passed through me at the site of the double barbed-wire fences. Why were there fences even within the camp, which itself was cut off from the outside world by other fences?

At the entrance, a large sign read, *Zwangsarbeitslager und Polizeiführer* (Forced labor camp and chief of police.)

It did not take long for the full meaning of Janover camp to enter deep into our hearts. We soon discovered that the human being was of no value

1. On Janover (Janowska), see part I, chapter 5, note 2.
2. The epigram "*Lasciate ogni speranza, voi ch'entrate*" comes from canto III, line 9 of Dante Alighieri's *Inferno* as Dante passes through the gate to Hell.

in this godforsaken area. All those transported here had a death sentence pronounced on them. Without their own awareness of it, they were already in the grave. The cross section of humanity here was large. All professions and craftsmen were represented here. There were mechanics, shoemakers, carpenters, tailors, furriers, locksmiths, welders, musicians, and veterinarians. There were also rabbis, lawyers, doctors, poets, druggists, and writers.

The German police, in their deliberate thoroughness, set about wiping out all vestiges of dignity and decency in the inmates. Every Jew's head was shaved, and two yellow rags were affixed to his jacket, one on the front and the other on the back. The back of the jacket was also smeared with a broad stripe from the collar to the bottom of the hem.

The Jews at Janover were forbidden to wear armlets with the Star of David, for it would then have become possible (although the chances were slight) for Jews to escape and mingle with Jews still at "liberty," who had to wear a Star of David. The Janover "insignia" was supposed to frustrate escape. There were non-Jews at Janover too, Polish and Ukrainian criminals who wore red rags, not yellow ones. They were distinguished from the Jews and, at the same time, separated from the Germans.

We were all put to work, some within the campgrounds, others outside. We were organized into brigades that were by no means fixed as to numbers. Some had twenty men, others more than eight hundred. The SS chose an inmate as a foreman and called him "brigadier." The larger brigades had a foreman plus one or two deputies.

The camp leader, Willhaus, was tall and lean, in his thirties, with a head too small for his extremely long neck. His voice was hoarse and always charged with excitement. He was an SS man, an *Obersturmführer*. So was his deputy, Rokita, who was about fifty years of age, medium-sized, and stout.[3] He had a clean-shaven head and an equally clean-shaven face and spoke softly. It was rumored that he had been a ragtime musician before the war. There were several others who made their rank and positions felt.

3. The commandant of the Janowska camp, Gustav Willhaus (1910–1945), and his deputy, Wilhelm Rokita, earned reputations for being especially cruel and bloodthirsty.

One was *Scharführer* Kolanko, who was unable to put together an intelligible sentence in any language, even German. His companion, Schönbach, was a fit companion for him.[4] The rest of the "staff" consisted of unranked SS men.

Each day began typically with the beating of prisoners who failed to awaken by themselves before roll call. There were no bells, no sirens, and no piercing whistles to announce the start of the day. There was no fixed hour for roll call. Our watches had been taken from us long ago. How could we tell time? We worked very hard and slept the sleep of the dead. The cracking of whips began the day. Whips on our flesh tore us from our sleep. Neither the early risers nor those who slept out of doors (there were three thousand places for twelve thousand inmates) escaped the blows.

It did not take long for the barracks to empty once the thirty-five troops pounced on us, swinging their long whips. It was quick for another reason: we never took off our clothes at night.

At the parade grounds, the brigades assembled, and the Jewish foreman of each brigade distributed three ounces of bread per man. Then the roll call began with the group leader announcing the various work chores. Now and again, that camp leader, in his hoarse voice, called to his dog, Arrow, who liked to scamper through the lines of men. As there were many inmates with lice and typhus, the leader did not want his dog to get too close to us.

Near the parade ground was the execution area, where all punishments were meted out. Penalties were meted out for the most minor offenses. If a man pushed forward a bit in the coffee line or was caught with a newspaper, a knife, a lighter, or a pencil, he was committing a crime. If he talked while working, sought shelter in the rain, or smoked a cigarette, he was violating rules. If a prisoner at work bent down for a cucumber peel or picked up a bit of an apple lying on the ground, this too was criminal and called for a punishment of twenty-five or fifty strokes on the bare

4. Adolf Kolanko was Willhaus's second assistant. SS-*Scharführer* Roman Schönbach served at Janowska between 1942 and 1943.

backside. Two SS men administered the beating and delivered their strokes
from opposite sides with short, hard truncheons. Those who gritted their
teeth and remained silent under the blows received the number of blows
intended for them. If a man cried out or tried to cover his backside with
his hands in an instinctive gesture of protection, he was given extra blows.

At times, Jewish "foremen" from the ranks were called on to help hold
down the victims, and if they—in their distaste at the job—did not grip
prisoners as prescribed, they too were beaten. And once or twice a week,
to intimidate the prisoners and keep them in a constant state of fear, they
randomly pulled an inmate from the ranks and shot him on the spot.

I became accustomed to shots ringing out all day long. The Germans
found causes. If an inmate was found to have dirty ears, an unwashed
neck, an unshaven face—these were causes enough. Under the conditions
existing at camp, how could we wash properly? There was one rusty water
pipe in front of the barracks with twelve or so perforations but little pressure. There were thousands of men, there was a long line, and the camp
was on a strict schedule. And even if one rose early enough for the washup,
where was he to obtain a cloth to dry himself?

Every day, during work detail, there was at least one casualty. This was
quite apart from the customary killings—the tests used by the SS men to
weed out the weak and the sick from the Jewish brigades—the beatings,
and the tortures. Every day, when the brigades returned from work, they
brought back dead men. We hauled back the corpses for a reason: the Germans kept a strict count of the prisoners when the columns returned to
camp. In the evenings, the Nazis counted the inmates—the living as well
as the dead—checking their count against the morning roll call. After the
count was over, the SS men walked among the ranks of the inmates and
selected for liquidation those who looked ill, whose shoulders drooped, or
who seemed on the point of collapse. The men were shot and, along with
the corpses, thrown into a ditch.

The "hot roll call" was a daily event. It remains as vivid in my mind
today as it was the first time I witnessed it. As I commit it to paper now,

doubts rise in my mind. Will those reading these lines believe me? Or will their credulity be strained?

It is dark in camp, and the watchtower reflectors focus their sharp beams on the brigades returning from their work and now assembling on the parade grounds. SS men examine the men to check if they are "properly" dressed. The camp officials march about, looking important, and the commanders give sharp orders. The troops, helmeted and armed, stand at stiff attention. There is a raised platform on which the commander moves about, and when he barks, "At ease!" to his men, we become rigid with fear, for it is at this moment that the Nazis will decide how many of us—and which of us—are to die.

For each man who has escaped this day, four prisoners will be killed. This ratio is known to us. There is no mystery about it. It is a terrible moment, and we stand in line, our bodies heavy with fatigue but our minds alert. The men on the stage are the masters of life and death. Twelve thousand of us wait for the word from the Nazi spokesman. The pious Jews among us mouth the *vidui*, the Jewish prayer before death, quietly and slowly to themselves: "*Ashamnu . . . Bogadnu . . . Gozalnu . . .*"[5]

The camp leader, Willhaus, descends and walks between the rows, flanked by SS men. He approaches a Jewish brigade leader and asks, "How many are missing here?"

In a trembling voice, the leader responds, "Two."

Slowly, Willhaus strips his glove off his right hand and barks, "Shoot eight!" And then, in his hoarse, excited voice, he cries out, "Come on! Come on! Quick!"

Eight victims, seized at random, are separated from the ranks and taken. Willhaus approaches the next brigade, where eight more Jews are taken from the ranks. Only the Polish and Ukrainian brigades are left alone.

---

5. The *vidui* is a Jewish prayer, a confession, phrased in the plural, made before dying. The sins are listed alphabetically. The first letters of each word in "*Ashamnu, bogadnu, gozalnu*" ("We have sinned, we have betrayed, we have stolen") correspond to the first three letters of the Hebrew alphabet: alef, bet, and gimel.

The victims are marched to the execution area and lined up in military fashion. Five SS men step forward, march to the back of the victims' formation, lift their rifles, and point them at the Jews. Five shots ring out; the victims drop to the ground, dead. The next group of condemned steps forward, and more shots rend the night air.

Sometimes it goes on like this all evening long. Germans will march, and guns will be fired, and Jews will be killed. Not all die at once. Some die slowly, writhing in agony, like worms in their own blood. At such times, Willhaus approaches the slowly dying man, aims his pistol at the back of his neck, and fires.

The "hot roll call" draws to a close.

A special unit called the "Death Brigade," under the command of Scheftelowitz, lays out the murdered inmates on stretchers and carries them into the valley behind the camp after first undressing them. The dead are tossed into a ditch. The execution area is strewn with sand to absorb the still warm blood.

Among the massed prisoners, not a whimper of protest is heard. Why do we submit passively? How does a handful of men control thousands? The question comes insistently to mind.

Examine the prisoners, if you will. We have been starved, some of us for months. We are emaciated, germ-ridden, barely able to stand. We have been stripped of our dignity. Hope has flown away from us like a frightened bird.

Many of us are psychologically ready for death. If there are those among us who flirt with the notion of rebelling, the barbed-wire enclosures and posted machine guns are sobering reminders. Keep in mind how we live. We have been worn down through lack of sleep. We have been beaten, dragged out of our homes, and our wives and children murdered before our eyes. We have been reduced to existence on a primitive level, our self-confidence destroyed and our instinct for self-preservation trampled on. To what end should a man fight? Death appeared inevitable in any case.

I saw behavior in this camp that is beyond description, involving the inhumanity of man to an extraordinary extent: the suffocating air in

the barracks, the constant hunger, the stomach ailments that developed as
a result of the putrid food, the robberies, the hygienic problems, and the
vermin. When a man died at night, it scarcely excited comment, so cal-
lous had we become to it all. The boundaries between life and death were
wiped away, and at times, the man who remained alive did not even move
away from what had become a corpse.

The Christian prisoners in the camp, hardened criminals who had originally been sentenced to death and were now in for life, were no better off
than the rest of us except that they were not shot—a difference of some
importance but not so major as it might seem to an outsider. The Christians, like the Jews, worked hard and were whipped and tortured. They
too were brought to the execution area, but they survived. If a Christian
became seriously ill, he was sent to the small camp hospital, while the same
illness contracted by a Jew spelled a death sentence. The Christian prisoners enjoyed the privilege of receiving packages from Polish and Ukrainian committees. They were permitted to visit home from time to time;
they could nurse hope of eventually being freed. Who was there to send us
packages that included food and cigarettes and greetings? We had no hope
for release except through death. We could derive comfort knowing that
nobody survived too long in Janover Camp.

~~~

# CHAPTER 7

# CLEAN RAGS
# FOR DIRTY ONES

Every second and third Saturday of the month, we were taken—driven like cattle is closer to the truth—to the Jewish bathing house in Lemberg for showers. Prior to showering, those of us fortunate enough to get inside surrendered our dirty clothes in exchange for laundered ones, keeping only our shoes. This might lead one to assume that we looked forward to the baths, we who were dirty and vermin-ridden. It should have been a welcome occasion, but it was quite the reverse. We dreaded the baths.

Why? To begin with, twelve thousand of us were lined up to be marched to the baths, guarded by SS men and Askaris, soldiers of the renegade General Vlasov, who betrayed the Soviets and joined the Germans several months after the outbreak of the Russo-German war in 1941.[1] In camp, the Askaris were employed as guards, escorting the brigades to work and back. No less cruel than the Germans, they participated as enthusiastically as their masters in the atrocities.

Their bayonets gleaming in the sun, the Askaris led us through Lemberg's deserted streets through an area blocked off earlier, past houses whose doors and windows were shut tight. Pressed closely together, we took care not to step out of line and receive a bullet as reward. Our guards

---

1. Most often used to describe local armies that served European colonial powers in Africa, an *askari* (Swahili for "soldier") here refers to a Soviet soldier who fought against the Soviet Red Army. Andrey Vlasov (1901–1946) was a Red Army general who switched allegiances and led the Russian Liberation Army, which fought under German command. Vlasov was tried and hanged for treason in 1946.

barked their marching orders, their oaths and obscenities. The only other sound was that of thousands of wooden-soled shoes striking the pavement.

As the columns entered the Jewish neighborhood of Lemberg, where we were to bathe, our guards ordered us to sit down. The veterans among us knew better than to dawdle when ordered to do something. We sat down on the sidewalk, on the pavement, in a puddle of water if we were standing in the rain. We were to sit still, not converse, not move, not turn our heads. Sometimes, I sat there for hours, all day and all night, until I felt myself turning to stone. Later, I could barely stand.

The bathhouse was small, consisting of three rooms. Yet there were many thousands of us! Now the fortunate ones among us entered the first room and undressed quickly, leaving all our clothes in a heap and taking only our shoes, coffee cups, and haversacks. In the second room, we lined up for the shower, waiting our turn, clutching our shoes.

Finally, I am under the shower, hot water coursing down my body, which is decorated with welts from whip-lashings. I live for the moment. What a delight to feel the hot water washing away the dirt and fatigue! If only I did not have to hold on to my shoes, which are getting wet!

In the third room, fresh underwear and clothing were issued by officials of the Lemberg Jewish Council; we received a pair of trousers, a jacket, and a shirt. The veterans among us did not mind exchanging old dirty clothes for old clean clothes. But for some, the newcomers, it was a comedown; they had yielded up decent clothing for disinfected rags. They were clean, but they were rags, and when one put them on, one looked like everyone else, like a Janover Camp inmate.

The prisoners who slept outside the barracks had kept free of vermin, but now, as they put on clean clothes, they picked up lice. The disinfectant did not kill the lice but only narcotized them. As soon as they came in contact with a human body, they came alive once more.

As we left the third room, Jewish women, members of the Lemberg Jewish Council, stood near long tables and served us a thick soup with bread. Each prisoner received a full portion of soup and a quarter of bread. It was this combination of events: the bath, the clean clothes, the soup and the bread, and a kindly smile and a good word from fellow human beings that made us—for a short spell—seem alive again. One prayed more for the friendliness and the smiles than for the food.

So far, this bathing experience, as described, went off without a hitch. Why, then, did we dread it?

Weigh the situation for a moment. Fifty men at a time entered the small rooms, and it took them nearly a half hour to take their baths or showers. The washing time was fixed from Saturday evening until Monday morning. If, within these thirty-two hours, one hundred men were bathed in an hour, then between four and five thousand could be processed. The remaining seven to eight thousand remained outside, squatting on the pavement for a day and a half, without moving, without food. Monday morning—dirty, unwashed, stiff in the joints, and hungry—these seven to eight thousand men, along with the more fortunate who had showered, were marched to their jobs by the Askaris. On the way back, along the deserted streets of Lemberg—lively, lovely Lemberg of my youth—my ears were filled with the clop-clopping of wooden soles on pavement and the occasional rifle shots of the Askaris, finishing off an inmate who had collapsed on the street from typhus or one with a weak heart, weakened further by the steaming heat of the shower, who tottered and fell. The rifle shots accompanied us all the way to the camp. Dead men were left lying along the road.

The angel of death lurked everywhere. I expected the angel to brush me with its wings. It was a miracle that I was still alive after a full month in camp. After four weeks, one was an old-timer who watched his friends and acquaintances being led away, waiting for his turn. At every roll call, friends were taken to the execution area. Following the roll call, I made my way to the spot where the killings had taken place and looked at the contorted and unrecognizable faces of my friends before they were carried away to the valley to be dumped in the pit.

It was now late autumn 1942. The Germans had swept through the towns of Galicia, driving before them thousands of new inmates to camps like Janover.

Over a period of two weeks, the Nazis drove fifty thousand Jews out of the town of Lemberg. Janover was the major collecting point of the Lemberg Jews. We saw the thousands pouring in—men, women, and children—lined up for execution or work. Families were separated; children were torn away from their mothers, who were beaten with truncheons and tortured as they cried for their children. It was not a new story, but this time we were direct observers, and the pain was nearly as great as if we were victims. In a sense, we were.

As I sit and write these lines, my flesh creeps recalling what happened a year ago. A year! Sometimes it seems to be a long time. And at other moments, it seems to me that what happened twelve months ago has just been experienced. My mind flies back to the past, one year ago.

We are at roll call, and the camp commander and his SS staff are approaching our brigade to select prisoners for execution. Suddenly, the commander seems to be pointing his finger at me, and he says, "Come on!" I am convinced that he means me. My time has come. I am neither excited nor upset. I am indifferent. But no, he doesn't mean me. He is pointing to some unfortunate behind me. Once again, his finger is pointed at me, and I am certain that I am being selected. Yet again I am wrong. Once more, it is another. Meanwhile, the commander steps back for an instant, and we have reason to believe the danger is over for the time being. But he changes his mind, comes back, and stands in front of me, his malevolent gaze on me. But he chooses another victim—three more victims. But I am still here.

The prisoners are marched to the execution area, murmuring "Shema Yisrael" on the way.[2] We hear the rifle shots. They are dead. I feel a deep compassion for the innocent dead but no fear. I have lost all my dear ones; I have nobody in the world. I am prepared to die.

---

2. The prayer "Shema Yisrael" ("Hear, O Israel") affirms one's faith in God. The prayer's name comes from Deuteronomy 6:4 ("Hear, O Israel: The Lord our God, the Lord is one.") It is said twice daily, at morning and at night, and, if possible, before death.

Nor was I an exception. For thousands of us in Janover Camp—fed two slices of bread daily, driven like animals to work and back, beaten and tortured—was there anything to look forward to but death? There was escape, but to what end? Where would one go? What would one do? I was reared with the notion that Jews can be depended on to come to the aid of their brethren. But the news filtering through to us, that inmates escaping from Janover were unable to find shelter among their fellow Jews in the Lemberg ghetto, put this theory to a severe test. The notion of escaping receded in my mind with each passing day.

Janover, surrounded by barbed wire, was an insulated world. We did not know what was going on outside; newspapers never reached us. We were nourished on rumors, most of them bad. The Germans were plunging further into Russia. We longed to hear about the second front opening in the West. Perhaps the Allied invasion had already begun? We had no way of knowing. A second front would bring new hope to the Jews in the ghettos, but I doubted that we in the death camps could be saved. It was too late for us; we could not survive until the Allied armies reached us in Lemberg. But it was cheering to contemplate that others out there, beyond the barbed wire, could be saved.

I remember talking to an inmate who had survived Dachau for two years before they transferred him to Janover.[3] "Even that hell, Dachau, is better than Janover," he told me. "Do you know of anyone who has survived this camp for two years? This place can break a man in two weeks!"

I remember another inmate, Dr. Schorr, a book-loving man who at one time possessed a flourishing medical practice in Sambor, taking me aside on a rock pile after our guards had gone berserk and shot several inmates. "The Germans will lose the war!" Dr. Schorr declared, as though this extraordinary thought had just occurred to him. "They'll lose even if they win more battles! And do you know why? They are no longer human!

3. The Dachau concentration camp outside of Munich, Germany, was the first concentration camp of the Germans' vast network of camps. It became a camp for political prisoners in March 1933.

What they are doing to us here is beyond sadism. They have lost their heads! Their demise is not far off! Mark my words!"

"But how long will that take?" I wanted to know. Even if one survived physically to see the day of German defeat, would the mind hold out? So many of the inmates in camp had been driven insane. Best able to retain their sanity were pious Jews, who stubbornly maintained faith in the face of the Nazi onslaught. "God will help," they said. "We do not understand Him. But he will help." Even when they were selected for execution in the daily roll calls, they prayed, reciting the *vidui*[4] on the way to the valley to be hanged or shot.

Despair raged like an epidemic among the rest of us, among the doctors, lawyers, musicians, and engineers—the educated, in other words. But the pious Jew put on his tefillin[5] when possible and recited his morning prayers, then went out to face the horrors of the day.

The pious Jews tried observing holidays, especially the major ones. On the first day of Rosh Hashanah 5703, we were marched to the bathing area in Lemberg. That night, unable to get inside, we were kept on the streets, awaiting our turn. Toward dawn, a large number in the crowd of squatting prisoners, myself among them, took out a little prayer book and greeted the incoming Rosh Hashanah in the traditional manner. On Yom Kippur, taking our lives in our hands, we met secretly in a loft for Kol Nidre.[6] There were twenty of us, including a rabbi who surprised us by coming with a prayer shawl—a miracle in itself—and conducting the service, albeit in a tearful voice.

We closed our eyes and saw the prayer houses in our native towns, overflowing with people. The Kol Nidre mood seized us even here, in a pathetic little loft, hidden from the prying eyes of the SS men. The words took on their deepest meanings, and we wondered how many of us would be alive

4. See part I, chapter 6, note 5.
5. Tefillin ("phylacteries") are a set of small black leather boxes that observant Jews wear on their foreheads and arms during morning prayers. They contain scrolls with Torah passages, including the Shema (See part I, chapter 7, note 2).
6. Kol Nidre ("all vows") is a declaration recited on the eve of Yom Kippur, the annual Jewish Day of Atonement. It ceremonially annuls all vows and oaths made before God.

eight days hence. But we banished these dark thoughts and carried on with
our prayers to God. We had once again participated in an immortal Jewish
service at what was, to us, a moment of utter misery for the Jewish people
as a collective entity.[7]

I recall periods of darkest despair when the light of hope appeared
briefly. It happened the day we were marched to move sand from one hill
to another. There were more than ten thousand of us but only two hundred wheelbarrows and twenty-five spades. Woe to those who were seen
without either spade or wheelbarrow. The inmates were assaulted with
truncheons; many were shot down.

Suddenly we heard the camp siren bellowing like a wounded boar.
"Back to the barracks!" the SS men cried, trying to herd us into some
semblance of formation, then fleeing, leaving us to shift for ourselves. We
heard the roar of engines and turned our faces to the sky. "Allied planes!"
one of the inmates shouted, his voice filled with exaltation. "Our planes!"

We lost our heads, began to dance in the sand and wave to the sky raiders. I gesticulated wildly, shouting, "Come down! Bomb us! Obliterate

7. [Thorne's note:] Quite coincidentally, I met this rabbi, who survived the war, in the
United States. He is Rabbi Israel Spira, the rabbi of Bluzhov, known by this title to his
many followers in Brooklyn, New York. How was it possible for a man to live through
his experiences in Janover Camp? The story is almost unbelievable. And this is it: When
he was a youngster of about seven or eight, his parents, who lived in a small Galician
town, took him along with them on vacation in Bad Kissingen, Germany. He played
there with many German children, including the son of the owner of the house in
which they were staying. More than thirty years passed, and the rabbi was now in
Janover Camp. He looked closely at one of the German SS men and had the impression
that the German was the boy with whom he had played, the son of the owners of the
house in which he and his parents vacationed. The rabbi tried to approach the SS man
and talk to him and finally succeeded when the German was alone. The rabbi asked
him whether his name was "thus and so" and whether he came from Bad Kissingen. At
first, the German could scarcely credit his ears but eventually realized that the rabbi was
his boyhood companion. And he helped the rabbi escape from the camp into the ghetto
of Lemberg. From there, the rabbi was shipped to many other camps and ghettos until
he finally arrived in Bergen-Belsen. When the American Army closed in, the SS men
packed about 2,800 Jews—men, women, and children—into wagons and drove them
off to be executed. On the way, the rabbi managed to contact the head of the German
police and promised him that if he helped save the Jews, he, the rabbi, would speak up
on his behalf to the Americans and point out that he had saved 2,800 Jews. The police
chief, realizing that the Americans would soon break through, agreed to the arrange-
ment. A few hours later, the Americans arrived, and the Jews were saved.

Janover!" I did not stop to consider that, if the camp were to be obliterated, I would be a casualty. But I was prepared to strike that bargain. To turn Janover to rubble was my first priority; what happened to me was of no consequence. All my dear ones dead; I felt like a leftover, guilty for having survived while the others perished.

Had I known at the time that my brother, David, was alive—a thing I only found out several days later—I would have been less cavalier about inviting the Allied planes to drop their bombs on me.

I found out about my brother from Aron Halberstam, who slipped me a piece of paper one morning. "It is from your brother!" he said.[8]

"He's alive?" I said, incredulous.

"The note is from him," Halberstam said.

I stuffed the paper in my pocket and waited impatiently for an opportunity to read it without being detected.

"They have killed everybody," my brother wrote. "I am the only survivor. They did not kill me; they saved me for a work detail. I suppose, that so long as I have the strength to use a pick and shovel, they will let me live. Can I dare hope for the day when we will be reunited, my brother?"

I was not alone. Once again, I yearned to live.

8. The Halberstams were a prominent Hasidic dynasty from Sandz (Polish: *Nowy Sącz*) founded in the mid-nineteenth century by Aryeh Leib Halberstam (1797/99–1876). Many of the dynasty's offshoots and subdynasties have active communities today. See also part II, chapter 3, note 5.

CHAPTER 8

# EVEN THE DEAD
# ARE NOT IMMUNE

The Germans followed a policy of crushing our spirits before they took our lives, robbing us of our last vestiges of dignity and self-worth and trampling us into docile nonpersons. But none of the blows rained on us humiliated me as much as being assigned to a work detail at the Jewish cemetery near Lemberg to smash the gravestones and monuments—some of them centuries old—and erase every vestige of Judaism. Marching to the cemetery, carrying spade and pick, my mind was in turmoil. I became obsessed with the notion of escaping. But how? Where would I hide? On more than one occasion, while desecrating a tombstone with a large pick, I toyed with the idea of killing a Nazi guard when he briefly turned his back on me. I could not sleep. Each time I raised a pick at a marble or granite tomb of some holy rabbi many years dead, I recited kaddish, calling out the name of the dead, asking forgiveness for disturbing his rest. "*El Malei Rachamim*," I cried. The cry, on the lips of all Jews in our detail, was heard throughout the day.[1]

Adolph, a *Volksdeutscher*[2] in charge of our detail, carried a whip in one hand and a wooden club in the other. He roamed the cemetery all day long, sometimes pouncing on us, bellowing, "No sentiment! No sentiment! This

1. Kaddish and "El Malei Rachamim" are both Jewish prayers of mourning and remembrance. The latter is typically recited at the graveside during burial.
2. The term *volksdeutsch* was used to describe ethnic Germans living beyond the national boundaries of Germany. Before World War II, an estimated thirty million ethnic Germans lived in Central and Eastern Europe, mostly in Ukraine, Poland, Romania, and the Baltic region.

is not a cemetery; it's a quarry!" He set one prisoner against another, ordering us to flog our brothers.

There was no avoiding the fiend's club and whip; there was no hiding from the work of desecration. Every day, the cemetery appeared more and more like a quarry. One morning, I was asked to level the tombstone of the great *Gaon*, Rabbi Joseph Saul Nathansohn—the illustrious rabbi of Lemberg and author of the responsa *Sho'el u-Meshiv*, known to those who studied the Talmud.[3] That morning, I reached the lowest depth of despair, vowing to escape at the first favorable opportunity. As I stood over the grave of the holy man, reciting kaddish, pleading for forgiveness, I became aware of someone nearby. It was not Adolph; I turned and recognized the cemetery watchman, a small man, a Jew, with a pair of gentle eyes. He nodded a greeting. I nodded gratefully in return. "I see you have on a good suit," he said barely above a whisper.

I said absently, "Yes. I received it from my brother," wondering why he'd brought it up.

"The reason I mention it," the watchman said, "Saturday, you will be taken to the baths. They'll take your nice suit and give you some clean rags in return. You've been here a long time and know what I'm saying."

"Of course I know," I said, lowering the heavy pick.

"If you want to avoid it," he suggested, "why not exchange your clothes for rags now instead of during the bathing period and get some money for them."

I readily agreed to the transaction, and it was thus we started to be friends.

It was a brief friendship. The watchman, whose name I never learned—we called him "The Shammes"—lived in a small room with his wife and two daughters near the cemetery gate.[4] All four of them were gentle

---

3. *Gaon* is an honorific title used to acknowledge those with great knowledge of the Torah. From 1857 until 1875, Rabbi Joseph Saul Nathansohn (1808–1875) was the rabbi of Lemberg. Nathansohn's most important work was a responsa, a legal commentary on the Talmud (Jewish law), called *Sho'el u-Meshiv*.
4. A shammes is the caretaker or sexton of a synagogue.

and soft-spoken, and when they were together, it was a pleasure to listen to their conversation, which in my ears, accustomed to the bellowing of Nazi guards, sounded like birdsong. I treasured the brief moments I spent in that room, where the watchman's wife ran a little clandestine lunchroom, selling a bowl of soup for five złotys to the inmates who worked on the cemetery detail. Her risk selling to us was as great as ours buying from her. But I took my chances to taste a little soup fit for human consumption and to spend a few precious moments with such a warmhearted family.

The first time I entered the watchman's dwelling and saw my face in a mirror, I was frightened by the sunken-faced image and the bloodshot eyes staring back at me. I could scarcely recognize myself, so radically had I changed.

It felt strange to sit at a table, to hold a spoon in my hand, to eat off of a plate. I had nearly forgotten how it felt to be a human being.

I ran to the watchman's shack whenever the opportunity presented itself. He kept me abreast of the world's news. I learned from him that the Americans had tried but failed to make a landing at Dieppe.[5] "But they'll make it next time," he assured me. "The Allies are determined to finish off the Germans," he said, sounding like an authority. Eager to grasp at any straw, I listened intently and muttered, "Amen."

One day, I confided to my friend that I was obsessed with the notion of escaping, that I could not go on desecrating holy gravestones and monuments, and that I would do something desperate unless there was some sudden change. I told him that my brother was sending me frantic notes, pleading with me to attempt escape. But I was understandably reluctant, having in mind the punishment meted out to those who'd been caught attempting escape. I wrote back to my brother, suggesting that he go from Sambor to Drohobycz, because the authorities knew I came from Sambor and would look for me there if I escaped from the camp.

5. On August 19, 1942, Allied forces assaulted the German-occupied port of Dieppe in northern France. The raid failed spectacularly and resulted in massive Allied casualties.

I told all this to the watchman. "I think I can be of help to you," he said. He informed me that in addition to his duties as a watchman, he served as a gravedigger and helped transport dead Jews from Lemberg to the cemetery. Even though the cemetery was in the process of being destroyed, new corpses were brought to it from the ghetto and buried without headstones or other identification. In addition, when Jewish inmates from Janover Camp were murdered during their bathing period, he was entrusted with bringing them to the cemetery for burial.

"I travel back and forth, you see," he informed me. "I don't make a habit of helping people escape; in all the months, I've tried it only two times. But I'll help you, friend."

It could be attempted only during the bathing period, he explained to me. He would drive his cart to the bathing house to pick up the dead who had been shot during the bathing period. With luck, one could spirit a live prisoner into the cart, treating him as though he were a corpse. "I'll discuss this with my assistant, Jonah," he promised me.

Several days later, I learned that my brother had fled Sambor to Drohobycz in the dead of night, arriving safely at his destination.

On Friday of that eventful week, the watchman informed me that the Jewish Council of Lemberg had been alerted to prepare the baths for the following day. "Do you want to try it then?" he asked me.

Although full of qualms, I said, "Yes, I'll do what you say. I'll see you tomorrow."

The next day, Saturday, with threatening clouds marching overhead, my pulse racing wildly, and my knees shaking as I stood over a headstone, shoveling soil away from its base, I saw the watchman coming toward me. His face appeared calm. "I brought you a bowl of soup," he said. We sat down, surrounded by gravestones, and he outlined to me our plan for escape. He told me where to go after we'd been marched to Lemberg, on what street corner to wait for him and his cart. I was to go limp when he arrived, lie on the ground, and make-believe I was dead when he lifted me and tossed me into the cart. If the suggested corner seemed impractical, he gave me an alternate one. This was to take place the following Monday, after the prisoners had been kept in front of the bathhouse a couple of days, too tired to observe what was going on around them.

If my group was led to the bathing rooms before Monday, I was to try to delay my entry by falling back to the end of the line. I hoped that I would manage to remain outside until the appointed hour.

The watchman shook my hand and said fervently, "Good luck."

At once, I was a bit more confident and believed that, with the help of God, all would go well.

That same evening, after the day's work, we assembled on the parade grounds of the camp. Oddly enough, we were not called and made ready for bathing. This meant there would be no bathing for us this week. As it had rained during the day and was wet everywhere, the inmates were pleased by the delay.

Following the roll call, I returned to the barracks with a fellow named Grob, who came from the town of Rzeszów. It was thanks to Grob that I was living in this barracks in the first place. The barracks leader, a well-known thief from Lemberg, was a friend of Grob's, and through Grob's good offices, I was permitted into this barracks. For some days now, I had noticed that Grob was not well. His complexion had changed, and when he slept, his breath came fast and hot. He generally rolled himself up in his jacket, which he used as a pillow; he seemed always to be cold, although it was very warm in the barracks.

Prisoners generally kept their indispositions to themselves; it was common for the Nazis to kill prisoners who were suspected of being ill. Even Grob, who must have known I would not report him, dared not tell me that he had typhus. He was afraid to utter a word. I left him alone, observing his pale, drawn face and feverish eyes. "I'm glad there's no bathing," he said. I well understood why he was pleased. Had he gone bathing, he could not have escaped the peering eyes of the Germans who would have killed him.

Finally, I slept. And then, as though it were a nightmare, I felt hundreds of pairs of wooden shoes stamping over me. I thought I heard shooting. I woke up with a start. It was no dream. SS men were storming through the barracks, striking out with their whips and clubs. The prisoners jumped off their beds, rushing about wildly.

I heard screams and the words "Roll call!"

"Let's not leave by the door!" Grob cried. "Let's go by the window and avoid their whips!"

Outside, the skies opened, and a heavy rain came pouring down, buffeted by a strong wind. We could scarcely make headway, bumping against one another, slipping in the mud. With strenuous effort, we finally reached the area where our brigade usually fell in. Some of us stood there numb, trembling in the cold. Others huddled together, seeking protection against the wind and rain.

Could this be morning roll call? It seemed to me that evening roll call had taken place not long ago. Rumors began flying through our ranks. "We're all going to be executed!" someone said. The powerful searchlight illuminated the area, turning night into day. We remained in the rain several hours, soaked to the bone. Finally, we heard a command, "East Station Brigade, march!" One brigade after another left the area, heading toward the exit gates.

We marched toward the city to the baths. "What will become of Grob?" I thought. Grob could barely walk. I realized that what lay ahead would mean death for him: we would have to wait more than thirty hours in the now-flooded streets where narrow lanes used to be. "Sit down!" an SS man barked, and at the familiar command, we squatted in the cold water.

In spite of the terrible night and the discomfort, I remembered my arrangements with the watchman, and I moved toward the corner we'd agreed on. But I sat and waited . . . and waited . . . and waited, until the day and the night had passed. But the cart did not come by.

On Monday morning, I saw the watchman again at the cemetery, and he signaled to me what I already knew: that the cart had not come. At noon, when I had my soup in his one-room dwelling, he told me that he had not gone out at all because of the miserable weather and because he had feared the violence of the SS men and the Askaris, their native helpers. He assured me that next time the plan would meet with success; he hoped that God would preserve me until then. Two weeks was a long time to wait, as we both well knew. To survive two weeks in Janover Camp was a great achievement; I would need the protection of God, who had preserved me until now. Poor Shammes. He had no way of knowing that God would leave his side in but a few days.

Some days later—it was difficult to keep track in the camp—I waited impatiently for noon, when I would go to the watchman's shack. Suddenly, a handful of prisoners came running up to us; then they ran back to the cemetery. Apparently, something had happened in the watchman's dwelling, but no one was quite certain what.

In the next instant, we heard the gunfire coming from the direction of the watchman's shack. Later in the day, we learned what had happened. Willhaus, the camp commander, had burst into the watchman's shack soon after noon and found two inmates eating at the table. He shot them both, then turned his gun on the watchman's wife and one of his daughters. The other daughter managed to escape through the window. Nobody knew what had happened to the watchman.

We learned something else: that Adolph, the German cemetery supervisor—our boss who, when angry, foamed at the mouth like a mad dog—had been threatened by Willhaus with being sent to the Russian front for his lapse. At that, Adolph fell on his knees to beg for mercy. All afternoon, he sat stolidly, like an idiot, on one of the graves, his head between his hands, staring into space. Before the day's end, though, he pulled himself together, waved his whip in our direction and cried; "I'll get even with you, Jews!"

Returning to camp, I was greeted by a sight that took my breath away. I saw my friend, the watchman, bound to the punishing pole, being tortured. His face, ripped by the whip strokes, was covered with blood. As I passed him, his eyes caught me, and he murmured; "I am in great pain, my friend, in great pain."

Willhaus appeared on the platform, calling out victims, men to be executed, in a hoarse voice. Soon, the whole execution area was covered with blood. But he continued calling out more names, and more shots rang out. I could not recall such a bloody roll call. Finally, exhausted, mopping his face with a handkerchief, Willhaus ordered the killing to stop, whereupon he began to harangue us. The executions, he declared, were due to the discovery of several prisoners in the cemetery watchman's dwelling. "A lesson will be taught to you! We, Germans, do not need you, Jews! We have enough Aryans to do our work—Poles, Ukrainians, Russians, Czechs, and Serbs. We have Greeks, Frenchmen, Dutchmen, and Belgians. If you Jews want to survive, even for a short time, you'd better obey camp rules!" He continued in the same vein, his voice rising to a high hysterical pitch, reminding me of Hitler's outbursts that I'd heard on the radio in the late 1930s. It had never occurred to me then that this madman would someday destroy my world. The imitation Hitler on the platform was trembling with rage, but after the carnage, his verbal blasts came as an anticlimax.

Concluding his tirade, he ordered that every brigade leader working in the cemetery receive fifty strokes and that the Jewish policemen be demoted to "common prisoners."

The counting of the brigades was then started, which usually meant the end of the shooting. This time, however, men were killed even as they counted. One prisoner, a little bearded man, accidentally called out his neighbor's number instead of his own. He was ordered to leave the brigade and stand near the kitchen wall and count to the number sixteen, sixteen times. Trembling with fear yet relieved to have come through alive, he started counting. Facing the wall, he recited the number, then turned around, as though expecting a bullet. Reaching sixteen, he turned around to rejoin his group. Just then, Rokita pulled his gun and fired. As the bearded prisoner lay writhing on the ground, Rokita shot him again.

That night, I could not sleep. From the window near my cot, I stared at the cemetery watchman, still fastened by wire to the post, trying to move. The wire had cut into his flesh, and his face had turned black. His eyes were large with pain and filled with blood. There was dirty foam dribbling from his mouth. His lips moved convulsively. He seemed to want to speak but was unable to. The upper part of his body was naked, and a few hours later, he was hanged from the gallows. He wore only trousers, and his tongue popped out of his mouth. His body swung in the wind. He had finally died; it was a relief for him. But the cemetery was now a real cemetery to me. I had lost my friend, as he had lost his life.

That autumn, it rained without cease. The air was wet and cold, and the earth was soaked. It did not take long before typhus began to spread. The prisoners, weakened and sick, were quickly infected. More than two-thirds of the camp's inmates were struck down by the disease. Every morning, working groups of men carried out the dead bodies of those who had succumbed during the night, placing them in front of the barracks so that they could be reported as dead during the roll call.

At about this time, I too became ill. I grew weak and rapidly lost strength. The hammer slipped from my grasp, and I fainted.

When I recovered, I found myself lying between two graves, out of sight of the other workers. Apparently, I had been placed there by my fellow workers, who intended to carry me back to the camp in the evening as another dead prisoner.

I attempted to stand on my feet and, after great effort, finally managed to drag myself back to the corps to return to work. If the guard saw that I was too weak to do my work, he would report me to the authorities, and I would be shot in the evening.

My friend, Dr. Schorr, examined me on the spot, and said I had typhus. The men would report me, and as the disease was widespread, the fact that I was sick alarmed nobody. Some sixty in our brigade were ill with typhus, and the brigade leader told me he would do all he could to cover for me. That night, while lying on my cot, I began to tremble violently. Grob, who lay near me, soon became aware of my condition and whispered to me that he himself had contracted the fever four weeks earlier. He instructed me how to comport myself when I left the camp with the other workers.

He told me about his pink painting stone, which he had obtained from his sister in the Lemberg ghetto. With this stone, one could paint one's cheeks after washing, making it difficult for the SS to notice how pale the victim was. While helping me, Grob said, "Don't tell this to anyone. It must be kept secret. If everybody learns this trick, the camp will be full of people with painted cheeks, and we'll all be caught." That same night, Dr. Schorr and another friend from Sambor, Dr. Reich, visited me at my barracks and told me that, as they had no medicine for me, I must develop a strong will to live if I wanted to survive.

A week later, I received from my brother a Russian coat lined with cotton wool, called a *fufaika*, and a pair of shoes. My trembling stopped, and my fever vanished. Once again, I was comparatively healthy.

I did have the will to live.

Autumn brought with it evil tidings. A massive deportation called "October Action" was undertaken by the Germans. Freight trains filled with Jews rolled day and night through Lemberg in the direction of Żółkiew— Rawa-Ruska. The people in the boxcars called out to us, desiring to learn where they were going and whether we could help them. But what could we do but shrug impotently? We were as ignorant as they about the ultimate destination of the transports. On occasion, someone jumped out of a boxcar; sometimes, whole families attempted it, jumping with their children, often without clothes. When apprehended, they were shot.

Each day, we picked up information about the evacuees: they were being transported to ghettos recently established by the Germans in every town in Poland. Several weeks later, I met a woman who had escaped, jumping to safety from one of the boxcars. She had wandered around the countryside without any clothes for three weeks and had found her husband in Drohobycz.

In August 1942, something new had been added to the armband of the ghetto Jew. A red letter *A* had been embroidered into the emblem of the Star of David, to signify that the wearer ranked as a worker.[6] The number of the person's working certificate was fixed behind the star, which also contained the German police seal. A person wearing the armband was

---

6. The *A* stood for *Arbeiter*, German for "worker."

reasonably immune from attack, as it was issued only to those Jews who worked in German establishments. Inhabitants of the ghetto who were not yet assigned to a job cast about desperately for work. Brokers, including both Jews and non-Jews, offered bands for sale. Many people sold their last possessions to acquire one.

But now, in October, Jews with bands as well as those without were hustled into boxcars and sent away to be killed.

# CHAPTER 9

# ESCAPE TO THE LEMBERG GHETTO

Jonah, the watchman's assistant, was now promoted to the full-fledged watchman of the cemetery. The hollows of his face filled out, he stood in the doorway of his one-room dwelling in the cemetery and regarded me. I asked, "Jonah, can we do something?" He replied suspiciously, "If you're thinking of escaping now, forget about it! It's too dangerous. I won't take a chance."

"I offer you twenty dollars, Jonah," I said.

"Do you think I'll make my wife a widow and my children orphans for a dog's price?" he demanded.

I offered him fifty dollars.

He looked at me challengingly and said, "Let me see the money!"

I led him to a remote corner of the cemetery, removed one of my shoes, and took out several American money notes that my brother had sent to me.

I gave him ten dollars in advance, which he hid quickly in his pocket. Then he said, "This is what I can do for you. Sunday night, when I pick up the dead near the bathhouse, I can pick you up too and bring you to the cemetery. Afterward, you'll have to shift for yourself. And it won't be easy. If you try to make it to Lemberg without identity papers, the Germans or the Ukrainian militia will get you. And even if you manage to make it to the Lemberg ghetto alive, how will you get inside? And even if you slip in, who will risk his life to hide you?"

"I've thought about it all," I said to Jonah. Actually, I'd thought only about escaping. I had no idea how to go about evading the Germans and Ukrainians or how I would get into the Lemberg ghetto. But I was determined to try it. "Whatever happens, I won't betray you," I said.

On Saturday morning, it was made known to us that we would be taken to the bathhouse that evening.

More than a full day has passed. I am on a street corner a short distance from the bathhouse, sitting and waiting. My bones are stiff. It has taken me twenty-four hours—Saturday night to Sunday night—to reach this corner. I am wearing a cap. I hope Jonah recognizes me. I am supposed to be lying down. When Jonah catches sight of me, he will pick me up as though I were dead and toss me on the cart. Jonah is not a big man, and I am not a small one; though I've lost a lot of weight, I'm still fairly husky. How will he manage it? Fortunately, the late October sun was warm the entire day, and I'm not uncomfortable. Had it rained, I would be miserable.

Jonah has passed here several times with his cart, but he has not recognized me.

It has been a quiet night. The SS men are walking about with grim faces. They have heard that the Germans are being driven from Stalingrad. The camp inmates who are sitting around me are tired and weak. We haven't been given any bread since Saturday morning. It is now Sunday night. We are all beginning to feel wretched; if we do not wash tonight, we will be marched to work from here tomorrow morning at six.

It must be after midnight already.

I hear the rolling of wheels. My heart begins to pound.

Cautiously, I look around me. There are no SS men around. I lie motionless. The carriage stops near me, and two men approach. I close my eyes, not daring to breathe. Strong hands lift me by my arms and legs. I let my head hang limply. There is a muttered command, and I am thrown into the cart, tossed on dead bodies. The cart cover closes over me, and the wheels roll on. I remember my instruction and keep my eyes shut, for the SS men usually stop the vehicle, examine the corpses, and scatter a few shots into the bodies. I think of what awaits me if I am recaptured. I recall the poor watchman. My flesh creeps.

At length, the rattling of the cart ceases. We have left the narrow streets behind us, and in fifteen minutes, we are in the cemetery. Meanwhile, I am curious to know how many bodies are in the cart with me. I let my hands move about. I feel one cold body, but another is still warm. Maybe he is still alive, I think. Carefully, I turn in his direction, and I speak in a low voice. "Are you alive? You have nothing to be afraid of. Are you living?" There is no answer. Loneliness grips me.

How pleased I would be if he were alive! We could have helped each other, for as yet, I have no real plan of escape. How will I manage to do it? My thoughts are interrupted as I become aware that the cart has stopped.

Jonah cracks his whip as a signal that we have arrived at the cemetery, our destination. From here on, I am on my own. I get off the cart. Jonah approaches me. I give him the forty dollars I owe.

"Where are you off to now?" Jonah asks.

"To the Lemberg ghetto," I reply with more assurance than I possess.

He offers me a Hungarian cigarette. I ask him if he can refer me to someone in the ghetto. He pretends not to know anyone there, the reason being, I think, that he is afraid I will be indiscreet and tell how much money I've given him. After all, fifty American dollars is two thousand złotys, a fortune!

At five in the morning, armed with a spade so that I may be taken for a street worker and the Jewish armband that Jonah has obtained for me on my jacket, I leave the cemetery.

I am no stranger to Lemberg. As a youth, I studied there and made many friends. I might just be fortunate enough to meet up with old friends willing to hide me.

As I leave the cemetery and enter an open field, I hesitate for an instant, trying to get my bearings. Suddenly I hear the barking of dogs. Dawn begins to break. I start toward the town and reach Rappaport Street, which is near the Jewish hospital.

As I look about me and see the familiar landmarks, warm sentiments rise in my heart; I spent the happiest days of my youth here as a member of the Zionist group called Tikvat Zion.[1] The religious Zionists were particularly active in Lemberg. One of the outstanding leaders of the religious Zionist group was Dr. Simon Federbusch, the Hebrew scholar.[2] Dr. Federbusch, who left a deep impression on us, was another reason for my love of Lemberg.

I pass Rappaport Street and enter the Zamarstynów district, where the Jewish ghetto is situated.[3]

I see scores of people wearing armbands, rushing to work. I walk on, spade on my shoulders, looking to neither the left nor the right. Finally, entering the ghetto gate, I feel safe for the moment.

As I write, I recall that seven months after I smuggled myself into the Lemberg ghetto, I heard that Jonah had been caught helping other Jews escape and hanged.

1. The group's name is Hebrew for "hope of Zion."
2. Simon Federbusch (1892–1969) was a prominent rabbi, scholar, and Zionist who, between the World Wars, had been a member of the Sejm (the Polish parliament). He moved to Finland in 1930 and to New York in 1940, where he continued his work as a rabbi and as an advocate for the Zionist cause.
3. The Germans established a ghetto in the Zamarstynów district in the northern part of Lemberg in November 1941 and liquidated it in June 1943. At its peak, the ghetto held more than 120,000 people, most of whom were murdered in Bełżec or Janowska or in mass shootings.

# CHAPTER 10

# IN THE GHETTO

Prior to the German invasion of Poland in 1939, more than one hundred thousand Jews lived in Lemberg. During the Soviet occupation, the Jewish population increased by fifty thousand.[1] In 1941, when the Germans gained control of the city, persecution of the Jews began, with three pogroms in the first few weeks.[2] As usual, the Ukrainians and the Poles played an active role in the persecutions in which thousands of Jews were killed, among them the famous Hasidic rabbi of Bobov, Ben Zion Halberstam, who had many thousands of followers in Poland and beyond its borders.[3] Also killed in the actions were Rabbi Aaron Levin of Rzeszów, a leader in the Agudath Israel[4] in Poland; his brother, Yechezkel Lewin, rabbi

---

1. Before the war, Lwów had Poland's third largest population of Jews, behind Warsaw and Łódź. After the Soviets occupied the city in September 1939, the Jewish population grew to two hundred thousand, of which half were refugees from German-occupied Poland.
2. After the Germans invaded the Soviet Union in June 1941, Ukrainians and Germans launched pogroms against the city's Jews. The violence culminated in the Petlura Days in late July, so named because Ukrainians justified them as vengeance for the 1926 murder of the antisemitic Ukrainian nationalist politician Simon Petlura (1879–1926) by the Yiddish poet Sholom Schwartzbard (1886–1938).
3. Ben Zion Halberstam (1874–1941) was the second Bobover rebbe and thus, at the time, the leader of the Bobover Hasidic dynasty.
4. Aaron Levin (1879–1941) was a rabbi, deputy to the Polish Sejm (parliament), and a leader of Agudath Israel, a political movement and umbrella organization of Orthodox Jews.

of Lemberg[5]; and Professor Allerhand, who was murdered in the *Aktion* of August 1942.[6]

In one particular *Aktion*, more than fifty thousand Jews were killed in Lemberg; forty thousand more were herded into the Zamarstynów ghetto. By the end of 1941, hundreds of Lemberg youngsters were taken to the Janover Camp, there to be liquidated.

Entering the Lemberg ghetto that late autumn morning, I was fully aware the place was a hellhole. But it could not be as bad as Janover Camp, I felt, where most of us had lost the semblance of human beings.

Having made my entry into the ghetto without being stopped, I adjusted my armband on the sleeve, took the spade from my shoulder and proceeded to paw the pavement, pick up fruit peelings and other refuse, working my way deeper into the ghetto. But after several hours of diligent work, I failed to encounter even one familiar face.

Ragged, dirty, I could scarcely count on being offered shelter by some kindly soul. It was necessary to clean up. But how? Taking my life in my hands, I extracted some money, hidden in my shoe, and made my way to a small shopping area, where I bought old clothing and supplies: trousers, a shirt, a tie, socks, a light overcoat, and even a hat, a bar of soap, cigarettes, and food.

Dragging the spade with me as though it were a passport, I entered a barbershop, sat down in the vacant chair, placing my purchases on the floor near my feet. The barber, a Jew, cut my hair, shaved the stubble off my face, scarcely uttering a word to me. But I could see by his glance that he understood my situation. When he had finished, I asked, "How much do I owe you?"

---

5. Yechezkel Lewin (1897–1941) was a reform rabbi and editor of a Jewish weekly newspaper. During the pogrom, he asked the head of the Ukrainian Greek Catholic Church, metropolitan archbishop Andrey Sheptytsky (1865–1944), to intervene to stop the violence to no avail. Sheptytsky was, however, instrumental in saving hundreds of Jews. See part II, chapter 3, note 10.

6. Moses (Maurycy) Allerhand (1868–1942) was a famous legal scholar and professor at the University of Lwów. The Germans initially asked him to head Lemberg's Jewish Council, but he refused the position on grounds of his ill health.

"Nothing," he replied.

"But I can afford to pay," I protested.

"Save it," he said, pushing away the złotys I offered him. "You will need it later."

I thanked him warmly; even as I write these words, I feel deeply obliged to him. After months in Janover Camp—a lifetime, really—where humans had been transformed into animals, often fighting for a slice of bread, a crumb, as though they were mad dogs, it was a deeply moving experience, a joy, a blinding revelation, to meet the Lemberg barber, who by his one generous act renewed my faith in humanity.

Still holding on to my spade, I ran to a bathhouse, paid, and was led to a tub that I filled with hot water. What pleasure! What delight! I sat in the water for what seemed like hours, shunting my worries to some remote part of the mind, aware only of the warmth, of being cleansed, of shedding not only the dirt but Janover as well. The fresh clothing renewed me and gave me courage.

Emerging on the ghetto street, seeing two SS men cross the street, walking in my direction, I came rudely awake. Where to take shelter? Where to spend the night?

I fled from the SS men. It was dark. The ghetto streets were virtually empty, as curfew was at seven o'clock. The police were out in force. A policeman crossed my path. I froze. If he demanded to see my papers, I would be lost. I possessed no papers of any kind. I saw a courtyard and a sign on an open gate: Łokietka Street 14. I entered the courtyard warily and hid until the policeman had passed. Could I seek shelter here? I looked around. The courtyard was littered with furniture, with beds; apparently people slept out in the yard. I heard voices. I found a stool in a corner and sat down. I was exhausted. It had been a long and eventful night and day. I had escaped from Janover. From Janover! But what was awaiting me here in the Lemberg ghetto? From the frying pan into the fire! I slept.

I heard (in my dreams?) the lovely chanting of Jews studying the Talmud. I did not dare open my eyes. Schodnica came to mind, the synagogue where as a boy I studied the Talmud from dawn to dusk. My father wanted

me to be a rabbi. Study the Talmud, son! He did not have to urge me. I
embraced the Talmud with all my might. Rabbi Abraham Merzel was my
teacher, a gentle man with a light touch, an inspiration. I recalled some of
my good friends: Meilich Backenroth, Max Gartner-Backenroth, Mendel
Merzel, Ben Eichenstein, and the many, many, others.

The Talmudic chanting continued. I opened my eyes. It was no dream. I
rose from the stool and walked in the direction of the singing, which came
from an area where blankets served as partitions. I pushed a blanket aside
and looked inside. An old man sat at a table that had a lighted candle on
it. He wore a skullcap, and he rocked to and fro as he studied the Talmud
treatise "Chullin."[7] A young man sat nearby, studying with him.

The old man saw me, interrupted his studying, and with a kind smile,
invited me in.

"I am sorry," I said, "but it has been such a long time since I have heard
these wonderful Talmud sounds, I had to come and see."

The old man asked me my name, where I came from, and how life was
on the outside. His name was Isaac Meier, and in spite of his advanced age,
he retained a freshness of spirit. The young man with him was his son, and
as we talked, we forgot for the moment the reality of our lives.

A young woman with sharp features and piercing eyes burst in. She was
the young man's wife. She questioned me closely, suspicion in her voice.
"Where are you from? What are you doing here?"

I told her the truth. But she was not satisfied. She wanted more details.
I rose quickly and told them that I did not plan to stay with them and that
they were not responsible for me. In the morning, I said, I would leave the
courtyard.

I left, although the old man pleaded with me to stay. I returned to the
cluttered corner where I had slept earlier, hoping the young woman would

---

7. The Talmudic tractate "Chullin" (meaning "ordinary" or "profane" things) addresses
kosher butchering and meat consumption. The swaying during Jewish prayer and
study known as "shuckling" is a long-standing practice understood to intensify concentration and heighten the emotional impact of the experience.

not report me. I was determined to remain awake, ready to flee, if necessary, but I was soon asleep.

Rudely awakened, I jumped to my feet, ready to run, but it was the
young woman who had interrogated me earlier, accompanied by her husband, the young Talmudist. I was about to plead with her to let me go, that
I meant no harm, but she said, "Come with us, young man; I'll make up
a bed for you. I frightened you with my questions. I'm sorry. Nowadays, a
Jew is afraid of his own shadow. We want to help you."

Impressed by the earnestness in her voice, I let the two of them lead me
to their stall, to an armchair where she placed a feather cushion for my
head and a feather cover for my body. It reminded me of home, of another
era now dead. To take off my shoes and remove my clothes before sleeping,
which I now proceeded to do, these habits too belonged to this other era.

I was awakened by shouts. Opening my eyes, I saw men and women
scurrying about, seeking shelter. "The SS entered the ghetto in force!" I
heard someone saying. I dressed quickly, an art I learned in Janover. In an
instant, I was ready to flee.

But it turned out to be a false alarm. Once again, I undressed and slept
fifteen hours.

The old man greeted me with a smile. "I've been thinking," he said,
"that you and I are related."

"Aren't all Jews related?" I said, moved by the man's friendly manner.
Before the end of the day, he managed to obtain a temporary shelter for
me some distance from the courtyard. We embraced, and I took my leave.

My landlady, a widow who lived in one room with her son and daughter and rented out space to persons who came only at night to sleep
took me in, although she knew I'd escaped from Janover; she needed the
money. Among her lodgers was the rabbi of Wadowice and his brother.[8] In

8. Wadowice is known best as the hometown of Karol Wojtyła (1920–2005), the future
Pope John Paul II. As a youth, Wojtyła had many friends from among the town's two
thousand Jews—most of whom died in the Holocaust. His positive relationships with
Jews before the Holocaust influenced his efforts as pope to improve relations between
Jews and Catholics.

addition to renting space in her room, the widow supported herself and her two children by buying butter and eggs outside the ghetto and selling them at a profit inside the ghetto.

Soon everybody in the shelter knew I had escaped from Janover. Nothing was said about it to me, but whenever a rumor spread that there was a policeman in the neighborhood, they fled, all except the landlady, who watched me hide under the bedcovers, a prayer on my lips. She sat down, folded her hands in her lap and waited for the worst. When the policeman had passed the house, she said, "You can come out now," and resumed her chores.

Five days passed. Would I ever get to Drohobycz? Was my brother still there, alive? In the evening, the rabbi's brother had some exciting news for me. A truck driver, a trustworthy man, according to the rabbi's brother, was preparing to drive to Drohobycz. "He's parked at the Żółkiew gate. He'll take a passenger."

"I'll go!" I said eagerly. "I'll pay him!" Putting on my coat, I left the shelter and started toward the gate.

All at once, I felt a heavy hand on my shoulder and heard a loud voice, ordering me to stop.

"Your identity card!"

I turned. Keiler, a Jewish militiaman, one of the most brutal and feared in Lemberg, stood there facing me, his malevolent little eyes regarding me mockingly, as if he knew that I did not possess an identity card, that I had escaped Janover Camp. "Come, come, identity card!" he repeated.

In a voice I tried very hard to control, I said, "What is it you want of me? Leave me alone; I'm in a hurry."

"Quit playing games with me," he said, taking hold of my arm to make certain I would not try to run away. "Either you show me your papers, if you have any, which I doubt, or you come with me to the *Kommandant* of the Jewish ghetto police."

By this time, a crowd of curious men and women had gathered around us as well as several more Jewish militiamen. Keiler, assisted by his fellow policemen, toadies of the Germans who were Jews in name only, who were in fact the dregs of society, pushed and shoved me in the direction of the Jewish militia headquarters.

I remember distinctly thinking, *You're in the net, brother. Only a miracle will get you out of it!* Although my mind was in a turmoil, I saw very clearly the camp gallows and the bullwhips. Some people carried cyanide pills to be put under the tongue for just such an occasion as this one; were I in possession of a pill, I would not have hesitated to use it.

The *Kommandant's* office, where the militiamen dragged me, was a large smoke-filled room. A dozen Jewish militiamen sat around idly, smoking, lashing whips against dirty black boots, hurling obscenities at one another. One of them looked up and asked in a bored tone of voice, "Who do we have here? Another bird that's escaped the Janover cage?"

Keiler, still gripping my arm, pushed me toward the desk, where an officer sat over a pile of papers, grimacing painfully. "What's up?" he demanded.

"He escaped Janover!" Keiler declared. "He—"

"Not true!" I interrupted. "The Jewish Council has given me a task to perform! I was on my way to perform it!"

"He's lying, chief!" Keiler cried. "He's from Janover! I can prove it!"

"Wait, wait," the *Kommandant* said, holding up his hand. Turning to me, he said, "If you have the proper documents, I'll let you go on your private mission. But if there are no identity papers, Keiler will take you back to Janover Camp."

"You cannot do it!" I said with mock indignation. "The fate of the Jewish community rests on me and the mission I must perform! Take me to the president of the Jewish Council! I demand to see the president of the council!" I was aware of my voice rising, demanding justice, of my fist thumping the desk, of my knees shaking, of saying to myself: this whole edifice of lies is built on shifting sands.

Keiler, tiring of the game, flung himself at me, trying to open my shirt, rip it off my back and point to welts and scars, which all inmates in camp possessed. But I pushed him away, almost sent him sprawling, surprised at my own strength.

I fully expected to be clubbed down, to be attacked by a dozen whips. I was surprised when the *Kommandant* restrained his men who were about to fling themselves on me and said in a calm voice, "The Jewish Council is closed for the night. Tomorrow morning, we'll take you to the headquarters and hear what they have to say about you and your mission. Tonight, you'll be locked up in the ghetto jail. What's your name?"

I gave him a false name. He then ordered me taken to the Bałuckiego ghetto prison to be held there until morning, when I would be brought before the Jewish Council, and if my tale proved false, they would return me to Janover.

I was placed in a tiny cell with a barred window and metal door. Two boys, the nature of whose crime I did not learn, shared the cell with me. They were absorbed in a card game and paid no attention to me. Later, a young mother with a young child was flung into the cell. "They are holding me for breaking the curfew and stealing," she announced, cradling the little girl in her lap. "My Rochele is skin and bones! I must feed her!" She fell silent.

I tried to take stock of my situation. The word *future* occurred to me, but I dismissed it. What future? It seemed to me that I'd reached the end of the road. Up to now, I'd been fortunate; I'd had many narrow escapes. Of our large family, only my brother and I were left. Nearly all my friends had perished. Oftentimes I attributed my still being alive to miracles, to intervention by a higher power. But why me? Why not my father, who had been more pious than me—a godly man, truly, who had prevailed on me to study for the rabbinate when I had sought to become a doctor? It was his guidance, his inspiration, that made it possible for me to be ordained at the age of nineteen! No, my survival up until now must be attributed to my physical endurance and agility. Even now, after these many months, subjected to beatings, tortures, and hunger, I could not consider myself physically a weakling. But in my present dilemma, my physical state did not count for anything. Only a miracle could save me.

Finally, I fell into a fitful slumber. When I awakened, it was daylight. The two boys were still absorbed in their card game, oblivious to all else, it seemed. I wondered: Weren't they worried about their fate? I envied them their lack of concern.

At noon, two Jewish policemen came for me, accompanied by a man dressed in civilian clothes, who introduced himself as deputy leader of the Jewish Council. He demanded to see my identification card and papers pertaining to my work for the council.

Suspecting a ruse, I refused. "Take me to council headquarters," I said. "There I will show them what has to be shown."

The policemen threatened me with Janover again, and the man in civilian clothes said I would regret my obstinacy. Finally, they left, threatening to be back.

After they had gone, I asked the two boys whether they knew anything about the man in civilian clothes. "Is he really deputy chairman of the Jewish Council?"

"No, no," one of the boys replied, amused by my naïveté. "The leaders of the Jewish Council have fat bellies and double chins. This skinny one is Rappaport, a nobody!"

Later in the afternoon, the vice chairman of the Lemberg Jewish Police, who was the deputy director of the Jewish Council, arrived with two policemen, summoned me to the prison courtyard, and declared that the ghetto council was prepared to accept my story on condition that I leave immediately with the promise that I would not return. Before leaving, the man said, I must bribe Keiler to prevent his exposing me to the Germans. "If, by chance, you're captured outside the ghetto," the official declared, "you are not to disclose that you'd been here. Is that agreeable?"

For the first time since being confronted by the Jewish Police of the Lemberg ghetto, I was at a loss for words. Should I leave the ghetto immediately or be delivered to Janover Camp? Where was I to go if I left the ghetto by myself? While life in Janover was fraught with peril, being caught outside the ghetto meant certain death.

I tried bargaining with them; I asked if it was possible for me to remain in the ghetto another eight days. They refused my request. In desperation,

I offered another proposal. Could I remain in the prison cell a few days longer? This too was refused me.

I shrugged, sighed, and said, "Take me to the gate."

"Remember," the council official said in parting, "you are not to mention us under any circumstances. If you do, we'll deny everything."

My destination was Drohobycz, but in view of the fact that the truck driver with whom I could have gone had left a long time ago, the railroad was my only alternative. It was not a practical alternative, as Jews were forbidden to ride trains. Nonetheless, I found out that a train was scheduled to leave at six thirty the following morning. I would attempt it.

Spending a sleepless night, I rose early, took off my armband. I would try to pass as an Aryan. I reached the station a little after six in the morning and asked the girl in the ticket booth for a ticket to Drohobycz. She told me that there were no more seat tickets and slammed the window shut. I was thunderstruck. I had never heard of special tickets. Again, I felt trapped and was certain that I would not emerge alive from this adventure.

As I stepped away from the window, a ragged boy approached me and asked in a high voice, "Where do you want to go?"

I ignored his question.

But the boy was persistent. "I have a ticket for a reserved seat to Stryj, which is near Drohobycz."

How clever, I thought. So that's how the boys make extra money. I paid him what he asked, and he whispered to me, "I know who you are, but I won't denounce you." And he disappeared.

I found a seat on the train, which was full of Poles and Ukrainians who, if they could but recognize me, would turn me in. But I was not approached by anyone, and as I sat in my seat, I managed to work myself into a more agreeable state of mind by the time the train reached Stryj.

Nearly all the passengers got off. I didn't want to be the first to leave and peeked through the window to see who was on the station. I noticed German policemen and railway guards and observed how they were examining documents. My heart sank. I had not thought that the Germans would be so thorough. I could not decide what to do, and then fate played a hand in my decision. The train began to move again in the direction of Drohobycz, and I realized that I would have to jump if I wanted to get off now. I remained where I was, even though I had a ticket only to Stryj. It was three more stations to Drohobycz, and in another forty minutes, we arrived.

Because there were policemen here too, I jumped out of the train from the opposite side to avoid them. I came upon a small group of Jewish workers who were loading lumber from a truck into a freight car. I rushed up to them and said, in a trembling voice, "*Ivri Anochi*, I am one of you. I've just come from Lemberg. How can I get into town?"

One of them replied, "Quick! Get your armband on, or they'll kill you." I began to work, and when it grew dark, I marched with them into the ghetto.

I was safe again. Here, I found my brother and many of my friends and acquaintances, and I told them of what had happened to me during the past weeks. I told them what the Germans were doing at Janover and how they were trying to liquidate the entire Jewish population. Although everything I said to them was true, even I could not anticipate how much more suffering faced me. Even as I lie here and write these words, I can scarcely realize how much misery the future would hold.

CHAPTER 11

# BLACK THURSDAY

There was no slaking the German thirst for Jewish blood. The hapless Drohobycz Jewish Council cast about for some stratagem that would lessen the severity of German brutality. Dr. Ruhrberg[1] suggested that bribery of the Gestapo leaders be tried. Nikolaus Tolle,[2] the chief German officer, seemed amenable, as were his henchmen.

And thus, the greasing of the palms began. And for a while, it worked. But the Nazi appetite was insatiable. It began with personal valuables; when those were exhausted, the representatives of the master race took textiles for suits, coats, and dresses; silverware and furniture; and foodstuffs like butter, eggs, coffee, and tea. It became a flourishing business, making it necessary for the council to set aside a purchasing office in order to fill the German orders. The office was managed by three distinguished men, Samuel Rothenberg, Nachum Petranker, and Moses Kartin, under whose leadership workshops were established for shoemakers, tailors, and furriers, all for the purpose of filling German orders.

The Security Police insisted that everything be of the highest and finest quality. Top Gestapo officials, who confiscated villas, demanded that the Jewish Council provide them with gardeners and landscape artists.

---

1. Maurycy Ruhrberg was the assistant to Isaac Rosenblatt, the head of the Drohobycz Jewish Council, although in some accounts, Ruhrberg was more influential. He was shot at the end of 1942. For more on Ruhrberg, see chapter 12 of part I.
2. SS-*Hauptsturmführer* Nikolaus Tolle (1899–1945) was the *Kommandant* of the German Security Police in Drohobycz.

Hermann Göring[3] is quoted as having said that all German indus-try must be geared for war production and that all other elements of the economy would have to suffer. In Drohobycz, the Germans lived in the lap of luxury, thanks to the Jewish Council, to whom every whim, every caprice of the Gestapo leaders was law.

No demand was too outlandish, too bizarre. I recall the case of the horse whip with a silver handle. A member of the Gestapo ordered the item from the council. None of the craftsmen had ever made a whip; the pur-chasing committee had no idea where to buy it. The committee, mindful of the German's threat that Jewish heads would roll unless his whims were satisfied, scurried about in town and environs, searching for a horse whip with a silver handle.

Another German, to whom crossword puzzles were an obsession, unable to solve a particular puzzle as one word eluded him, telephoned the Jewish Council, demanding that it supply him with the proper word. A steady caller, he had once asked for a five-letter word for an extinct tribe. Another time, he needed a three-letter Turkish word and, on yet another, a three-letter word for a particular species of antelope. Each demand was accompanied by a threat of execution. Teachers, doctors, and lawyers were pressed into service by the council; maps, dictionaries, and reference books were made available for any eventuality that might arise.

I recall an instance of a Nazi, bent on improving his vocabulary, who demanded that the council supply him with a ten-letter word for *teacher*. He gave the staff fifteen minutes to come up with the answer. At the end of the allotted time, with no answer in sight, though the staff had tried man-fully, Dr. Ruhrberg telephoned the Nazi and pleaded for an extension of time. The adamant Gestapo officer warned the president of the council that if he failed to come up with the proper word, he would be held responsible.

Panic spread in the office. Some officials fled; others hid in the loft and cellar. Dr. Ruhrberg, threatened with execution, sent out an appeal

3. To bolster the German economy and prepare Germany for war, Adolf Hitler intro-duced a Four Year Plan in 1936 and gave control of it to the leading Nazi politician, Hermann Göring (1893–1946).

to members of the Jewish community to help him and his staff to find an answer, a ten-letter word for *teacher*. He offered prizes—loaves of bread—to the person or persons who came up with the proper word, but the search proved fruitless and Dr. Ruhrberg, prepared for the worst, went to his office to call the German. Just then, a young girl about ten years old knocked on the president's door and said, "I heard your appeal and came running. Perhaps the word *Schullehrer* (instructor) fits?" Dr. Ruhrberg and the staff, whom he summoned to his office, began counting the letters. They concluded that if the *ch* or the double *l* could be counted as a single letter, it would fit. Dr. Ruhrberg telephoned the German, gave him the missing word, and anxiously waited. But when the Gestapo officer failed to call him back after an hour had passed, it became apparent that this particular crisis had passed.

But there were others. A major problem was supplying the Germans with pornographic material, "literature" and dirty pictures, which they were constantly ordering. The books they desired had to be written in German, the only language they understood. So the Jewish Council was forced to import them from Germany. The smut proved expensive. Yet somehow, the council managed to comply. Dr. Ruhrberg was kept busy. His talent to appease the Gestapo officers, whose demands were endless and whose tastes bizarre, gave the Jews of Drohobycz a brief respite.

Dr. Ruhrberg's efforts notwithstanding, there were constant killings. The case of a man named Fliegner was a case in point. He was working in the gardens of the SS man Felix Landau,[4] on 12 Jana Street, attending to his chores and minding his own business, when Landau saw him. At that moment, the German was entertaining his mistress, Trude Segall, when he decided to test her accuracy with a pistol.

---

4. [Thorne's note:] Landau had received from Hitler the Blutorden Medal as one of the assassins of the Austrian Chancellor, Dr. Dollfuss. [Editor's note:] The Blutorden (Blood Order) was one of the Nazi Party's most prestigious decorations. Engelbert Dollfuss (1892–1934) was the authoritarian ruler of Austria whom Nazi agents assassinated on July 25, 1934, as part of a failed coup attempt.

She shot at Fliegner a number of times but missed him. Laughing glee-fully, Landau grabbed the pistol from her and shot Fliegner through the head. The next day, when Dr. Ruhrberg asked Landau why he had killed the harmless Jew, the Nazi replied, "Why not? Others are killing thousands of Jews. Can't I shoot at least one?"

Another incident that is etched sharply on my mind is the murder of three teenage girls: Sternbach, Kupferberg, and Zuckerman. The pretty and lively youngsters, employed as bricklayer helpers, were joking with one another as they went about their work. A Gestapo officer named Gün-ther[5] came by, stood awhile and observed them at their work, then took out a gun and, for no reason at all, shot them dead. The father of one of the girls, Kupferberg, was a barber who cut Günther's hair. After the shoot-ing, the Gestapo officer sent for Kupferberg because he wanted a shave. When the barber finished with his task, Günther said, "Kupferberg, a half hour ago, I shot your daughter." Kupferberg fainted.

Such cases can be multiplied again and again. In Borysław, seven hun-dred Jews who had gathered in the woods to pray were murdered by the Nazis. At Turka on the Stryj, three hundred Jews were killed. There, Ger-mans entered the town, knocked on doors, and inquired where Jews lived. When the desired information was received, they proceeded to shoot every Jew in sight.

In one day alone, 1,100 Jews in Stryj were rounded up and thrown in jail. Dr. Ruhrberg and engineer Naftali Backenroth[6] worked heroically to save them. In spite of their efforts, 850 of those arrested were shipped to another area and shot.

In November 1941, and later in March, August, and October 1942, the Germans took violent action against the Jews of Drohobycz. Lieberman was the representative of the Jewish *Arbeitsamt* (Employment Office).

5. The Gestapo officer Karl Günther is known primarily for murdering the famous writer and artist Bruno Schulz (1892–1942). Günther shot Schulz to spite Felix Landau (1910–1983), who liked Schulz's paintings and protected him. Landau had shot Gün-ther's Jewish servant.
6. Chapter 22 of part I explains in greater detail the rescue efforts of Leon Thorne's cousin Naftali Backenroth (1905–1993).

He was empowered to issue certificates of invalidism to Jews who were too sick to work. Those who possessed such certificates were ordered to the Drohobycz office. More than three hundred of them crowded into the office building and courtyard. Suddenly, German trucks filled with Security Police rumbled up to the office, seized all the Jews, drove them to the nearby village of Bronica, and executed them. By early spring, the Jews of Drohobycz became fully aware that Dr. Ruhrberg's heroic efforts notwithstanding, they were facing extinction.

During this period, the chief of the Drohobycz Security Service informed the Jewish Council that farmhands were needed for work in Volhynia and Podolia and requested one thousand Jews from the town.

The council, charged with the responsibility of selecting the Jews, announced it would welcome volunteers. Some, considering this an opportunity to improve their situation, volunteered. But although a large number signed up to go, there weren't enough to fill the quota. As a result, the council selected dozens of thieves and informers for the trip, thereby doing their duty and ridding the area of undesirable elements.

Weeks passed without a word. After a month of silence, the leaders of the Jewish Council asked the chief of the Security Police if there was anything wrong with the mail, as none of the Jews had received any letters from those who left. The chief laughed. "How stupid can you be? For more than one thousand years, people believed you Jews were smart. Can't you guess what's happened to them?"

In July of 1942, the Germans went to work on the children of the area. A special kitchen had been established for them by the Jewish Council. The Gestapo commissioner, a man named Haeckel, had often assured Dr. Ruhrberg that the Germans would not molest the youngsters when they came to eat. But one day, when hundreds of them were gathered in the kitchen, German Police entered the area, grabbed dozens of helpless, crying children, and threw them on the trucks. Some managed to escape, but they were not to be free for long, as the Nazis hunted them down, killing 150. During this period, the parents of the children lived in great anxiety, waiting to see if any had survived. There were heartbreaking scenes in town when the fortunate youngsters who lived through this pogrom returned to their parents.

In August and October, the Nazis instituted new pogroms, but the Jews of Drohobycz were more fortunate than those in the other Galician towns. In other areas, the Germans wiped out half of the Jewish population; in Drohobycz "only" one-fourth of the Jews, or four thousand, were butchered.

Dr. Ruhrberg and Naftali Backenroth played key roles in the saving of Jewish lives at this time. They, like some other members of the Jewish Council, tried helping their brethren, although the Germans had set up the council, here and in other Polish cities and towns, for the purpose of serving the invaders' interest. But by the middle of 1942, the Jewish Council in Drohobycz and other communities had lost what little leverage it possessed with the Germans and lent itself as an instrument of Jewish liquidation.

I will go one step further: none of the members of the Jewish Council of Drohobycz would, under normal conditions, be elected by the Jews to represent them. With rare exceptions, as in the case of Dr. Ruhrberg and Naftali Backenroth, the people who sat on the Jewish Councils were corrupt men who represented themselves only and served their own interests, doing the bidding of the Germans and hoping that they and their families would survive.

The Jewish Police were even worse. An instrument of repression often as brutal as their German masters, their main goal was survival for themselves and their families.

On November 4, 1942, the assault against the Jews of Drohobycz began in earnest. The intended victims, sensing the magnitude of the peril, fled to previously prepared hiding places. The German dragnet found disappointingly few victims during the early days of the *Aktion*. Frustrated, they brought up their artillery, flushing many Jews out of their hiding places. Tanks stood ready to back up the artillery, in the event that they proved necessary. The Jewish Police volunteered its services for what later became known as the "November Action," arresting numbers of old people. It was a cold wintry month. The old were not expected to survive; certainly, they would not live through the war.

The prisoners were moved to a large building, the Komarner Synagogue, whose windows were barred and doors bolted. German police and Ukrainian militias guarded this ancient house of worship-turned-prison.

For more than three weeks, the Jewish Police ran around town with axes and mattocks, searching for victims. Doors were smashed, floor planks uprooted, and hundreds of elderly Jews were found and arrested.

Soon, typhoid fever broke out in the Komarner Synagogue. Hundreds of people died like flies. The Jewish Police were empowered with the task of supplying Jews to replace the dead. The more Jews they brought in, the more deaths there were.

At first, the prisoners had received bread and soup twice daily, which was brought from the Jewish kitchens. The latrines were cleaned regularly. When a person died, the corpse was immediately transported to the cemetery. But after the outbreak of typhoid, nobody wanted to take the risk of bringing food to the area; the prisoners were no longer led to the latrines, and the dead were no longer isolated from them. The dead lay in heaps in the mud. The stench was horrible, and lice and fever abounded. Many of the prisoners went mad. Day and night, one heard crying and moaning. Some of those who lost their minds stripped themselves of their clothing and danced wildly in the knee-deep mud.

Edward Galotti, the chief of the Jewish Police in Drohobycz and the only decent Jewish policeman whom I knew, was in charge of providing the necessary Jewish quota and lost control of the situation. He pleaded with the Gestapo to do something about it, but the Germans were not interested. To them, this was the easiest and cheapest mass liquidation of the Jews. Some of them even enjoyed it and came in large numbers to the area to see the mad Jews dancing about. The Gestapo man Gildner brought his children to see the "spectacle."

After three weeks, the Jewish Council and the Jewish Police decided to run the risk of refusing to cooperate with the Germans any longer. Tanks and grenades were less painful than slow torture. The Germans invaded the ghetto, captured thousands of Jews, and placed them in boxcars scheduled to go to Lemberg. Among those who died in this fashion was Leo Spanndoerfer, for many years one of the leaders of the Jewish community in Drohobycz.

This same tragedy was repeated in the surrounding communities, as the Germans went wild and massacred all the Jews they could seize.

Thursday, November 19, 1942, was one of the blackest days of this terrible period. A Gestapo man, Huebner, was friendly with Max Reiner, a Jewish druggist's assistant. A month earlier, Reiner had lost his wife, child, and parents. It was obvious that Huebner had not been able to help him. Reiner, upset by the tragedy, was no longer seen with Huebner. The tension between the two men grew in intensity. Then on the morning of November 19, they met in the chemist's shop. They quarreled. Huebner drew his pistol and killed Reiner.

Huebner, aroused and bloodthirsty, quickly called a few Gestapo men to his side and with them invaded the office of the Jewish Council, shooting down everyone in sight. They entered the ghetto and thus began the day that was later called "Bloody Thursday."

The Germans stood at the corners of the Jewish quarter and shot down everyone who happened to come along. At that moment, traffic was heavy in the area, and soon there was a heap of corpses piled in every ghetto lane.

By midafternoon, their bloody work finished, the murderers invaded the offices of the Jewish Council and demanded brandy to help them celebrate.

Among the many victims of the madmen, I must single out one, the noted Polish Jewish writer, Professor Bruno Schulz. Pride of the Jews of Drohobycz and all of Galicia, Professor Schulz, in addition to his writing, which included poetry, was also a painter of note. During the occupation, he did numerous portraits of Gestapo officers' girlfriends. He was killed by accident, walking through the ghetto on the way to visit his mother, bringing her food. As he neared the ghetto, the Gestapo man Günther shot him down.

Several days later, we learned that a mass killing had also taken place in Lemberg.

# CHAPTER 12

# DESPAIR IN THE JEWISH QUARTER

As the murders continued, despair gripped the entire Jewish population. It began on December 7, 1942, when the entire Jewish Council, including Dr. Ruhrberg, suddenly disappeared. The only exception was Dr. Gerstenfeld.[1] The others had the money they needed in order to help them escape; only Dr. Gerstenfeld, shy and fearful, was unable to obtain enough money to get away. He came to the council office as usual on the morning of December 8 and found none of his colleagues. The safe had been ransacked and contained only a torn five złoty note. Dr. Gerstenfeld looked about in shocked amazement. The whole world seemed to have crashed down on him. In a few moments, Gestapo officers rushed into the office and demanded an explanation as to what had happened to the others. Finally convinced that he had nothing to do with planning the escape, they named him chairman of the council, ordering him to appoint new members as soon as possible.

When we heard what had happened, we were convinced our liquidation was at hand. Rumors abounded that we were to be killed immediately. We heard we would be tortured. The stories grew more terrible with each telling, but meanwhile we waited.

---

1. Jacob Gerstenfeld (1890–1943) was appointed head of the Drohobycz *Judenrat* on December 30, 1942, and shot in 1943.

At Drohobycz, there were three groups of workers. The first unit of armament workers, wearing an R sign, was employed mainly in the oil refineries called Beskiden. The R stood for *Rüstungsarbeiter.*[2]

The second group, working for army establishments, wore the W sign. The W stood for *Wehrmachtsbetrieb.*[3] The workers were kept busy in sawmills and municipal workshops.

The third group wore no signs at all. They were on call by the Gestapo and led by Engineer Backenroth. A fourth group was later established and forced to labor in the ceramic works.

When the rumors began as to who would be liquidated and who spared, we understood that the only Jews with any chance of survival were those who wore the R and W signs. The Beskiden management arranged for housing for its workers, who were lodged in requisitioned Jewish-owned dwellings, situated on Jagiellońska Street near the Sadigurer Synagogue. Surrounded by a high wall, the unit was guarded by the Jewish Police.

R and W workers were considered SS property. Money was paid to the SS at a daily rate of five złotys for a man and four złotys for a woman. The laborers were "fed" by the camp administration. The meals were skimpy indeed, consisting of a weekly allotment of soup and bread. The SS was charged for this food at a cost of 1.40 złotys per day. At this rate, the net profit to the SS was 3.60 złotys for a man and 2.60 złotys for a woman.

When the workers were moved from the ghetto to the barracks, many of them brought their families with them and hid them in lofts and cellars. In this fashion, each camp barracks became a miniature ghetto.

---

2. German oil companies founded the Beskiden-Erdölgesellschaft (Beskid Mountains Oil Company) in November 1939 to exploit Polish oil resources for the German war effort. Jews became forced laborers in the *Arbeitslager Beskiden* (Beskiden Work Camp), which Thorne mentions later in chapters 13 and 20 of part I. A *Rüstungsarbeiter* sign designated that a person was an armaments worker and thus important to the German war effort, which increased chances of survival.
3. The designation *Wehrmachtsbetrieb* indicated that a company produced goods for the military.

Those remaining in the ghetto were now more isolated than ever; in their despair, there followed a wave of suicides. People who still possessed money bought potassium cyanide, a tube of which cost eight hundred to one thousand złotys. The poison trade flourished. Often persons, families, who'd invested their last złotys on cyanide discovered that they'd been sold placebos. Those who could not afford cyanide (whose prices rose before an *Aktion* and declined after it) gassed themselves to death. And those who were too poor to obtain gas hanged themselves.

Suicide was discussed frequently and openly. One could hear men and women talking about it in the streets, saying, "Today, I will put an end to it. I'll kill myself and my family." Nobody tried to dissuade anybody from committing suicide. The young as well as the old talked about it.

But there were men and women among us who possessed the courage to live and to contemplate escape. To escape, one had to have money and look like an Aryan. One had to obtain forged papers to pass as an Aryan or hide in Christian dwellings. Some tried crossing the Carpathian Mountains into Hungary; some attempted to build permanent underground hideouts.

Forged papers became a brisk commerce, making it possible for a large number of Jews to escape. Some who had connections with Catholic priests were provided certificates of baptism.

Escape from the ghetto was no guarantee of safety. We learned, in time, that many who had succeeded in getting out were hunted down on the outside and murdered.

With the introduction of the Reich identity cards, it became necessary for one to prove in six different ways that he was of Aryan descent, which required two certificates for his parents and four for his grandparents.

In every town, there were extortionists who took the last money from Jews, assuring them that they would help them escape and delivering them instead to the Gestapo. They earned money from two sources and became rich in the process.

The Jews who managed to hide in Polish or Ukrainian dwellings suffered even more than those who tried to escape. The Poles and Ukrainians would trick the Jews out of all their money and valuables and then turn them over to the police, who executed them on the spot or in the woods. The Jewish Council was then ordered to bury the victims in the Jewish cemetery.

The Jews who planned to cross the border into Hungary had their troubles. Normally, getting across the border was not difficult, as the towns of Drohobycz, Sambor, and Stryj were only some eighty to one hundred kilometers from the border. But most Jews were not familiar with the thick Carpathian forests and were dependent on guides to lead them. More often than not, the guides betrayed them, turning them over to armed peasants, who killed them.

Later, the Jews grew wiser and marched in armed groups. In most cases, they were defeated by the peasants who outnumbered them. Those who survived the shootings were marched back to the ghettos.

The handfuls who crossed the border successfully were faced with major obstacles. The Hungarian authorities had forbidden anyone to shelter strangers. As a result, the Jews who managed to reach Hungary were eventually picked up by Hungarian police and returned to the Germans, who shot them on the border between Hungary and occupied Poland, called the "General Government."[4]

The bitter experiences led the Jews to trust no one. They learned to rely on themselves alone. At great expense and under extreme secrecy, many of them managed to build comfortable hiding places, some with electric or gas lights, water and fresh air supplies, and radios and food stores. The hideouts were well camouflaged.

Although it is not easy for me to write in this condition, I must say a few words about Dr. Maurice Ruhrberg, whom thousands of Jews in Drohobycz and its surroundings considered their leader from the first day of the German occupation until December 1942, when he escaped from the ghetto. He was called Maciek, the name his parents and close friends gave him. His father, Wilhelm Ruhrberg, had been the chairman of the Jewish community for many

4. The *Generalgouvernement* (General Government) was the official name of the German zone of occupied Poland. The seat of government was in Kraków, and from its establishment on October 26, 1939, until its dissolution in January 1945, the National Socialist lawyer Hans Frank (1900–1946) served as governor. Frank was hanged as a war criminal in 1946.

years. Maciek was given a good education and, after gaining his degree, was sent to Trieste to study economics, where he earned his doctorate. When he returned to Poland and became aware that his degree could not help him earn a livelihood, he studied law. Although he received his master of law degree, he did not get very far in the profession. For years, he worked as a legal assistant, and even when he went out on his own, he did not do too well.

His parents' connections made it possible for Maciek to get a job as a reporter for the *Chwila*, a Zionist newspaper in Lemberg,[5] but here too, he did not establish himself as outstanding. He made more money by keeping certain scandalous items out of the newspaper than by reporting them. He probably would have managed a degree of success somehow through journalism and the law had it not been for the outbreak of the war in June 1941. This cataclysmic event changed his life as well as the lives of millions of others. From the moment he joined the Jewish Council, which was a creature of the Germans, Dr. Ruhrberg proved how agile he was, how adept, at handling his masters. He knew almost by instinct the susceptibility of these corrupt men to bribery. He bribed on a large scale, giving a certain present to one official, then another to the second one. Often, he kept the gifts secret to avoid arousing jealousy among the recipients. Unlike many Jews, whose dealing with the Gestapo was often an exercise in self-effacement, in groveling, Dr. Ruhrberg maintained his dignity, his aristocratic bearing, even in a room full of Gestapo officers. And he helped the Jews, whom he divided into two distinct groups: those from Drohobycz and its environs whom he considered "his" Jews and those from distant places. He was prepared to sacrifice four Jews from the outside to save one from Drohobycz.

When negotiating with the Germans on how many Jews were to be murdered, Dr. Ruhrberg tried to persuade the representatives of the Thousand-Year Reich[6] to take their victims from other communities.

5. *Chwila* (Polish for "moment") was a daily newspaper published in Lwów (Lemberg) from 1919 to 1939. As a Zionist publication, it criticized the idea that Jews could assimilate into Polish society and instead advocated establishing a Jewish state in Palestine.
6. Chapter 20 of the Book of Revelation mentions a one-thousand-year reign of Christ when the world would be at peace. National Socialist propagandists adopted this phrase and used it to describe the Third Reich as the *tausendjähriges Reich* (thousand-year empire).

Called on to intercede on behalf of the intended victims, he expected to be paid. If he received no payment, he could be quite indifferent to the fate of an entire Jewish village.

Dr. Ruhrberg was the right man in the right place at the right time. He suffered from delusions of grandeur, believing himself to be a diplomat, a statesman, a prince of Israel. Relishing his role as a savior of the Jews, he could not perceive the stark realities of ghetto life, the grave danger in which the Jews found themselves, the gravest in their long history. He persuaded himself that he could go on palliating the Gestapo, saving "his" Jews almost single-handedly, while elsewhere they perished.

But in December 1942, Dr. Ruhrberg fled Drohobycz, an abdicating monarch going into exile, convinced the populace would recall his reign with reverence. He made a solemn speech before departing to a small group of his constituents and the Jewish Police who stood in review like an honor guard. He looked a little absurd.

Dr. Ruhrberg's escape was not a sudden one. He had said on numerous occasions that the Gestapo killed all those who bribed them. When the news spread in Drohobycz that he had fled, a wave of suicides followed.

He fled toward the Carpathian Mountains, accompanied by his wife and some close friends, driving in the direction of Maidan. There, between the high mountains and the thick woods, he had built a hiding place for his family, a comfortable one, with plenty of food laid in for a long stay. Soon after the arrival at his destination, Dr. Ruhrberg was traced by the Germans and forced to flee, reaching Borysław, where he stayed for a short period. Obtaining "Aryan" papers for himself and his wife, he drove to Warsaw, where he remained for six months, passing as an Aryan in the Christian sector of the city. A suspicious landlord denounced him to the Gestapo, who arrested him. He told the Germans all they wanted to know. The Gestapo in Drohobycz was informed of his capture. With his wife, Dr. Ruhrberg was brought back to Drohobycz and shot to death.

---

# CHAPTER 13

# THE POOR CANNOT
# AFFORD SUICIDE

My joy at having escaped the Janover Camp was short lived. My arrival at Drohobycz coincided with the bloody November Action that virtually wiped out the town's Jewish populace.[1]

Having no employment, I was constantly on the alert. Like my brother, with whom I was reunited, I kept off the streets, venturing out only in the dark of night, walking through streets and alleys emptied by the curfew. Of our once large and flourishing family, only a few relatives were left, taking shelter in cellars and attics. In former days, these men, without exception, had been rich and influential, possessing fine homes, employing hundreds of workers and craftsmen. Now they huddled in wretched cellars.

One night, my brother and I fled Drohobycz, making our way to the village of Rołów, where, according to rumor, work might be less difficult to find. Although the Security Police had confiscated all the dwellings and lands, a handful of Jews apparently was allowed to live there.

A German policeman, a *Volksdeutscher*[2] named Fleischer, one of a group put in charge of the confiscated property, made no trouble for the Jews, who showered him with small bribes. Appearing on the farm every two or three days, the German sat down on a wooden bench and waited. The Jews did not let him wait long. Soon they brought him presents, which he took quietly and left.

---

1. Beginning on November 6–7, 1942, the Gestapo demanded that one hundred Jews be rounded up each day and delivered to the Komarner Synagogue in Drohobycz.
2. See part I, chapter 8, note 2.

One of the dwellings was occupied by the Lorberbaum family, whom we knew from Drohobycz. Three other families lived with them: the Kammermanns, Richters, and Teppers. We began to talk about what was uppermost in our minds—of a place to hide not just for a night or a week but for the duration. Such places were difficult to find, but they were worth their weight in gold. Kammermann, in a confiding mood, revealed to me that he had a friend in the village, a Ukrainian named Parashtchak, who boasted of a large cellar where he offered to hide not only the Kammermann family but the others as well. He made the offer out of the goodness of his heart and not for a profit, but Kammermann and his friends insisted they would pay, turning over to the peasant all the money and valuables they possessed. "We had a most difficult time convincing him to take anything from us," Kammermann said. "How do you like that for a decent peasant?"

Kammermann further revealed that they expected to move in within three weeks and generously suggested that my brother and I move in with them. "It won't cost you a groschen,"[3] he said, outlining to me the advantages of the place. The cellar was stocked with 2,500 pounds of flour and fat. Soap was already on hand as well as toothpaste, cigarettes, matches, and even medicine. "I require one thing from you," he declared solemnly, "that you keep a record of all the events that transpired during the German occupation so that the world would know what we lived through."

I was deeply moved by the generous offer and accepted for my brother and myself. "I'll pay you, of course," I said, but he refused to take money. "Not being a businessman, you'll need the money after the war is over. But the record you must promise me to keep."

I made a solemn promise, and I have kept it. What had started out as a commitment on my part to make the record of German crimes against my people has long since become an obsession. Each time I sit down to add to my ledger, I think of Kammermann, who after making the generous

3. *Groschen* is a colloquial German word for "cent." The Polish złoty is divided into one hundred *groszy*.

offer to me, spoke to the peasant, who in my presence refused to take me
in. He could not be moved, saying he was ready to help his friends but
not strangers. Kammermann was disappointed at the peasant's obdu-
racy, but as I recall it, I was not. To tell the truth, I disliked Parashtchak
from the moment I laid eyes on him. His eyes were cold and cruel. I had
imagined that a man eager to help save lives would have a kindly look. I
told Kammermann about my mistrust of the Ukrainian, but he laughed
at me and said, "I've known him for a long time. A more reliable man you
won't find!"

Early in December, all the Jews working in villages surrounding
Drohobycz were ordered to move to the town's Jewish quarter. Prior to
our departure from Rołów, Kammermann again brought up the subject
of hiding, assuring me he would try to prevail on the Ukrainian to take in
my brother and me.

I thanked my friend. Perhaps I had judged the peasant too harshly. First
impressions can be deceiving. I prayed that all would turn out well, that
Parashtchak would heed my friend's plea and permit us to hide in his cellar. Otherwise, our chances of survival were zero.

Three weeks passed. One day, while at Jewish Council headquarters, I
heard that several corpses had been found in the woods between Rołów
and Gaje. When the bodies were brought in—thirteen, including men,
women, and children—it was revealed that they were the Kammermanns,
Richters, and Teppers. All thirteen, we learned, had been shot to death by
Parashtchak and Fleischer.

Mourning my friend, I recalled the wise words of Rabbi Mendele of
Kotzk.[4] On the Sabbath before the new moon, we say the prayer, "Fulfill, O Lord, our heart's wishes for the best." The rabbi explained why the
words "for the best" are used. After all, can a man wish for evil? Nor can a
man foretell if his wishes will lead to good or evil, for many wishes lead to
destruction. That is why the words "for the best" are employed. It means

4. Menachem Mendel Morgensztern (1787–1859), known as the Kotzker Rebbe, was an
early nineteenth-century rabbi and Hasidic leader. In 1839, he withdrew from society
and lived in seclusion for two more decades until his death.

that God should protect man when he makes a wish, and when he asks for a favor, it should end well.

I remembered the parable as I stood at the cemetery, looking down at the dead face of Kammermann.

Even now it is not clear to me why Parashtchak had not wanted to take in my brother and me. Perhaps he did not think we were worth his bullets. Perhaps he had been reluctant to deal with two young Jews.

We buried our friends and returned to Drohobycz, where life was becoming more unbearable with each passing day. Roundups of Jews were now a daily occurrence. The flight of Dr. Ruhrberg and other council members made life even more difficult for those who remained. Attempts to escape became more frequent, and many of those who had not the means to run killed themselves.

A suicide epidemic held Drohobycz in its grip. Daily, I scanned the lists of persons who had taken their own lives, hoping not to find names of friends and acquaintances. One became inured to this new phenomenon in our daily lives, but on occasion an incident came to one's attention that stunned and shocked. One such incident concerned two families occupying one room. The Hausmanns were old and childless; the Birnbaums, who I'd known back home, had two children. One day, I heard loud weeping in the room adjacent to ours, where the two families lived. I ran to find out what had happened. Entering, I saw Mrs. Birnbaum and her eleven-year-old son, Janek, lying dead on the sofa. The two Hausmanns, husband and wife, stood near the sofa looking down at the two corpses, wailing loudly. I tried consoling them—after all, suicides were such a commonplace occurrence. Perhaps they were better off, I said. But the two mourners paid no attention to me, raising the pitch of their wails. Then Hausmann turned his tear-stained face to me and said in a sepulchral tone, "They used the cyanide we bought for ourselves! It was *our* poison! We saved and saved, we skimped, and we didn't eat to save for the cyanide. Now it's gone!"

"And I thought she was a friend," the Hausmann woman moaned. "I thought she could be trusted."

"What can we do now, without the poison?" the husband demanded.

At this point, Elias Birnbaum entered the room. Seeing his wife and child dead on the sofa, his face turned ashen, and his body seemed to contract as though in this one terrible moment he'd shrunk. He tried saying something but couldn't, finally whispering, "What happened? When did this happen? Why didn't she say anything about this to me? With what did she kill herself?"

Hausmann, who with his wife burst into tears again, said, "With our cyanide she killed herself! She did it with our poison!"

Birnbaum, crushed, sank into a chair. "She didn't tell me and our daughter. Why didn't she tell us? What are we two going to do?"

I tried consoling the grieving man. "Don't cry," I said. "Maybe they're better off." But Birnbaum's mind was elsewhere. "Why did they go without me, without us?" he demanded.

"Maybe Hausmann can tell you where he got the cyanide," I said.

Birnbaum shook his head. "The chemist ran away from the ghetto; now it's impossible to get cyanide."

Suddenly Birnbaum's sixteen-year-old daughter came running. Crying "I heard about Mama!" she flung herself at the two corpses, kissed them violently, and embraced them. She opened a pocket knife that she clasped in her hand and tried stabbing herself. We wrested the knife from her, but she tried reclaiming it to kill the Hausmanns. "If you hadn't left the poison in the room," she cried, "my mother and brother would not be dead!" We tried restraining the poor girl, whose hysterical cries could be heard in the street. That night, the Hausmanns went elsewhere to sleep, fearing another violent outburst from the girl. The next day, when the Jewish Council undertakers came for the bodies, the girl tried preventing them.

The above incident happened in December 1942, when we in the ghetto were reaching our nadir of despair. Each person was now interested only in himself.

While we, the remnant of the once-flourishing Jewish community of Drohobycz, were waiting for the final crushing blow, the Aryans, the Ukrainians and Poles, were also waiting—to seize, steal, and grab our remaining

possessions. Like vultures circling in the sky about to swoop down on carrion, they eagerly came in their carts from neighboring villages, hundreds
of them, expecting to cart away every object left behind by the Jews.

Late in December 1942, a series of events took place—some of them
thousands of miles away from the ghetto—that seemed to affect our lives
in Drohobycz. The Americans landed in Africa and occupied French
Morocco and Algeria.[5] For the first time, the hitherto unconquerable
Wehrmacht was retreating in Libya and Tunisia. A whole German army
was surrounded in Stalingrad and tasting defeat after defeat elsewhere on
the Eastern Front. We, in Drohobycz, became aware of this extraordinary
series of events when the Gestapo, seemingly determined to liquidate the
remaining Jews in a December Action, called it off. We wondered: Had
the killers lost their zest for killing? We hoped the lull would endure.

Naftali Backenroth, knowledgeable about such matters, left his secure
shelter, appeared in the ghetto, and declared in a loud voice, "For the time
being, we are safe, there will be no liquidation."

People emerged, warily, from their cellars and attics and entered the
ghetto. And indeed, nobody intercepted them; nobody arrested them.
Every day, more old familiar faces were seen in the ghetto, smiling, bewildered, stunned by the turn of events, embracing friends and strangers
alike. People I had long thought dead held out a hand to be shaken. How
eagerly I grasped those hands!

The price of poisons dropped; the suicides ceased. We now felt sorry
for those who had killed themselves. Those who had been within a hair's
breadth of killing themselves thanked God for stopping them at the last
moment. Wilner's was one such case. He could not wait to tell it to an
old friend. "You should hear it!" he said. "My family is alive today by a
miracle!" His little daughter, Blumele, had performed the miracle.

---

5. The joint Anglo-American invasion of North Africa, code-named "Operation Torch,"
began on November 8, 1942.

"It happened early in December," Wilner said, eagerly beginning his tale, holding me by the arm lest I decided to escape, "during Chanukah,[6] when we celebrate the great victories of the Maccabees. My mind was almost constantly on Palestine, berating myself for never having tried to go there with my family. In the past two decades, there had been opportunities to go. But I'm not a doer; I let things slide. Still, once in a while, when things got really bad, I thought of Palestine, how happy all of us could have been there, working for some kind of future. For more than a thousand years, we Jews have been living in Europe, deceiving ourselves that this was our home. We invested our lives in Europe. Why didn't we return to our mother country, Palestine, where we could have created the good life for ourselves and a bright future for our children? Even after Palestine was opened to the Jews through the Balfour Declaration, we preferred to remain, living among Poles and Ukrainians, thinking of Palestine only during morning and evening prayers."[7]

Wilner paused, tightened his grip on my arm. "Even during the worst terror, I couldn't get the lost opportunity of Palestine out of my mind. Then it got so bad, my mother who lived with us said she'd be better off dead. My wife and my sisters started talking about wanting to kill themselves, trying to convince me that I should try to live and that a man alone would have a better chance of surviving. That's when I began thinking of suicide. But I, who was once a wealthy man, who inherited properties from both father and father-in-law, didn't have enough money to buy poison for the whole family."

"Then one day, I fell on the idea of buying coal, heating the oven, and inhaling the fumes. I talked it over with the family; we all agreed to go

6. Chanukah (or Hanukkah, Hebrew for "dedication" or "consecration"), also known as the "Festival of Lights," is the eight-day celebration that commemorates Judah Maccabee's successful revolt in 165 BCE against the Seleucid monarchy, which resulted in the recovery and rededication of the Second Temple in Jerusalem.
7. The Balfour Declaration of November 2, 1917, was contained in a letter from foreign secretary Arthur Balfour to the Zionist leader Lord Walter Rothschild. In it, Balfour affirmed the British government's support for the establishment of a Jewish homeland in Palestine.

through with it. Die together. The very next day I bought the coal, heated the oven, and closed the chimney, and we got ourselves ready to die. We said our farewells, embraced, cried, and lay down on the floor, waiting for death.

"I lay on the floor next to my loved ones. It was so quiet in the room that I could hear the others breathing. Once in a while, my mother sighed. I thought, Why did the people of Europe hate us and persecute us? What had we done to deserve this?

"I don't remember how long we lay on the floor. Suddenly, I was startled by my little Blumele's voice. 'Papa.' A shock ran through my body. Should I respond? Then she began sobbing. 'Papa, Mama, I don't want to die! I'm afraid! Help me.' In an instant, I was on my feet. I ran to the window and opened it wide and let the air come in."

Wilner finished his tale and let go of my arm. "Now maybe we can live on. At least they've stopped killing."

Seven months later, on June 27, 1943, on the twentieth day of Tammuz, in the year 5603 according to the Jewish calendar, Israel Wilner and his entire family were murdered in Camp Beskiden.

But at the time Wilner had told me his story of the miracle, things were quiet in the ghetto. The peasants returned to their villages with empty carts.

I should point out that even when life in Drohobycz was comparatively calm, the actions suspended, the Germans continued stripping us of our remaining belongings, setting up "Robbers Commissions" such as were active in Sambor and other places.

Methodically, they went from one dwelling to another, taking everything that they could lay their hands on. No house or apartment escaped them. First, they took only first-class goods: fine furniture, good carpeting, high-quality men's and women's clothing. On their second trip, they were less particular; the third and fourth times around, the homes were stripped of everything. By May 1943, there was nothing more to loot. The dwellings were bare, with the exception of old bottles, broken pots, rags, and paper.

Jewish property was considered war booty belonging to the German state.

The Jewish homes outside the ghetto were handled in a rather different way. There, the Germans confiscated the best houses, declaring them property of the state. The ordinary dwellings were sold to the local populace at very cheap prices.

This wholesale plundering deprived the Jews of their only source of income, their personal belongings. Those who did fairly well were the few merchants and shopkeepers of the ghetto. There were constant demands for food and clothing, and as a result, they suffered far less than the rest of us.

In the ghetto, there was an active "underground" stock exchange, with gold, jewels, and foreign currency being bought and sold. Life, as you see, continued along some of its "normal" paths.

I should say that some of these illegal businesses were owned jointly by Jews and non-Jews. From time to time, the non-Jewish partners betrayed the Jew, and as a result, all his property would be taken by the non-Jew. The Jew would be content to get away with his life. Meanwhile, the peasants themselves had looted so heavily that they were able to undersell the Jews. The Jewish merchants sometimes gave away their goods before the Robbers Commission made its appearance to cart everything away.

Outside the ghetto, Jews in partnership with non-Jews opened clothing stores. Naturally, the place was owned officially by the Aryan. The Jewish partners bought clothes in the ghetto and transported them in the dark of night. For a brief period, this business flourished. But soon the Gestapo got wind of it, and trucks were dispatched to the stores and emptied them of all their merchandise.

Taking advantage of the "relaxed" period, we established a sick fund, tax office, communal kitchen, Jewish hospital, and other organizations that flourished among us before the war. There were always long lines at the kitchen, where one hundred grams of bread and a plate of soup were issued once a day. Formerly wealthy and influential people stood in that line to receive their only nourishment for the day.

The Jewish hospital had been founded by the Jewish Council. When the Gestapo invaded the ghetto, they drove the sick into the streets, loaded them onto trucks, and took them away. During the November Action, instead of driving the sick into the streets, the Germans marched through the wards and shot everybody in their beds.

Jewish intellectual life was crushed. German authorities forbade the establishment of Jewish schools; the only way to teach the children was for persons to visit homes and give private lessons. No lectures on Jewish subjects were given, for life was too hard, too bitter for people to care about Jewish history, religion, and cultural themes.

Until August 1942, the only Jewish newspaper we saw was the *Gazeta Żydowska*, which was sent on from Warsaw and consisted of four small pages written in Polish. It appeared three times a week and was not as good as prewar Jewish newspapers, but we were all happy to read it. We followed with special interest the work of Dr. Edmund Weiss and Dr. Hillel Seidman.[8]

Jewish books, which were held in great respect, were torn apart by non-Jews and used as packing paper. When the Jews were forced to move to the ghetto, they were unable to take their books, and so the volumes were left behind and collected by the poor, who sold them for packing paper. You can imagine how many books were destroyed from the fact that the price of packing paper decreased from two złotys to fifteen groszy per pound.

As death lived so closely to us, the young people tried hard to enjoy life. As a result, respect for morality diminished. Jewish women, who felt they might die any day, women who had been chaste and proper all their lives, sold themselves in order to survive. During the various actions, the most beautiful women in the ghetto became mistresses of the German and Ukrainian policemen. When their lovers tired of them, they were sent into the streets during an *Aktion* or shipped to a collecting point and sent to their death.

---

8. The *Gazeta Żydowska* ("Jewish newspaper") was the official German-sanctioned, Polish-language newspaper for all Jewish ghettos in German-occupied Poland. The journalists and religious scholars Edmund Weiss and Hillel Seidman were regular contributors.

The men who did not work played cards in the ghetto and drank heavily in an effort to conquer their boredom. They too tried to forget the conditions under which they lived.

As of November 1942, 10,000 Jews had managed to survive. About 1,000 had escaped into the woods, with 1,500 more working for the Germans. Another 1,500 had managed to find hiding places. This left about 6,000 Jews in the Drohobycz ghetto.

The streets were usually empty as the young worked, while the old preferred to remain indoors. Only on Sundays were the streets crowded. The workers received passes to leave the camps in the morning and return in the evenings. Later, the Germans abolished the passes, issuing them only to a handful of Jewish Council members. Sunday was bathing day, when the Jews were marched to the bathhouse. We eagerly looked forward to Sunday.

During the early months of the occupation, many babies were born, but the rate decreased radically. As far as I know, only one marriage took place after the August Action. The couple was wed in the cemetery, a custom originating during the Middle Ages when plagues were prevalent. It was believed that marriage in a cemetery made people immune from further disaster.[9] If I remember correctly, this particular marriage was performed by Zalel Bartfeld.

---

9. Well before the Holocaust, Jews sometimes performed marriage ceremonies in cemeteries, which were known as *shvartse khupes* or *shvartse khasenes* ("black weddings"). Through them, afflicted communities aimed to ingratiate themselves with the dead and encourage God to stop epidemics.

# CHAPTER 14

# THE SITUATION OF THE CHRISTIANS

The non-Jews, the so-called Aryans, Ukrainians and Poles, were not much better off than Jews. They participated in the looting and profited at our expense, but the Germans treated them almost as harshly as the Jews. Christians were subject to compulsory labor service from the ages of eighteen to sixty. Younger boys and girls were put to work and housed in barracks. Those unwilling to work were sent to concentration camps in Germany. The Ukrainians who had hoped the Germans would liberate them from the Poles were bitterly disappointed.

Peasants were ordered to deliver most of their produce to the occupation forces. In the beginning they were not pressured, but when the deadline came and deliveries were not made, German police entered the villages, selected ten of the finest homes and set them afire. The local mayor was forced to make a statement to the villagers, informing them that if they did not meet their quotas within three days, the entire village would be razed. As a result, the peasants delivered up their cattle, horses, and pigs. Each young pig was registered, and the peasant was forced to slaughter it, with half going to the Germans, the other half remaining with him. The same held true for cattle. The Germans were eager to obtain milk, and depending on the number of cows a farmer owned, a milk quota was set for him. If the quota was too high, as often happened, the peasant had to buy milk from his neighbor to fill it. The milk was carefully examined for its fat content, the Germans punishing those who watered it down.

Deliberately and arrogantly, the Germans manifested in every possible way that they were conquerors. They avoided any contact with the native populace. They rode in railway cars bearing "For Germans Only" signs. On the doors of hotels and cafes, there appeared the warning "Jews and Poles Forbidden." Movie houses and theaters were opened three times a week for Germans, twice a week for Poles, and one day a week for Ukrainians.

Shops established for Germans displayed products that were not available to the natives but were available to the invaders for trifling sums.

When the Gestapo was not busy persecuting Jews, they kept active by executing gypsies and beggars, all of whom were thrown into mass graves like the Jews.

When Soviet prisoners were brought to our area, there were no Jews among them. They had been separated from the Russians and were shot on sight by their captors. The Germans also brought a large group from the Volga German Republic in Russia, most of whom—originally of German descent—were elderly men and women who had lived in their homeland all their lives and whose parents and grandparents had been reared on Russian soil on the Volga.[1] By the end of 1942, more than 250 of these Russo-Germans had come to Drohobycz. They had no idea of the meaning of Nazism and were ignorant of the German theory of racial purity. Learning what the Germans were doing to Jews, they began to fear that they too would be liquidated. They were right.

Several weeks later, a large group of Russians, about 150 of them, were led to Bronica and shot.[2] Before the executions, brigades of laborers were ordered to dig large pits; it was at this point that we all became panicky, believing mass murders were about to take place. However, this time, they were digging for the Russians.

1. The Volga Germans were ethnic Germans recruited to Russia as farmers in the eighteenth century by Russian empress Catherine the Great. Stalin aggressively persecuted the Volga Germans as potential collaborators during World War II.
2. The Bronica forest northwest of Drohobycz was the site of mass executions during 1942–1943. Approximately eleven thousand Jews were murdered there.

During this period, my brother and I were employed in the Hyrawka Gardens.[3] My brother was ordered into a special barracks, while I, in addition to the barracks, held on to my place in the ghetto.

In the ghetto, everyone possessed a hiding place, without which a Jew was lost. Finally, I found one for my brother and myself with a man named Schnall, who checked on us very carefully before letting us in to make certain he was not running a risk.

On a cold Sunday in February, panic broke out in the ghetto. People scurried about, searching for a place to hide. I ran to Schnall's hiding place, and when I arrived there, out of breath, it was already crowded with men, women, and children. Schnall had let the children in only after he had made sure their parents had brought along the necessary tranquilizing drugs to keep them quiet. From past experience, it was known that children often panicked, screamed, and gave everybody away. People continued knocking on Schnall's door, but he let in only those who had prior reservations.

As we sat in the cellar, crowded like herring in a barrel, we heard loud screams upstairs. We were petrified. After a long wait, some of us pushed our way to the ladder, which led to the main floor. A woman in the upstairs room told us what had happened. In order to get to the cellar from the kitchen, we'd had to crawl through a large baking oven. While I and some others managed to get to the cellar, people had jammed in the oven, which had collapsed under the pressure of overcrowding. Most of those people now jammed the cellar, which no longer remained a hiding place. We were now fair game for the German and Ukrainian police.

We wondered: Should we stay or look for another place? Some argued that the German and Ukrainian police would not look behind a collapsed oven. Finally, we all agreed to leave the cellar. I was the last one out.

3. In October 1941, the Drohobycz *Judenrat* and SS-*Hauptscharführer* Felix Landau, who was in charge of Jewish labor assignments, agreed to open a dairy, fruit, and vegetable farm in Hyrawka to supply the German military with agricultural products. Its leader, Naftali Backenroth, helped save many Jews by employing them at the facility, thereby making them essential to the German war effort. For more on Hyrawka, see part I, chapter 20.

Emerging into the street, I was met by deathly silence. No human was to be seen. The houses were dark and desolate, with no smoke rising from their chimneys. I saw a frightened cat crawl along the wall, but it smelled death and hurried away.

I stood there, not knowing where to go. I thought I would follow the others, but it seemed as if they had been swallowed up by the earth. I walked from house to house, knocking on doors, but received no answer.

The echo of my steps pursued me, and I was seized with panic. Finally, I reached the building of the Jewish Council.

All was desolate . . .

I came to the *Kommandantura* (Commandant's Office) of the Jewish Police, which was nearby. I opened the door and found myself in a darkened room filled with cigarette smoke. Here, there were many Jewish policemen, wearing their blue caps with a Star of Zion. My entrance caused a commotion. What was a civilian doing here before an *Aktion* was to take place? They all crowded around me.

Finally, I discovered one officer I knew, a man named Licht. "What are you doing here?" he asked. "Why don't you hide? The *Aktion* may begin at any minute. The Germans have been drinking for hours, and they may strike soon."

I asked him if it was possible for me to hide there until evening. Then, I said, I would slip into my brother's camp at dark.

He replied that this was not a sound idea, as the place was being watched.

"If you have money," another policeman said, "I can manage to hide you."

My friend assured him that I did. "Where can you hide him, and how much will it cost?" Licht asked. Both men moved into a corner and consulted. Then they motioned for me to follow them. Licht assured me that they were taking me to a safe place. We went into the street, walked from one lane to another to the Komarner Synagogue. We entered a garden and walked through it to a small house. The door was padlocked. One of them stepped forward and opened it, and as we entered, we found ourselves in a large narrow passageway. Here, I paid the money agreed on and walked into the kitchen. From there, we entered a room that had some wooden beds. The policemen moved one of the beds from the wall. He knocked several times on the floor, speaking in a loud voice to someone I could not see. We heard movement, and suddenly two boards of the floor were raised.

A voice called up, "What's going on up there? Can we come out?"

"No, I want to know if you can take in a friend of mine who has no place to hide."

The voice replied, "What do you expect of me? We're suffocating down here, and you're bringing us another one?"

They argued briefly, then I was shoved down through the opening. I could see the cellar was very small, its dozen occupants seated on benches along the wall and on the floor, where several women were holding their sleeping children. The planks were slammed down, and I stood in the darkness, not daring to move, fearing I might step on someone.

A heavy silence smothered the dark room. Nobody offered to move and make room for me. Obviously, I was not welcome, having been forced on them, yet the man who had brought me here was in control; they could not turn him down.

I found a tiny space on the floor and sat down. It was hot in the cellar; I thought we would suffocate. I felt particularly sorry for the little children.

At five in the morning, when most of us were stiff from sitting still, we heard the first shots, faint at first, but becoming louder and more frequent. We could hear the rattling of machine guns.

The *Aktion* has begun. The mothers are told to stifle their children's cries. We adults take care not to utter a sound, cough, or clear our throats.

Suddenly, we hear the rattling of a door. We hear heavy blows, and the door is broken open. There are steps overhead, coming closer. Beds are moved aside, and wardrobes are toppled. We crouch and hold our breath. Then the steps recede and withdraw and after a while—silence. We begin to relax and move about.

Hardly twenty minutes pass. We hear those heavy ominous footsteps above us. This time, not only are the beds moved, but the floorboards are pulled up. We stiffen with fear, certain they will find us. But soon—it seems to me like eternity—the footsteps retreat. But the respite is a brief one; another dozen jackals appear, sniffing for Jewish blood, to be followed by several more. This goes on for seven hours. The raids cease; the firing stops. We are exhausted, but we're alive! Maybe we're destined to survive . . .

But at two in the afternoon, the firing resumes. From past experience, I judge the *Aktion* will last about four hours. Fear works its way to the surface again like some poisonous plant. In four hours, they can snuff out a great many innocent lives. We hear their cleated boots. The search begins. We hear objects crashing to the floor. My heart beats violently. They are more thorough than the previous groups. In their search for the entrance to the cellar, they move the beds and thump the boards, listening for a hollow sound.

Can we hope for them to overlook the two boards that can betray us? They have taken note of the hollow sound! They knock repeatedly, seemingly convinced there is an opening. They proceed to chop with axes, but the wood is well-bolted from the inside and does not give way.

They shout, "Open! Open up!"

We observe the silence of the dead. A mother next to me clasps a hand on her little boy's mouth; his eyes, filled with terror, are fixed on the ceiling. The axes resume chopping; the wood is beginning to give. The chinks become wider; rays of light now filter through. Then the boards give way altogether, and we are bathed in daylight.

We have been discovered! All is lost!

We hear a German. "Is anyone down there?"

A Ukrainian declares, "It's full of Jews."

We hear someone leave the house. In a few minutes, reinforcements arrive, and we are ordered up. We do not move. Suddenly, a shot is fired into our hiding place. The noise shocks us into activity. We jump up from our seats. Children begin to scream. One man lies dead in the cellar, his brains blown out. A young woman, apparently the dead man's daughter, pulls at him and cries, "Father, Father, come, we must go up." But of course, the dead man does not hear her anguished cries.

Slowly, we all climb up the ladder. Four Nazi policemen and a group of Ukrainian militia are armed with guns, ready to fire.

I look about me, and for the first time, I see the people with whom I have spent the last twenty-four hours. Faces are flushed and bloody. A woman carrying a child tries to open a window to escape. A shot is fired, and she falls back into the room. She tries to rise again, but a second bullet kills her. Another woman picks up the weeping child.

After the Germans batter a few more women and children, we are all marched into the street. I am surprised to see that it is a clear winter day, with a light-blue mist floating over the ghetto. The sun is sinking, and its rays are especially attractive to us who have been trapped in a dark cellar. How good it would be if we were free!

There are police at every corner, ready to shoot should we make a false step. Every once in a while, a German shoots a Jew, but meanwhile we are kept marching. As we leave the ghetto, there are joyful crowds of Poles and Ukrainians watching us being herded to what everyone believes is our death.

We finally arrive at the prison of the court of justice. Here, a Gestapo group leader named Gabriel[4] takes charge, and we are divided into two groups: women and children are locked into one cell, men into another.

---

4. For his active role in the murder of Jews in East Galicia, Gestapo official and SS-*Oberscharführer* Josef Gabriel (1907–fl. 1968) was tried and sentenced to life imprisonment in March 1959. He was, however, released in 1968.

—∕—

# CHAPTER 15

# IN THE SHADOW
# OF DEATH

I am thrust into a crowded cell with not a single bench or chair on which to sit. The walls are covered with inscriptions, names of those who had passed through on their way to their deaths. There are rows and rows of names as well as dates of imprisonment and probably execution. I speculate why a man so close to death should bother engraving his name on a prison wall. Man refuses to believe he will be obliterated from the world, his memory erased. Great men are more fortunate. They leave their works behind: symphonies, novels, graceful buildings, and colorful paintings. But the men who passed through this prison, average men, had to content themselves with their names scratched on the damp wall, aware there would be no tombstone. The writer hopes those who come after him will see his name and think of him, if only for an instant.

In addition to names, angry words are scratched in Yiddish. "Murderers! Our blood will not be silent. Amalek![1] Bitter will be your end! Lord, that you may do ill, we see best ourselves. But do not forget the criminals of the Gestapo and the Ukrainian Militia!"

As we look about us, some recognize acquaintances and friends. Men embrace one another, weeping bitterly.

---

1. In the Hebrew Bible, Amalek is a descendant of Esau. The Book of Exodus describes the Amalekites as a tribe that attacked the ancient Israelites without provocation, and in Jewish tradition, they epitomize hostility to the Jews.

Sitting in a corner reading is Rabbi Wolf Nussenbaum, the spiritual leader of Drohobycz, author of many books and dean of the *yeshiva*[2] in Lublin. The rabbi's face is furrowed with grief, and he looks as though he himself is responsible for the misery in the cell. For more than thirty years, he taught Jews ethics and morality, urging them to believe in God. And now? He looks as though he wants to hide. Rabbi Nussenbaum rises, draws his prayer belt tight, and turns his face to the wall in silent prayer. Some of us who are close by ask him respectfully, "May we pray together?"

"Of course," the rabbi says. "I haven't invited anyone to join me because of the great bitterness I sense in this cell."

A voice cries out, "We want to pray. Is anyone opposed to it?"

Someone replies, "Why should we oppose prayer? We've prayed all our lives and will be faithful to the Lord until our last breaths."

We all rise, and the rabbi recites the kaddish, the prayer for the dead. We join in the silent prayer, the *shemoneh esreh*.[3] Pious Jews throughout the world recite this prayer three times a day, but it sounds strange in this cell. Even the words seem to have different meanings. Why should we pray now? What does it mean to pray for a "good year"? In our minds, we are practically dead. As we recite, we sigh and groan. Finally, the silent prayer becomes a single, united cry. We no longer repeat the words of the Hebrew text. Instead we ask, "Oh Lord, what do you want of us? How have we sinned that such fate should befall us? Oh Lord, we have renounced the joys of life, according to your doctrine. What have we done to deserve this fate?"

Our lamenting carries to the other cells; soon the entire prison resounds with the cries.

A German slides open a panel at the door and calls out, "Be silent, you damn Jewish pigs! If you don't shut up, we'll beat you all."

2. A *yeshiva* is an Orthodox Jewish college or rabbinical academy. Rabbi Wolf Nussenbaum (1877–1943) died in the mass executions described in the next chapter.

3. Although *shemoneh esreh* means "eighteen" in Hebrew, it is actually a series of nineteen benedictions that is a central component of Jewish liturgy. In traditional congregations, it is said silently.

We struggle to control ourselves. We cease praying. It grows dark. I close my eyes and try to sleep.

In the morning, Polish guards provide us with water, and we pool our money, bribing them to bring us bread and cigarettes. They tell us that within the last twenty-four hours, more than one thousand Jews have been arrested and imprisoned. We are told that the Germans will not bother transporting us and that we will be killed in the Bronica forest near Drohobycz. They tell us it might happen within a day or two.

Before we are to be killed, the guards will take us to the prison office, where we will be searched all over and all our possessions, except clothing, taken away. Then we will be driven to the execution area. The Polish guards, eager to get our money before the Germans confiscate it, offer to do us favors. They unlock the cell doors and allow prisoners to visit one another to make their farewells. I wander from cell to cell, looking for friends and relatives. We embrace, telling each other that we hope to die without too much pain. We dread the idea of being wounded and tossed into graves while still alive. There are rumors that living men and women are thrown into mass graves, covered by earth.

We arrange for messages to be delivered to friends and relatives on the outside. I write a farewell note to my brother: "As you're the last surviving member of our family, I hope you manage to live through the war and through this hell. I'm now prepared for the worst. In my mind, I've been living on borrowed time the last few months, since the day of my arrival at Janover Camp. How many more miraculous escapes can I hope for? Man cannot live forever; I've suffered much, but the end to my suffering is near. When you hear about the executions, you will know I'm dead. Stay alive at all costs! You are the last remaining member of the whole family. You must stay alive and carry our name. Never forget what the cursed Germans have done to us. If God spares you, settle in a Jewish community, marry a Jewish woman,[4] and if you are blessed with children, name them after those who

---

4. Especially among Orthodox Jews, intermarriage is forbidden and considered a violation of the biblical prohibition in Deuteronomy 7:3–4. Chapter 13 of part II, "The Story of Simon Becker," concerns a Jew who married outside the faith.

have been killed, so that we will live on through them. I assure you that my last thoughts are of you."

I feel better, knowing my brother will read these final words. I am ready to die.

As the first group is led to the prison office, we try to get rid of everything of value still in our possession. Gold and jewelry are flung into toilets, papers destroyed. It does not surprise me seeing men assigned to cleaning the toilets dig through the muck to recover what they can.

We are led to the office. Gestapo authorities order us to empty our pockets into a large box. They warn us that we will be searched afterward, and if anything is found, our tongues will be cut out, our eyes pierced, and our limbs severed. We are convinced that they are capable of doing it; we have heard of such things.

We empty our pockets, throwing everything into the box. Searched, we are led into another cell. Here, we are under strict surveillance. On occasion, a prisoner timidly asks for water. But the only response is a curse. "Soon you won't need water!" they tell us. This bit of information does not surprise any of us. I know we will be shot; I'm reconciled, yet I'm terrified. How I cling to this wretched life!

I wonder if death will come as hard to others as it will to me. Do I feel this way because I'm still young? A glance at other faces convinces me that they too are suffering at the thought of death, regardless of age.

The old rabbi rises and begins to talk to us. He attempts to offer consolation. He tells of the vanity of life on earth and that we are about to enter a new, more glorious life.

"For thirty years, I have been leading you in the ways of God. I have been guiding you on matters of morality, manners, and grace. These teachings will be valuable to you in the hours ahead."

He gazes at the men who are listening to him in silence. Suddenly, his voice breaks, and his eyes flash. He raises his arms and cries out in a loud voice, "Damned be the Amalek of today who is aiming to destroy the ancient house of Israel! May he be cursed for the murders of innocent men, harmless women, and children! All traces and signs of him will be wiped out by God for all generations."

He assures us that we will be sainted martyrs who possess a divine idea that our enemies cannot fathom. He asks us to rise and repeat the words of the *vidui*, the prayer of death.[5] He recites each word methodically, and we repeat after him: "*Ashamnu...Bogadnu...Gozalnu.*"

"We have done wrong."

"We were faithless."

"We have robbed."

As we recite, a Polish guard opens the sliding panel and watches us. From the other cell, the women entreat us to write down the words of the *vidui*, as they wish to recite it. The Pole cooperates and passes through paper and pencil, and soon the women join us.

The rabbi's speech and the recitation of the *vidui* calm us, and we now wait for our final moments.

Outside, we hear automobile engines, and once more terror grips us. The women begin to scream, a guard fires a shot, and there is silence once more. Heavy steps are heard in the corridor. Our cell door is flung open, and the Germans drive us through two lines of police into the open courtyard.

The day of doom is here. They are beating us with whips; we make a feeble effort to protect our heads by clasping our hands over them. But our bodies absorb the fierce blows.

We reach the waiting trucks, bruised, climb in, and lie down on the floor.

The trucks begin moving.

5. See part I, chapter 6, note 5.

CHAPTER 16

# THE EXECUTIONS

The truck is filled with prisoners, some of whom are lying on top of me while I lie on others. The weight crushes me; I can scarcely breathe. The ride on the bumpy road is interminable. Finally, the screeching brakes bring the truck to a stop. We are in Bronica.

We are ordered out, and I see nearby a large clearing in the middle of the thick forest. The trees are laden with icicles that bring to mind frozen tears. At the edge of the clearing, there are two long, deep trenches.

The first group is ordered to undress. Soon they are stark naked; their bodies turn blue from the cold. They are herded toward the trenches, over which the executioners have put down long planks on which several people can stand. Machine guns are lined up at the other end.

The first group of five on the plank are shot; their bodies fall into the trench. Five more are brought up to stand on the plank and are shot.

I look around desperately and see that the whole area is surrounded by armed guards. This is the end; there is no escaping it.

The shooting of adults continues. The children are not shot; taken from their parents, they are flung into the trenches to be buried alive. The first trench is filled with corpses. Some victims are still alive and twitching convulsively. But it does not make any difference; dirt is being tossed into the mass grave.

The machine guns continue firing. Now my group prepares for death. I am ordered to take a man who was killed by a German bullet from the truck and remove his clothing. I work as though in a nightmare.

I finish and begin to undress. I get one shoe off, but the lace on the other is knotted. As I try to loosen it, I lose my balance and fall on the huge heap of clothing. As I struggle with my clothes, I find myself buried in the heap. I creep deeper into what is suddenly a hiding place. There is shooting around me, but as I crouch in the clothing, the noise becomes duller. I do not think at all. I act instinctively, like an animal. Now, the shooting and crying have ceased; the noise of the truck engines has died away.

Finally, the clothes covering me are being taken away, and the weight on my body grows lighter. Should I creep out now or wait until I am discovered? Or should I pretend I am dead?

In a moment, I will be discovered. I decide to act. I throw off the few remaining pieces of clothing that cover me and rise as though I were a diver emerging from the depths of the sea. I look around me. The guards are busy searching for valuables, but when they see me, they begin to beat me.

The trenches are now filled with earth. More than one thousand Jews are buried here, and it is a miracle that I am still alive.

One of the guards snarls, "Come on! Dig a grave for yourself."

They will not leave a corpse lying about, and so I am ordered to work on my own grave. I dig a hole alongside the trenches, shoveling the icy yellow earth that will soon cover me. The guards nearby are busy rummaging through heaps of clothing, searching for valuables. One of them discovers gold coins, and the two guards standing over me are distracted by the find.

To this day, I am baffled by what came over me and made me leap like a madman at the guard nearest me and strike him with the shovel. He fell, the gun dropping from his hands. I jumped over him and sprinted toward the clump of trees nearby. In an instant, I was in the woods, my ears filled with the guards' shouts, warning me to stop. But I was fleeing for my life. I continued running. I leaped over fallen trees, dragged my feet over marshy ground. I stumbled, fell, rose, ran, aware of the crunchy snow underfoot. They were behind me, but I did not dare turn and lose momentum. *I must not stop, must not be taken*, I said to myself. *I must survive to tell the story of what happened in the woods in Bronica.*

My heart pounding, I grew dizzy, bayonets jabbed at my lungs, but I was determined to survive.

Suddenly, before me spread a clearing. Was I at the edge of the woods? I was wrong; it was a ravine packed with snow. I tried jumping over it, fell short, and landed in the snow. I was sinking. Hardly able to catch my breath, I thought I would die there. Picking up a handful of snow, I put it to my temples and in my mouth. I felt somewhat revived. Could I dare hope I would survive? I recalled the story of a girl who had escaped from a situation similar to mine several months ago, staggering back into the ghetto naked and raving mad. Would I pay a similar price? Would I go mad? How could one continue to live with the memory of what one had witnessed in Bronica and remain sane?

Hours passed. I was numb with cold, wearing only a pair of trousers, one stocking, and one shoe. Suddenly, as though responding to some inner command that said "You will not die here!" I began moving my arms and legs vigorously. Slowly the circulation was returning. I grabbed the root of a large tree and began hoisting myself out of the ravine. It had turned dark. The sky was filled with stars; a light wind was blowing. Skirting the ravine, I reached the woods again and stopped.

Where should I go? If I went to Drohobycz, the Jewish Council, most likely informed of my escape, might grab me. Were I not famished—not having eaten in five days—I would have set out to distant Sambor.

I decided to retrace my steps in the woods and try Drohobycz.

It was quiet here—deserted, abandoned—but I moved warily, making sure I would not step on dry branches and call attention to myself.

After an hour, I was back at the clearing where the executions had taken place. It was peaceful here now, the graves covered with soil, the cries stilled. I was suddenly assailed by guilt for being alive while the others had perished.

Pausing over the mass grave, I recalled the names and faces of some of the persons alive only yesterday: the hairdresser who told his cellmates how prosperous he had been before the Germans came, how much in love he was with his wife; the coachman who told us about the joyous Sabbaths of yesteryear spent with his wife and children after a long week's labor. Vivid in my mind was the pretty girl of nineteen who embraced her father an instant before they had perished, content to die with him. I began walking again, unable to rid myself of the guilt—torment that crushed me with its weight until I found it necessary to rest. Reaching the ghetto's narrow streets, I sat down near a familiar house. I wondered how much longer I could go on. How many more miraculous escapes could I expect? Bone-weary, life-weary, I sat there under a dark sky, on a deserted ghetto street, as though waiting to be taken by a passing German, Ukrainian, or Pole. Not many years ago, while still in rabbinical school, I held firmly to the notion that the Jewish people, having survived Egypt, Persia, Babylonia, and Rome, were indestructible. But to have been in Janover Camp, to have witnessed Bronica, was to learn differently.

I walked toward a familiar house and knocked. I heard Cousin Chuma's voice and called back, almost choking on my words. She opened, and I almost fell in. She reached for me, aided by Cyla and Rose, who led me inside. They gazed at me, at my bloodshot eyes, my face blue with cold and that strange attire, consisting of a pair of pants, a shoe on one foot, and a stocking on the other. Mercifully, they did not seek explanations but put me to bed.

I slept, and then I was awake. Shivering although covered, it seemed to me I was colder in bed than I had been in the ravine. Nightmares crowded my brain.

Awakening, I was surprised to find my brother sleeping in the bed next to mine. I woke him, we embraced, and I asked why he was asleep. "It's daytime now," I said, pointing to the curtained window and the sun shining outside. My brother smiled and replied, "During the nights, I've been busy tending to you."

"Why? What was the matter with me?" I wanted to know. "You slept two days around the clock," he explained. "You were burning up with fever;

you screamed in your sleep. You could not be left unattended. I think you are recovering now."

I nodded. "I must tell you about Bronica!" I said, feeling I would go mad unless I unburdened myself.

It was decided to keep my escape a secret. Clothes were found for me. Some visitors came, among them Schnall, who pumped my hand and told me how pleased he was at my being alive. "I'm planning to build another hiding place," he said, "and I want you and your brother to come in with us."

From Schnall, I learned there was another survivor besides me of the Bronica massacre, a nineteen-year-old girl, Amalia Stock, whose parents had been killed earlier. Her survival, like mine, was a miracle. She had managed to hide under a pile of clothing in the truck that took them to the execution area. She remained in the truck, which was later driven to a Jewish labor camp. When the clothes were unloaded by the Jewish laborers, she was found and aided in her escape. "Now she's in the ghetto with her sister. She saw one thing you missed," Schnall concluded, "photographers taking pictures of the massacre."

The next day, Amalia Stock, thin but still pretty, her burning black eyes like live coals, came to see me. "Of the many thousands, we are the only two survivors," she said, adding, "It must have been fated."

Poor Amalia! She died in Bronica four months later, when the Drohobycz ghetto was liquidated.

I sit here in the cellar, and I write. But I realize that I will never be able to recapture on paper and make the reader see the horrors of Janover and Bronica. Words, even if I were skillful with them, which I am not, cannot convey the reality of that period. Maybe if I were a Count Leo Tolstoy . . . So I will confine myself to facts; the events themselves will supply the drama.

# CHAPTER 17

# LAST DAYS OF THE SAMBOR GHETTO

The passage of time dulls pain and cauterizes wounds. It is one of the marvels of nature. If it were not so, man could not endure the agonies.

In the same fashion, my own life continued. One evening, I went to the house where only recently Rabbi Wolf Nussenbaum had lived, hoping to reclaim a manuscript he had borrowed from me, one dealing with Talmudic matters, in which he was so well versed. I found the manuscript on the floor in a pile of books and papers. I felt as though this saintly man were still alive, although I vividly remembered him dying in the mass killing at Bronica.

We tried to establish some kind of normalcy in our lives, even to the extent of making plans for the future, unrealistic though they may have been. The young people began frequenting the woods, looking for partisans, while the older ones tried to exchange their temporary hiding places for more permanent ones.

While this was going on, the Germans continued implementing their Final Solution plans. One day, an order was issued to liquidate the Jewish post office, which served as a communication center for all Jews in every ghetto. Now the ghettos were separated from one another. Jews were forbidden to telephone other Jews, wire, or write to them. If a Jew wished to contact a fellow Jew in another town, he would usually get in touch with two Christians, one of whom would have to deliver the message to the other, who in turn, gave the letter to the addressee.

During this period, I received a letter from my brother-in-law, Moses Mandelbaum, who wrote from the Sambor ghetto that he was planning to cross the Carpathian Mountains and flee to Hungary and from there immigrate to Palestine. The person who guided the escapees across the Carpathians, my brother-in-law wrote, had come highly recommended to him as a skilled group leader who had guided a group only recently. Would my brother and I be interested? The notion excited me; it appealed to me immensely. Without wasting time, I sent a message to my brother in camp, suggesting that he meet me.

My brother came in; we talked about the matter and decided to risk it and return to Sambor. I got in touch with Schnall, told him of our plan, and asked him to reserve space for us both in his new hideout should our mission to Sambor fail. He agreed, and we left Drohobycz at dawn and passed the town and across the woods, reaching Sambor two days later.

The Sambor ghetto was a small one, consisting of one main street called Mnishcha Lane, about eighty meters long. Several small lanes branched out of it. The entire ghetto area, called "The *Blich*," was surrounded by barbed wire.[1] There was a synagogue on the bleaching ground of the town, which was not a part of the ghetto, its entrance leading to a street outside the ghetto proper. A second synagogue, much smaller in size, served as a hospital.

The Jewish cemetery served other purposes besides burial; the living took refuge there, sitting on the grass on a balmy spring evening, the young daring to dream of brighter tomorrows.

Approximately three thousand people were herded into the ghetto, many of them from nearby towns—from Stary Sambor, Felsztyn, Turka, and others.

The Germans had two aims in establishing ghettos: First, this placed the Jews in one area, so when they staged an *Aktion*, the intended victims were readily available. Second, it was a simpler matter to starve the Jews within the ghetto, where the victims could survive only as long as the food

---

1. Blich was the area of Sambor at the town's edge where the ghetto was established in March 1942. It was so named because it was the site of a bleachery (*blichowanie*), a building where the cleansing, disinfecting, and whitening process of textile manufacture known as bleaching occurs.

supply held out. Once the supplies were used up, the Jews would perish. To some extent, the Germans miscalculated; weeks passed, but the Jews, though emaciated, managed to hang on.

How did this happen?

In the beginning, supplies were used up quickly, but after a while, young men began escaping the ghetto through the sewers and coming back with food. In addition, local peasants openly traded and bartered with the Jews near the barbed wire that separated the ghetto from the rest of Sambor. Fowl was available as well as vegetables—but no meat.

Unlike the Drohobycz ghetto where the German police and local militia stole, plundered, and killed Jews daily, Sambor had only one Gestapo agent, a thug named Wüstner (who was later shot by his fellow Germans when he went mad).[2]

The Sambor ghetto prided itself on its rabbis, among whom were Rabbi Pinchas Twersky of Ostilla; Rabbi Simcha Rubin-Horowitz of Sądowa Wisznia; the rabbis of Komarno, Dębica, Zagórz, Cieszyn, and Bukowsko; Rabbi Mieses of Sambor; Rabbi Kalman Jolles; and the renowned scholar, Rabbi Jakob Turkel. All of them were later wiped out by the Germans. But while still alive, these esteemed men made life in the Sambor ghetto a little easier to endure.

After the establishment of the ghetto, a number of Jews who had converted to Christianity—some a long time ago and others during the German occupation—were sent there. Many of the converts, particularly the more recent ones, had hoped to escape persecutions through baptism. It did not work. Although they had been left alone in the early stages of the war, they were now receiving the same treatment as the rest of us. In Sambor, for example, the converts had only to be registered; in other places, they were forced to wear Jewish armbands. Wealthy converts managed to avoid trouble by selling their homes and shops and hiding out with

2. SS-*Hauptscharführer* Karl Ulrich Wüstner (1909–1943) was the chief of police in Sambor until 1943.

Christian relatives (through marriage) in the larger towns. Life became unbearable for those sent to the ghetto. They had not counted on being treated like Jews. Some of them expected hostility, even violence, from the ghetto Jews. But we in the ghetto had more pressing concerns. The converts were accepted as fellow Jews; however, they kept to themselves, gathering near the barbed-wire fence in the evenings to pass the time with Christian members of their families who remained outside.

We left the converts alone to their own devices. But among ourselves, we acted as though we were our brothers' keepers, sharing what little we possessed, worrying together in times of trouble, and rejoicing on those rare occasions when there was good news for others.

And then, on a Sunday in mid-April 1943, the lull in the killing came to an abrupt end. Hundreds of German policemen, led by the thug Wüstner, descended on the ghetto. Within a short time, a thousand Jews were trapped and dragged to the town prison. Two days later, Ukrainian workmen were brought in and put to work in the cemetery, digging a huge pit thirty meters long and three meters deep. On Wednesday, the prisoners were driven to the area, ordered to strip, and forced to lie down in the pit, facedown. Those who refused were ordered to stand aside to be dealt with later. About sixty people, lying in the grave, formed one layer. Policemen walked along the length of the grave and shot everyone in the back of the head. Behind walked other policemen, making certain no one remained alive. Then a second layer of Jews covered the corpses, and they too were disposed of in the same fashion. The process was repeated until all the prisoners had been murdered.

The Germans then went to work on those who had refused to lie in the pit. They cut off their hands and feet, threw them in the pit while still alive, and covered them with earth.

In a few hours, a thousand Jews had been liquidated.

With the massacres resuming, fear gripped the Jews of Sambor. People slept with one eye open; every household posted a guard at night to alert the sleepers in the event the Germans were staging a raid.

It was during this period that my brother and I entered the Sambor ghetto. We had come at Moses Mandelbaum's urging, to be briefed by him about escaping to Hungary.

He was glad to see us and enthusiastically filled us in on details of his plan. He was leaving within several days, he told us. His group would include five men, three women, and a twelve-year-old boy. Some of them had members of their families in Hungary who had gone on earlier. The group leader, who was most "reliable," according to Mandelbaum, demanded one thousand dollars for taking them to Munkács.[3]

He introduced us to the group leader, whom we liked. Stefan was a slender man with a swarthy face, sparkling eyes, and a relaxed manner. He was neither Polish nor Ukrainian but probably descended from the Turks. A smuggler by profession, he told us many stories of his "professional" life.

During the Russian occupation,[4] from 1939 to 1941, his smuggling had been fairly active, but now that the Germans were in control, he was far busier. Two or three times a week, he crossed the border to Hungary and returned with large quantities of Hungarian cigarettes.

He was not keen on smuggling Jews into Hungary, as he would be placed into a forced labor camp if caught. It was less hazardous smuggling contraband goods from one country to another. He was willing to help Jews, he said, only because he felt an obligation to a Jew named Weiss who had once done him a favor. On his most recent trip to Hungary, he had taken Weiss's eldest son. This particular group was to include his wife and two children, with Weiss himself scheduled to leave on the following trip.

On May 6, at midnight, we accompanied the group to the ghetto fence. Stefan signaled, and the group followed him out of the ghetto. They were soon swallowed up in the dark. We prayed for their safe arrival in Budapest.

---

3. Located today in the Subcarpathian Rus region of Ukraine, the small city of Munkács (Mukačevo in Czech and Slovak) was part of Czechoslovakia until Hungary annexed it in November 1938. By the time Germany occupied Hungary in March 1944, the town's Jewish population numbered roughly fifteen thousand. The Germans immediately concentrated these Jews in a ghetto and deported them to Auschwitz in mid-May 1944.
4. See part I, chapter 4, note 1.

Scheduled to follow in eleven days, we were busy with preparations. Rabbi Pinchas Twersky, the Ostiller rabbi, and his two sons were leaving with us. The rabbi had just recovered from a bout with typhoid, and we were to carry him on a stretcher across the Carpathians.

But things do not always work out according to plan. Nine days after Mandelbaum left, one of Rabbi Twersky's sons came to me with terrible news. A militiaman had just entered the ghetto and reported that a group of people, on their way to Hungary, had been captured and brought to the Sambor prison. They were to be shot.

Convinced this was the Mandelbaum group, I ran to the headquarters of the Jewish Council and told the story to Dr. Schneidscher, who went to the Gestapo. He returned an hour later, followed by several persons, among them Mandelbaum. There were only five in the group. The others had been shot.

Returning to my room, Mandelbaum, seemingly unaffected by their costly failure, said, "We'll try again next week." He did not blame Stefan for what happened to them. "I'll go with him again," he said. Stefan was a good man, he said, who knew the mountains well. For days, he'd led the group through thick shrubbery and virgin forest, as well as over hedges and ditches. Even as the path had become steeper and the mountains higher, Stefan had remained confident in his ability to reach Hungary. German patrols did not intimidate him. They marched by day and rested at night.

On the evening of the third day, they had come to a gorge, and it had appeared that they would soon be within striking distance of their goal. They'd slept there. But the next morning, heavy fog encircled them, and Stefan appeared concerned for the first time. He'd asked the group to pack their belongings and follow him to the top of the mountain. There, the vapor had been impenetrable. Stefan had suggested that they wait until the fog lifted, but the group, having great confidence in him, had urged him to continue. They'd marched for several hours through the fog, and finally Stefan had announced that they were lost. They waited for two days and two nights, cold and uncomfortable, hoping that they would find their way to Hungary. On the third day, they'd decided to move on. Stefan told them to walk on while he went back to find someone to help him. A few hours passed, and he'd returned with a young peasant, a cousin of his. Everyone had been relieved; they would be safe. In a couple of hours, they'd expected to reach a village where the peasant and his father lived. When they came to the home of the peasant, they had eaten, drunk, and hidden in a loft.

The next morning, they had been awakened by noise. They'd looked into the courtyard and seen that the house had been surrounded by the entire village population. There were cries of "Jews! Jews!" They had been betrayed, but no one knew who was responsible. Escape was out of the question, as militiamen had been informed of their presence.

The farmers had rushed at them with scythes, robbing them of all valuables. Soon Ukrainian militia arrived from a neighboring village. The group said that they had discovered the farmhouse by accident and had taken shelter there. Having no valuables, they had not been able to bribe them, and the Ukrainians had paid no attention to their pleas. They had delivered them to the Germans in Sianky.

Arriving in Sianky, they were led to the cellar of the building from which the border police operated. That evening, Gestapo agents beat them and later killed three of them.

The next morning, the survivors were manacled and transported to Sambor.

This was the story as Mandelbaum told it.

Failure of the mission notwithstanding, we decided to go on with the preparation of escaping to Hungary. Weiss helped organize the groups, the first of which included those who had failed in the recent attempt. My brother and I would go with the second group. Stefan was to be our guide. We planned to leave on the twenty-second of May. Several days before our flight, a striking bit of news reached us in the Sambor ghetto—that the Allied armies had routed the Germans in North Africa.[5] It was Thursday,

---

5. With the surrender of Axis forces on May 13, 1943, the Allies concluded their military campaign in North Africa.

May 20, a lovely day, and we were in a hopeful mood, celebrating the Nazi debacle a little prematurely. That very evening, while we were raising a symbolic toast to the Allies, Gestapo agents were arriving in large numbers, planning an *Aktion* against us the next day.

They struck Friday morning. The widow Karp, in whose house my brother and I were staying, woke us early and called our attention to the strange noises in the street. An instant later, one of our guards came running, warning us that a Gestapo *Aktion* was imminent. "Run! Hide!" he cried.

We dressed quickly and started for Sommer's house, where my brother and I had reserved a hiding place. Out in the streets, there was pandemonium, people running in all directions, trying to get to their hideouts before the raiders struck; we reached ours just as the door was shutting.

The cellar where we took refuge was well camouflaged. Although the Gestapo failed to find us, they demolished the structure above us. When we finally emerged, we found the house in shambles.

At the Jewish Council headquarters, we found out later that the Germans had taken seven hundred people from their hideouts and flung them in prison. Now people were milling around headquarters, pleading with Dr. Schneidscher to rescue those who had been seized, among them Weiss's daughter.

"I'll see what I can do," Dr. Schneidscher said as he left for Gestapo headquarters. He returned at midnight, empty-handed. Not one prisoner had been freed.

Disconsolate, we returned to our quarters to find that of the thirty persons living in the Karp house, only six had escaped arrest. The widow and her three children were among those taken. My brother, brother-in-law, three other men, and I were the only survivors.

Rifle shots awakened me in the morning. My brother was still asleep, but my brother-in-law's bed was empty. I looked out the window and saw Gestapo agents arresting Jews. Three of them approached our house and knocked. We made no move. Instead of smashing our door, as I fully expected, they proceeded to knock down the door of the next house. An instant later, they dragged three young men into the street. The youngsters tried tearing themselves away; two of them were shot and the third recaptured. I later discovered that the police had not gone into our place because it was locked from the outside, and they probably assumed it was empty. My brother-in-law, on leaving the room, had locked it from the outside.

That morning, the Germans shot eighty people, taking most of the dead with them. Informed that some corpses had been left near the ghetto fence, I went there to find my friend Aaron Orlander among them. Weiss and his wife were missing. I never saw them again.

That same day, 750 Jewish prisoners were driven in boxcars to Lemberg. The last car was loaded with corpses. I later talked with a Jewish policeman who had helped fill the cars with Jews. He told me that he had talked with Rabbi Twersky of Ostilla, who had said that the ways of God were inscrutable. The Lord had helped him recover from typhoid and was now handing him over to the bitterest enemies of the Jewish people. "But," the rabbi said, "we are all subject to God's will and must not question his ways."

During the next few days, an unbearable stench pervaded the ghetto. The gutter canal had been totally blocked by corpses, and water was pouring out of the gutter, overflowing the streets. People were standing about, trying to identify the decomposed bodies. While looking on, I saw a young girl, wearing horribly soiled clothing, turn up in the ghetto to find her parents. She had lived for five days in the sewers and was fortunate to find her parents still alive. People tried to save themselves. Some of the young men managed to obtain guns and fled to the woods. Others talked of escaping but did little more than discuss the matter. The peasants told them their days were numbered. Falling prey to the mood of despair, my brother and I heard the flapping of death's wings over our heads.

On Thursday, May 27, 1943, my brother and I walked to the ghetto fence, crept under it in the darkness, and managed to reach the railroad tracks. We followed the rails all night long and, at daybreak, reached the Jewish quarter of Drohobycz.

My brother went to the camp where he had previously been working while I wandered into the ghetto.

# CHAPTER 18

# THE LAST DAYS OF THE DROHOBYCZ GHETTO

Like the Jews of Sambor, the ghetto dwellers of Drohobycz were convinced that they were next to be liquidated. Time being of the essence, they worked feverishly on their hiding places; many of the young fled to the forests, some to join partisans. Those who possessed money, influence, and connections had left the ghetto a long time ago. Backenroth, the only influential Jew to remain in the ghetto, decided to stay to the end to help his people in every way possible. Dr. Gerstenfeld, who previously headed the Jewish Council, had been thrown out by the Germans and succeeded by an engineer named Borgman who could do nothing for us. The Jewish Council was impotent.

But Backenroth still possessed some influence. Familiar with Nazi methods and tactics, he now warned the remaining Jews in the ghetto that liquidation was imminent. The Jewish craftsmen, usually exempted by the Germans from actions, even when mass murders were taking place, were now being imprisoned, a sure sign, Backenroth said, that the ghetto was about to be wiped out.

We had no reason to doubt Backenroth's warning. The craftsmen were indeed being rounded up. Panic spread among the populace; we began to look to our hiding places.

My brother and I were to be part of a group comprising eighteen persons to hide with Schnall, who suggested we not put it off, not wait until the German *Aktion* started. But we bribed some militiamen and expected to be warned of an impending *Aktion* ahead of time.

Finally, after days of preparation, in which we gathered much food
and other provisions, I entered the shelter, reciting the Psalms and asking
God's blessing that we might survive and see the children of Israel live and
prosper once again. My brother, who was in the camp, was to come later.

The cellar was familiar to me, having been there several months ago.
Since that time, many alterations had been made. The floor was now
covered with wooden boards; there were beds for us all. In the middle
of the cellar, there was a table and two armchairs; a radio stood in the
corner. Electricity had been brought in, a gas stove, running water. Fresh
air circulated from the fireplace. In the adjacent room, our food was
stored. According to our calculations, we had enough food for a year. All
of us—eleven men, five women, and two children—expected to remain in
the cellar indefinitely.

Yet the feeling that we were trapped never left me. We ate our meals
silently, leaving the table soon after we finished, and returned to our
assigned places, our beds and bunks, to brood in private. We observed
the Sabbath in the customary fashion, praying and eating Sabbath food.
Occasionally we heard shooting, heard footsteps and the rumble of wheels.
During prolonged periods of quiet, we speculated that the ghetto had been
liquidated.

On Tuesday, the lights suddenly failed. We thought at first that it was
a short circuit and lighted our Sabbath candles. But soon we discovered
that we no longer possessed running water. We were stunned: How could
we go on without water, electricity, and gas? Worse still: Had the supply
lines leading to the Jewish quarter been cut? Had the house above us been
destroyed? Did the Gestapo suspect we were hiding under this house?

We waited for the calamity to overtake us. After several hours, during
which no suspicious movement was heard overhead, some of us calmed
down, declaring we could hold out for weeks, while others talked of committing suicide. I proposed that we not wait, take a chance, and escape
through the canal. Only one other, a man named Jonas Fischer, volunteered to try the canal with me. The others, content to remain, hoping
for the best, wrote letters to relatives, asking us to deliver them.

Fischer and I entered the canal on Thursday night. Fischer, armed with a map and a flashlight, led the way. We crept along slowly in this utterly black, ill-smelling, confined place, up to our waists in muck. Fischer held on to his map and flashlight and rucksack, his arms raised above his head. Occasionally, he studied the map. After what seemed like hours, he whispered to me that we were approaching Listopad Lane, where we planned to surface. He proved right. We stopped, and Fischer cautiously lifted the metal sewer cover. We crept out, greeted by a pitch-black night. Reaching a field, we sat down, took off our wet clothes, and put on dry ones we had carried in our rucksacks.

Suddenly, two men appeared out of the dark. We rose and approached them slowly. I asked, in Hebrew, "*Amcha?*[1] Are you Jews?"

They were the Schachter brothers from Rołów. Behind them was a child and the wife of one of the men. They said their experience was similar to ours, only their food had run out. They had not eaten four days and now were on their way to Rołów in the hope that a peasant they knew would put them up. When they learned that we were trying to enter my brother's camp, they asked us to take the woman and child until they found out how they would be treated by the peasant.

We agreed, and together we went into the field, slept for a while, and at dawn, reached the camp of Zuckerberg, the so-called Hyrawka Lumber Camp.

---

1. *Amcha* means "your people" or "your nation."

# CHAPTER 19

‒‒

# THE CAMP

The large piece of property we came to once belonged to a man named Zuckerberg, a Jew. It was now owned by Kunicia, a Ukrainian, who worked for the German army. Originally a lumber camp, the place was situated behind the new Jewish cemetery, three kilometers from town. The Jews employed in the camp were supposed to wear the *W* sign to show they were under the control of the SS. But very few of the camp inmates wore the sign, and about a dozen wore no sign at all. Kunicia paid five złotys for the *W* Jews, but the SS did not know of the existence of the others, for whom no payment was made. It was assumed that if the Nazis wanted the latter group, Kunicia would insist that they were needed here to fulfill his obligations to the German army and they would be left alone. There was another group in camp, relatives of the workers, who lived in cellars and hideouts or barracks. In addition, one hundred Ukrainians were employed in the camp.

The men lived in barracks, which were inspected by Jungermann, who was Jewish. Two policemen, Kammermann and Hallemann, acted as guards to make certain the workers did not escape. However, nobody ever tried to escape, as the workers lived in comparative safety.

The police led the men to work at six thirty in the morning. The workers were given soup twice a day and bread once a week.

The entire camp was surrounded by a high wooden fence that had two entrances from the street, one leading to the barracks, the other to the camp itself. Leaving the area was forbidden under a penalty of death.

Reaching the camp, we crept under the big wooden gate and cautiously walked to the barracks. The doors were locked and the windows camouflaged. We entered a nearby stable, waiting for an opportunity to get into the barracks. Before long, the barracks door creaked open, and a man came out. I approached, telling him my brother's name and asking where my brother slept. The man pointed to a window on the ground floor.

I tapped on the window. The camouflaged paper covering was lifted, and I saw my brother's face. He was overjoyed to see me and leaped out of the window, dressed in his nightshirt. He took me and Fischer to his room. The Schachter brothers and their family stayed behind in the stable.

In the camp, there were a large number of Jews who had managed to escape the ghetto. Many were here illegally and had no security whatsoever. At any moment, they might be found out. Jungermann was responsible for all inmates. If any of them were found, he would be put to death. Although he was not an evil man, he was understandably distraught, having hidden his parents, wife, and child in the camp. A few times a day, he went to the hiding place to see his one-year-old child, Mendele.

The two hiding places were already overcrowded with more than one hundred people. Where would the new refugees go? Jungermann ran desperately from one hiding place to another, pleading with Jews to leave the camp. He informed them about the woods nearby where they could hide, at least during the day. But no one left. He began to abuse the fugitives, and in response, they told him to send his own relatives to the woods. Jungermann became hysterical, and soon the quarreling became violent. Some of the more reasonable people tried to calm the others. What was the sense of fighting among themselves? Wasn't it enough that their archenemies were trying to destroy them?

Eventually, they calmed down and decided to build a third hiding place under the camp barracks. Until complete, the overflow could hide in the nearby forest to evade the Gestapo. I was among those who hid in the forest, returning to camp at night. I learned, one night, that friends had interceded on my behalf and gotten me a job. There was a job for tailors, a second for cobblers, and a third for brush makers. Saul Barsam, a relative of mine who was the foreman of the brush shop, helped place me in his establishment.

Meanwhile, the Schachter brothers decided to leave for the home of their peasant friend. They bribed the camp chief and were permitted to leave the woman and child for a few days. If their luck held, they planned to send for the woman and child.

I met Schnall's son in camp and told him of the difficulties under which his parents were living in the cellar. They could not survive much longer without water, electricity, and gas. He said he would try to bring his parents to the camp.

We worked hard during the day; we worked equally as hard at night, building the new hiding place under the barracks. Within a few days, it was ready; those who hid there felt safe for the time being. Three days later, they were discovered and arrested.

What comes to mind, as I write about the camp, are the Sabbaths. Remembering with an ache in our hearts the incomparably beautiful Sabbaths of our youths, we worked poorly on Saturdays, showing no interest in our labors.[1] In SS camps, the guards often went on a murder spree on Saturdays, claiming the Jewish inmates did not want to do their work. The camp's new director, a Russian, Moskalenko, was ignorant of the special meaning of the Sabbath. During the week, he drove the Jews hard, but he soon learned that he could not get them to do work on the Sabbath. So he kept away from us on Saturdays, and we were able to sit around quietly, reflecting on our past lives.

On one particular Saturday, we were sitting around talking when a young Ukrainian broke into our room and cried, "The Gestapo is here! You'd better get out quickly!"

We ran to the window to see what was happening. In the courtyard, we saw German policemen and Ukrainian militia armed with machine guns.

---

1. Work is forbidden during the Jewish Sabbath, which begins at sundown on Friday and lasts until sundown on Saturday.

Panic ensued. Some attempted to tear up planks from the floor to hide; some scampered up into the loft.

An armed German policeman approached our room and cried, "All Jews, out! Roll call!"

We followed the order, assembled in the courtyard, and fell into two ranks. The roll call was read by an SS man named Minkus.[2] Looking at his bloodshot eyes and his puffy face, we realized he was drunk.

After roll call, it was discovered that four men were missing. Minkus snarled at the director that if the four men were not found, he would be taken away. The frightened director ordered the Ukrainian workers to search for the missing Jews, and in a few moments, three of them were found. A while later, the fourth was discovered. Now every Jew was accounted for. Some eighty of them, listed as Ws, were lined up as well as twenty others who had no sign but were registered. They were separated from the rest.

Minkus, staggering drunk, with a pistol in each hand, ordered the director to read aloud the names of the Ws. When their names were called, they were to fall in a separate group. The work went slowly, and Minkus was impatient. Finally, he grabbed the list, reading the names himself. As both hands were occupied, he could not hold the list until he put one pistol between his teeth. Because he was drunk, he could not read or pronounce the names, especially as the gun in his mouth made it impossible for him to talk. He went into a frenzy, threw away the list, and ordered the director to pick it up and finish reading it. But now the list was so badly mutilated that the director was unable to read the names. He rushed to the office for another copy and came back, reading nervously because Minkus kept waving his pistols at him.

When the name of a coworker of mine was called, he hurried to the group where he belonged. Quickly, I followed him. My brother, whose name had already been called, was standing near me.

2. SS-*Unterscharführer* Erich Minkus (1903–1945) had a reputation of being a heavy drinker.

The director finished the list, and twenty men still remained in a segregated group. Before Minkus had an opportunity to issue any orders concerning this group, the director pointed out that if these men were taken from him, it would be impossible for the camp to fulfill its commitments to the German army. Minkus stared at him uncomprehendingly and finally began to understand the meaning of what the director said. He suddenly jumped among the twenty men and pushed some of them into our group. The rest were led through the factory gate, and we watched them until they disappeared. We stood silently, looking trancelike at the gate without realizing quite what was happening. Soon, however, we awoke to reality, and those who had relatives hiding in camp asked the director for permission to return to the barracks, fearing that they had been discovered.

We were marched from the gate of the lumber yard across the street to the barracks. As we neared the barracks' entrance, we saw a group of people surrounded by police. The hiding places had been found! The Jewish Police ordered us to stop, but those who saw relatives in the group, their wives and children, pleaded that we be allowed to continue walking. The police, after brief consultation among themselves, permitted us another twenty steps. As we neared the group, there were cries of despair from those who saw their loved ones about to be taken away. Sixty persons had been seized, among them the Schachter woman and her child and a Hebrew teacher, Feingold, who knew and loved Bialik's poems and recited them with such feeling! Bialik's celebrated poem "To the Slaughter" came to mind; I wondered whether Feingold too was thinking about it at this terrible moment.[3]

We were led away and soon lost sight of the group. Entering the camp, we were startled by loud cries. I climbed a high fence to have a better look at what was happening. I could see the nearby woods—the people taking off their clothes, mothers undressing their children. The policemen

---

3. The national poet of Israel Hayim Nahman Bialik (1873–1934) is considered the foremost of modern Hebrew poets. The poem that Thorne cites and calls "To the Slaughter" is actually called "In the City of Slaughter," which Bialik wrote in response to the April 1903 Kishinev pogroms.

loaded their rifles. Then the shrieks and the cries and the wails rent the air. Hearing the laments, we ran toward the woods, getting only as far as the gate, where we were stopped by police. The executions began, the victims offering no resistance, many of them apparently awaiting an end to their suffering. But one person, a girl of fourteen who refused to line up with the rest in front of a tree, was shoved to the ground, stomped, and shot. Feingold was next. I recalled Bialik's lines as Feingold stood there calmly, facing his executioners: "The sun was shining and the murderer killed."

We were ordered to dig a deep pit in which to lay the dead in rows of three. If we were not quick and were sloppy in placing the corpses the way the Germans ordered, we would be shot.

Several days later, a group of orphaned ghetto children, ranging from nine to twelve years of age, entered the camp. The group consisted of about twenty children from the ghetto of Drohobycz. Their parents had been killed, their neighbors were gone, and they could not expect help from Jews who were themselves in constant danger.

Life in the woods had hardened these children and made them independent. They had a fierce desire to live. Their leader, an eleven-year-old boy named Janek, had popped up from nowhere and made himself their spokesman and guide. It was believed that he and his parents had been loaded into a boxcar for execution and that he had jumped out of the train while his parents traveled on to their fate. Janek had wandered through villages and towns, across fields, and through woods, looking for a group to which to attach himself. He'd reached Drohobycz but had not intended to stay there. His dream was to cross the border into a country where there were no Germans. But at Drohobycz, he'd met this group of children and become their leader. When the children traded with the townsfolk and ghetto dwellers, he was the middleman. They always had to be on the alert, for the Germans were on the lookout for them. They vanished like ghosts, reappearing when they were needed.

They had disappeared into the woods on a Thursday, the day before the liquidation of the ghetto. A few days later, they found out the ghetto had been wiped out. Orphaned, homeless, dressed in rags, rain-soaked, they

emerged from the forest in search of food and warmth. The high stack rising above our camp attracted their attention. They guessed correctly that
this was a working area and some Jews might be found there.

This is how they found us—two weeks after the destruction of the
ghetto. Their joy was unbounded when they came in and found us, and
we too wept, welcoming them. It had been a long time since we had seen
Jewish children! We shared our food with them and suggested there might
be other ways in which we could help them. We offered to build a hiding
place for them, but they would not have it, suggesting they preferred shelter in the forest, where they would be less vulnerable.

Losing no time, we formed a committee and called it "For the Welfare
of the Children." It was a well-functioning committee. Every few days, a
delegation of children would arrive in camp, and we supplied them with
their needs. They did not remain in camp longer than was necessary, being
wary of it. But in the course of time, being bored with the forest, they came
more often and stayed longer. It was from these orphaned Jewish children
that we learned what was going on outside our hermetically sealed existence, that the Tarnopol and Stanisławów ghettos, and Lemberg's as well,
had been wiped out.

The children were not the only visitors. Others who had found refuge
in the woods came to us and asked for food, which we were glad to share
with them. One visitor, a sixteen-year-old girl, came every other day for
bread and milk for her group. She was a sad girl, always downcast, without
hope or faith. She would enter the camp through an opening in the high
fence, accept the rations, and vanish quickly into the woods. Her sorrow
was so heavy that some of us tried to cheer her up, but we failed. Her face
was pale, her eyes dark, and her grief deep. The only time I remember
her smiling was when we told her that the Allies had invaded Italy.[4] Rumors
prevailed; the Germans sometimes started false ones, knowing we would
become depressed on learning they were untrue. We did believe, however,
that the invasion had taken place; it was no lie. We informed the girl of this

4. The Allied invasion of Italy began on September 3, 1943.

news, and she uttered a gasp of joy. She thanked us and ran quickly to the woods to pass along the news. We were pleased that she had something to be happy about.

And then, it happened.

One day, Kammermann, the Jewish policeman, approached us and asked if we would volunteer to join a group that was burying a Jewish woman who had been shot not far from the camp. We were given spades and marched to the area designated. We soon came to a potato field and saw, lying on the ground, a young girl, dead, covered with dried blood, bullet wounds in her head and bosom. It was our girl! Her bread and empty milk pitcher were nearby.

Kammermann told us that he had been ordered to have the girl buried where she died. We dug a grave in a corner of the field near an old willow tree. As we laid her in the grave, we broke down and wept. We could not bring ourselves to cover her with earth. One of the men descended into the grave and covered her face with a cloth, and only then did we fill the grave.

But Jews, even when dead, were not left alone. The owner of the field where we buried the girl came to the camp and demanded that the dead girl be removed. He did not want a corpse on his property. We tried to prevail on him to let her rest. A corpse could not interfere with his farming; we even offered to pay him for letting her lie there. But he was adamant. He left and came back with a note from the Germans, ordering us to remove the body. We dug her up, carried her to the forest near the mass pits, dug a separate grave, and buried her. May she rest in eternal peace.

With time, the visits of the Jews who lived in the forests decreased. We soon found out the reason. The Germans were combing the area, capturing and murdering the refugees. Janek's group too was suffering casualties, though we hoped some of them were alive. Of the whole group, only four children were left. Soon we lost touch with them altogether.

Rochele Kupferberg became our new concern. Four years old, Rochele had been left behind by her Christian foster parents, who apparently were unwilling to keep her any longer. We found the child in the courtyard one morning, a note attached to her clothes, "Rochele Kupferberg, four years old." What to do with her? She was too young to be placed in a hide-out. We decided to keep her in the "upstairs" area instead, where we could keep an eye on her and play with her.

Not a day passed without some incident. One afternoon, the Ukrainian workers came to the fence, smiling maliciously. We became curious and expected the worst. Had the Gestapo come for us? We looked out the window and saw an elderly peasant on the road, carrying a child. A German policeman and two Ukrainian militiamen followed behind, together with a young peasant woman who was weeping. We soon learned what had happened.

The young woman, married, had borne this child to a Jew a year ago. The Gestapo heard of the case, ascertained that the child was illegitimate, of Jewish blood, and therefore was to be destroyed. The elderly peasant was the child's grandfather. The woman cried that she no longer was involved with the child's father and begged that her infant be spared. We were told the next day that the child was shot by the Germans in the Jewish cemetery.

# CHAPTER 20

# HYRAWKA

Adjacent to our camp was an agricultural center, a place where 350 Jewish boys and girls worked, surviving, by some miracle, the selections and liquidations. The director of Hyrawka, Millbusch, a liberal German, was responsible for the project, giving the young Jews the entire area, stretching from a brewery to the new Jewish cemetery at Drohobycz. But the actual leadership of the place was under two Jews: Altman and Dr. Reittman. Altman was bad; Reittman was worse.[1]

When the young Jews took over, they found two ancient brewing houses with deep cellars. One of the houses was converted to a store and the other to a barn for cattle.

In six months, the place was transformed. Dozens of plants, vegetables, and herbs were grown employing the most up-to-date methods. Horse, cattle, and sheep breeding was going on apace. Rabbits were raised; beehives flourished. Workshops were established for locksmiths, glaziers, plumbers, and brush makers. Excellent work was done in the pottery shop.

For the Germans, Hyrawka served a particular purpose. They made a showplace of it, bringing foreign journalists and important guests to view it to impress upon them their benevolent rule in the occupied territories.

---

1. Little is known about these two leaders except that Reittman was a credentialed agronomist and Altman was an experienced administrator and refugee from Vienna.

I cannot recall the exact date—it was probably in April 1943—when the special order was issued for the young people to abandon their gardening and cattle and move to the pottery and ceramic works.

The young people were stunned. They were reluctant to leave their fields and nurseries. The girls hugged the animals because they had become so attached to them. A few of them were so broken up over the order that they threatened to commit suicide, but they were dissuaded by Luki Schiller. Born to Jewish parents who had converted to Christianity, Schiller was considered Jewish by the Germans and wore an armband. He was a grandson of Dr. Feuerstein and was related to the Gartenberg family, the Galician "Rothschilds" who had done so much for the town of Drohobycz.[2]

Only ten young Jews were allowed to remain in the agricultural area for the purpose of training replacements. The rest, some with tears in their eyes, others sobbing loudly, were sent away. Ukrainians and Poles, passing along the road, stopped to gape at the sad procession of young Jews, at the tear-stained faces of the girls and the boys, some of whom protested loudly, and wondered why all the fuss, as it was apparent the youngsters were not being taken away to prison or to be shot.

Soon after the Hyrawka episode, our turn came. One morning—it was still dark—we heard cries: "Roll call!" I sat up in my bunk. The words *roll call* I associated with Janover Camp! Had I dreamed them now? "Roll call!" I heard the words repeated. I was not dreaming, for a German appeared at the barracks door, shouting and motioning with his rifle for us to fall out.

We dressed hurriedly and ran out and assembled in the courtyard. Soon we were surrounded by German police, Ukrainian militiamen, and police dogs. We were counted (eighty-two) and led to prison, along with ten others from the Hyrawka Gardens.

---

2. Moses (Moishe) Gartenberg (1841–1916) and his brother Lazar (1833–1898) were foundational figures of the oil boom in Galicia. Moses and his wife, Ottilie (1843–1902), were also well known as philanthropists. The Rothschilds were a Jewish family of bankers and philanthropists, one of the world's richest in the nineteenth century.

My brother and I were placed in cell number two, which was so over-crowded, one could hardly move. The entire prison was jammed with men wearing the *W* insignia, once cherished for the immunity it conferred on its wearer. It was apparent, at a glance, that the *W* camps were being dis-solved. Hundreds of men were locked in the cells.

A member of the Jewish Police—an *ex-member* is the more appropriate term, for he was seized with the rest of us—found a spot on the wall that was unmarked and wrote, "I, Bernard Hallemann, was brought here today, Tuesday, the 20th of July 1943, the 17th of Tammuz 5703, the Jewish era. The day of my execution will probably be the 22nd or 23rd of July."

Although many prisoners engraved such inscriptions on the walls, this one remains clear in my mind because of two errors. The writer did not die on July 22 or 23 but on July 20, the day of his capture. And he was not executed.

On the afternoon of the day we were imprisoned, we were ordered to fall out of our cells into the corridor. Here, Hallemann met a Ukrainian militiaman with whom he had served as a cop. The Ukrainian secretly handed Hallemann a badge of the Ukrainian secret police, and when we were driven back to our cells, Hallemann was not among us. The guards had mistaken him for a Ukrainian, and he could have escaped, had he had the courage to walk out of the prison. Instead, he dawdled about. The Ger-mans picked him up and beat him. The same day, he died of the beating.

Hallemann was whipped to death; other inmates were beaten regu-larly, although they were not killed. Now and again, some tried to escape, difficult though it was. When they were recaptured, the beatings were administered.

For the past five months, I had been living with older people; in this cell, I was among youngsters. When I moved about with the older folks, I heard laments and wailing. Now I listened mainly to young men singing Jewish songs. The handful of old people squatted in corners and wept. The young prisoners managed to get together some money to bribe the wardens and buy brandy, food, and cigarettes. They ate heartily and drank and talked about Palestine, a free Jewish homeland. They called for Hitler's defeat and his early demise. Those who could afford it bribed the wardens to permit them a few precious minutes with their girls who were in nearby cells. They met briefly in the hall and embraced. I gazed in wide-eyed wonder at the couples—their displays of affection, their brave smiles, and their capacity for self-delusion. One couple, both in their early twenties, clung to each other and talked of the "future." Suddenly, as they looked into one another's eyes, tears began to course down their cheeks. The warden called "time" and separated them. "Good-bye, my love. See you soon!" he said, being led away to his cell.

"Good-bye, my love. See you soon!" she echoed his words.

They never saw each other again.

Among those seized was Janek, the boy who had led the children in the forest. He had been caught and jailed, and when I saw him, he told me a vivid dream he had had last night. His mother had come to him in the dream, dressed in white, her face pale. She reproached him for having jumped out of the boxcar, leaving her alone. He asked forgiveness. I looked at him. He was tired, hungry, and broken in spirit. Sitting beside him were two small boys, members of his group. They were even more woebegone than Janek.

One of the men in our cell, Romek Miodownik, possessed a revolver with three bullets. He planned to shoot two Germans, he said, then himself. In his twenties, Miodownik had little patience with those in the cell who bemoaned their fate. He was determined not to die passively. "What will the world think of us, dying like sheep?" he demanded. "Will they understand how the victims let themselves be slaughtered without offering any resistance?" His anger rose as he spoke; he began to scream. "We did not lift a finger! Why didn't we?"

"Not so loud," someone said. The others tried to calm him. One man said, "How can we stand against the might of a country that has beaten Poland, Denmark, Norway, Holland, Belgium, France, Yugoslavia, and Greece? How can we fight effectively against an enemy that has attacked mighty Russia? Are you out of your mind?"

"Why don't the Russian prisoners resist?" another said. "Why didn't the twelve thousand Polish officers of Katyń fight back?[3] They were trained to fight—and look at them! They *really* went to their deaths like sheep. What can we do, who don't know how to use weapons? What can our wives and children do?"

"That's no excuse!" Miodownik shouted back. "Jewish history is full of heroes who fought back! Bar Kochba, for instance, and the Hasmoneans."[4]

Thursday afternoon, the killings began. The Germans started with cell number one, taking out ten people to be shot. An hour later, our turn came. Miodownik was among the first group. Five minutes after he had been led out, we heard the sharp report of a pistol; we waited for the second and third shots—he possessed three bullets—but we did not hear them. We were told later that a Ukrainian, standing next to Miodownik, had noticed the prisoner taking a weapon out of his pocket and seized his hand. The first bullet was deflected, and that was that.

Our cell door was flung open. I thought our time had come. Instead, a German officer, holding a slip of paper in his hand, called out five names. My brother and I were on the list. We were ordered to step into the corridor, where Moses Backenroth joined us along with Saul Barsam and a Dr. Spiro from Warsaw, who in the last few years had lived in Drohobycz.

We learned that the five of us had been selected as good workers and were to report to an establishment where workers were badly needed. The man who ran the place had good Gestapo connections and, as a result, could obtain men when he needed them.

Dr. Spiro refused the offer.

3. In April and May of 1940, on Joseph Stalin's orders, the NKVD (Soviet secret police) executed approximately twenty-two thousand Poles, including large numbers of military officers, intellectuals, lawyers, priests, and other elites. The Soviet Union long blamed Nazi Germany for the crime and only officially acknowledged its complicity in the massacre at Katyń forest in 1990.
4. Between approximately 132 and 136 CE, Jews in the province of Judea rebelled against the Roman Emperor Hadrian. Their revolt takes its name from its leader, Shimon Bar Kochba. The Hasmonean Dynasty was established as a result of the Maccabeans' successful rebellion against the Seleucid Dynasty, which began in 167 BCE.

"What do you mean, you won't go?" the prison director said. "Tomorrow, everybody here will be executed, and you will be alive."

"I want to be executed and will not leave," Dr. Spiro said.

His action puzzled and amazed the director, who went into a huddle with a Gestapo man and told him what was happening.

The German approached Dr. Spiro. "Why don't you want to leave this prison?" he asked. "You will be liberated if you do."

Dr. Spiro replied, "I don't believe that. Perhaps my death will be delayed three or four weeks. But I don't need these extra weeks to prolong my misery. This way, everything will be finished in twelve or fourteen hours. I am not interested in this extra time."

"You are right, Jew," the German said. We, in any case, went along with the director, as he ordered, and wondered uneasily whether Dr. Spiro was right after all.

We were taken to the Beskiden Camp[5] passing streets, once crowded, now deserted.

In the camp, we found out that Dr. Ruhrberg, the former vice president of the Jewish Council of Drohobycz, and his wife were here in Drohobycz. They were shot that same day.

5. See part I, chapter 12, note 2.

# CHAPTER 21

# WHY THERE WAS NO RESISTANCE

I sit here in the cellar and reflect: Why didn't we resist? What made it impossible for us to resist was the fact that we were opposed by a foe who possessed all the weapons, while we had none. Even if we had been armed with pistols, rifles, and bayonets, we might have fought, not to win—we could not hope to win against *Stukas* and tanks and flamethrowers and poison gas—but to take thousands of the enemy with us. But they possessed the armor, and we were armed with a prayer. We were helpless, but whole nations, attacked by our common enemy, were equally as helpless. Could we hope to hold back the evil tide that the nations of Europe could not—we, the ghetto Jews, who had been reared not to live by the sword but by the spirit, according to the Lord's word?

The enemy, in addition to being so strong, is devilishly clever. He picked us off, ghetto by ghetto. While one ghetto was in the process of liquidation, another was permitted to live until its turn came. Members of the Jewish Councils were promised immunity to help the enemy destroy their brethren. Jew was set against Jew.

As though that were not enough, the Poles and Ukrainians, among whom we lived, cooperated with the Germans, many of them joining in the plundering and the killing. Many of those who did not join in the massacres were glad to be rid of us because Jewish doctors, engineers, lawyers, and businessmen were their competitors. When our young men pleaded to be allowed to join the Polish partisans in acts of sabotage, they were turned away. Jews who asked for weapons were denounced and turned over to the Germans.

These are the reasons we, in the small towns, did not resist. Perhaps in the larger cities in Poland, there was (is) resistance. We are completely cut off here and do not know what goes on in other places.

On occasion, we do get news. The German defeat at Stalingrad in the winter of 1942 buoyed our spirits considerably.[1] Perhaps the German can be defeated after all. But now a year has passed, and they are still going strong. Will this ever end? Will we ever emerge from the darkness of this cellar and see the sun once more?

1. The German surrender at Stalingrad, considered a key turning point of World War II, took place on February 2, 1943.

─✦

# CHAPTER 22

# NAFTALI BACKENROTH[1]

A word about my cousin Naftali Backenroth, one of nature's noblemen, in my estimation. A highly educated man, he studied agriculture, chemistry, geology, and engineering. Appointed a lecturer at a polytechnical school in France at the age of twenty-three, he worked on a plan to connect the Mediterranean with the Red Sea by canal. He won a prize for his plan, though the project later fell through. A good-looking man, naturally gifted, and charismatic, he moved swiftly and purposefully, like an athlete. He was well liked in Drohobycz, popular among young and old alike. When the war broke out in 1939, he was connected with the naphtha works in Drohobycz.[2] In 1941, the Germans took over. One of their first orders was to mobilize Jewish intellectuals to clean latrines in the prisons, barracks, and municipal buildings. Backenroth's coworkers in the latrine detail were doctors, lawyers, professors, and engineers. Understandably, many grumbled, but not Backenroth, who said, "Let us get on with the work and finish it as soon as possible."

The Germans took note that he was a hard worker. When they discovered that he had studied agriculture, they sent him to work in the garden of a Gestapo officer. In this fashion, Backenroth made contact with the Gestapo. Soon he was able to do little favors for fellow Jews. At about

1. Sometimes called the "Jewish Schindler," Naftali Backenroth (1905–1993) was posthumously honored for his efforts to save Jews, which he did by making them indispensable to the German war effort. For more on Backenroth's remarkable story, see Mordecai Paldiel, *Saving One's Own: Jewish Rescuers during the Holocaust* (Lincoln: University of Nebraska Press, 2017), 59–67.
2. Naphtha is a liquid distilled from petroleum and used as a solvent and fuel. Naphtha refineries were a major part of the oil industry in Eastern Galicia.

that time, Jews began disappearing, taken off somewhere in a black automobile, never to return. It was Backenroth who found out that they were
imprisoned in the cellar of the Gestapo building to be shot the following
day. Backenroth managed to get some of them free. As more Germans
came to Drohobycz and took over apartments and houses, Backenroth
had more work to do. The Germans were pleased with the way in which he
laid out and took care of their gardens. He became popular with them too
and gained a measure of influence over them.

Backenroth was an unselfish man and an honest one. He cared little
about his own comfort. The Germans as well as the Jews respected him.
When he saved people, he did not ask for gifts or thanks. Those who
offered him money or presents soon learned that he would not accept a
thing from them.

Then Backenroth, in the midst of mounting trouble and misery, made
a startling proposal to the Germans. He offered to organize a Jewish work
group to complete projects that would be of permanent value, even after
the Germans left the country. He proposed to build hothouses, movie
houses, riding schools, social clubs, and gardens. The Gestapo agreed, and
Backenroth obtained seven hundred workers and one hundred administrative officers. He involved nearly 25 percent of all the Jews and established
workshops where children could learn various skills. Until March 1943, all
the people working with Backenroth were relatively secure and under no
persecution. Living conditions were not bad, and the food was adequate.
While Jews elsewhere—since mid-1942—were badly off, in Drohobycz
under Backenroth, life was bearable. So successful was his management that the property of the village Jews—outside of Drohobycz—was
handled by the Jews in the village. The village Jews were allowed to remain
on their property. They had to produce a good harvest, but at least they
were permitted to keep part of it, and Backenroth saw to it that some was
distributed among the Jewish workers in Drohobycz. Under his care, the
village Jews also felt safer. In time, all the Jews in the vicinity came to Backenroth with their problems. He helped everyone and became a leader, an
important leader, among them.

In his own house, there was poverty as elsewhere. He did not take advantage of his position to improve the lot of his own family. They ate stale bread and drank ersatz coffee. He felt his family must live like other Jews. In order for me to describe every noble act of his would require an entire book. But for the future historians of this era, I should like to tell this story, which I heard from Dr. Isidor Friedman, who is hiding in the cellar with me.

In the winter of 1941–1942, Dr. Friedman was passing through Mick-iewicz Street to go to work in the library of the Jesuit monastery of Chyrów, where he was helping sort books with Professor Bruno Schulz. He saw a column of trucks loaded with machine guns and manned by Gestapo men. The Gestapo crew was drunk, and Backenroth was standing there talking with them, asking them and pleading with them not to undertake the *Aktion* they were planning against the Jews in Turka on the Stryj. The Gestapo men laughed derisively, paying no attention to Backen-roth. One of them said something about "Martell cognac, but only genuine Martell cognac."[3] Obviously, the Germans wanted something from the Jew. Backenroth asked them to wait. He would bring them what they wanted. He disappeared and then came back with two bottles of the genuine pre-war cognac they wanted. That day, three hundred Jews were killed in Turka and not five hundred. Backenroth saved two hundred—one hundred Jews for each bottle of the cognac. That was our value in this period!

When the time came for the liquidation of the ghetto, everyone watched out for himself, and those who had contacts and influence man-aged to escape. The Jews had no leaders left except Backenroth. Alone with his family, he remained in the ghetto. During the liquidation of the ghetto, Backenroth was seized by Gestapo men who did not know him and imprisoned. The Drohobycz Gestapo came to the prison where he was held to release him. He declined the offer, agreeing to leave only if one

3. Founded in 1715, Martell is one of France's oldest and most prestigious cognac distilleries.

hundred Jews were freed with him. The Gestapo acceded to his wishes and freed one hundred Jews.

The liquidation continued apace, and even Backenroth, always buoyant, always optimistic in the past, surrendered to gloom and apathy.

I remember one incident of this period, the final chapter in the life of the Drohobycz Jews. It was Thursday, July 22, 1943. With others, I was brought to the Beskiden Camp to work. The massacres were going on, and the remaining Jews, a dejected lot, crowded around Backenroth, asking what he could do for them. One woman, distraught, tears in her eyes, pleaded with Backenroth to save her two children who had been seized. Backenroth stood there, listening to her but not responding. Not a muscle in his face moved; he seemed to be far away. He seemed crushed by the weight that had been his to carry all these many months. But the woman, seizing him by the wrists, cried in a trembling voice, "At least save *one* of my children!"

Backenroth started, straightened his sagging shoulders, and ran to the gate. An hour later, he returned with both her children. He led them to the camp gate, turned, and walked away. It was his final noble deed in the ghetto.

As I write these lines, my cousin Naftali Backenroth is still alive.

CHAPTER 23

# BEGINNING OF THE END

In the Beskiden Camp, there were seven hundred of us, all employed in the naphtha refineries and workshops. We worked all day, returning to camp in the evening. The camp was a miniature ghetto; life was grim. We all had at least one relative in prison; executions were taking place daily. Our minds dwelt often on escape. But where to?

One day, working in the Dereżyce refinery, my brother and I saw a Pole passing on the road, a man we knew by name of Stanisław Nendza. The time for obliqueness having passed long ago, I asked him point-blank whether he knew of a hiding place for us.

Nendza took his time replying. He had in fact built a hiding place with his friend Francizek Janiewski, he said, where three Jews were now staying. But he didn't know whether he could help the two of us. I offered him money; I said he could name his price. Nendza became a little more receptive but said he would have to talk this over with his partner and his wife.

Two days later, we saw him again, and Nendza had good news for us. He had talked it over with his wife and his partner and the three persons he was hiding, and they all were receptive. He demanded a large sum of money, which fortunately we were in a position to pay.

The negotiation, of such importance to us, took no more than ten minutes.

On Sunday, we crept out of camp after dark and started in the direction of Schodnica. We walked all night, finally reaching the Carpathian Mountains, where we hid in a ravine during the daylight hours. In the evening, we resumed walking until we reached Nendza's house, situated in a naphtha pit.

Entering, we saw a comfortable home with fine furniture, a cradle, pictures on the wall, and a cat. We had been uprooted such a long time, both of us felt as though this modest home was in fact a royal palace. Nendza closed the door behind us, quickly looked out the window to make certain we had not been followed, and said, "Come with me." He led us to the stable, part of which was partitioned off as a pigsty. He drove out the pig, pushed aside some straw, lifted a board, and opened a trap. We saw an opening large enough for one person to creep through. Nendza told us to go down; we obeyed. The opening above us was shut and the plank replaced. Above, the straw was being replaced and the pig driven back into the sty.

We went down and joined the three already there. And here we've been a year. One day has been like another. Our watches have stopped keeping time long ago. If we forget to strike a day off the calendar, that day does not exist. During this year, we have not seen the sky, sun or moon, snow, rain, blossoms, or fruit.

Our lives are monotonous, but the days roll on. One day resembles the one before—and the one after. Here, nothing happens—for which, I suppose, we should be grateful—time stands still. We are hungry for news, for progress reports on the war. We feel it in our bones that the Germans are losing, but hard proof is lacking; if it exists, it has not yet trickled down to this damp cellar and the one flickering candle.

Recently, we have been told a sad tale about two Jewish girls hiding in Schodnica who were discovered through mere chance. Two firemen had noticed smoke coming from a chimney in one of the houses. Believing there was a fire, they knocked on the door and, receiving no reply, broke in. Inside, they found the oven heated to make bread and two Jewish girls hiding in a room. They notified the police who killed the two girls and their peasant landlady.

Several days later, we heard another frightening tale. A small group of young Jews had armed themselves and pushed their way through the woods. Just as they approached Schodnica, the Germans saw them. Both sides opened fire. Seven Germans were killed, some wounded. A few of the Jewish partisans managed to escape, but those who were caught were tortured before the eyes of the villagers, then murdered.

The incidents mentioned above panicked the Ukrainians who organized into posses and went from house to house in search of Jews in hiding.

Our days of boredom were transformed into days of fear. We trembled at each strange sound, at footsteps in the stable above. We prayed that our landlords would not lose their nerve, that they would hold out. At about this time, Nendza's aunt came to the house and took away her niece—"To make certain," she said, "that the child escaped the fate of her foolhardy parents who would surely be caught hiding Jews."

The Carpathian mountain chain stretches like a protective rampart across Middle Europe. The icy eastern winds from Siberia go no further than the Carpathians, where the winters are severe, where the ancient huge trees crack in the forest and the snow is very deep. Our stable was covered with snow, but inside it was warm. The cold air coming down the chimney was easier to breathe than the sticky summer air. Being entombed brought with it the feeling that we were secure, that we were indeed dead to the world, where a titanic struggle was raging and good was gaining the upper hand over evil. It was only a matter of time. Would we be alive when the end came?

In midwinter, there was more trouble. Transmission belts belonging to the workshops of the naphtha pits had been stolen, and the Germans began a search of the homes of all the men who worked there. One of our landlords, Janiewski, a technician at the pits, was due to have his house searched. The five of us in the cellar had been warned to make as little noise as possible or we might be discovered. Then all of us, the landlords and their wives included, would face the firing squad.

We offered to go into the woods, but our landlords would not hear of it, saying the arctic air would kill us. We were touched by their generosity, their humanness—qualities rarely manifested during this period. Decent people. At the outset, monetary gain may have been the primary reason for their taking us in. But others have taken money and then denounced their charges to the Germans. Fearful for their lives though they are, Nendza and his partner have never asked us to leave.

This time, when the Germans searching for the thieves who had taken the transmission belts came closer, the two landlords themselves fled to the woods, leaving their wives behind.

To add to our woes, the Mahler woman's bleeding grew worse. Unable to get off her bed, she was fed and washed by Esther Backenroth. As carrot juice was the only available nourishment, it was given the sick woman after it was warmed in a small tin can over a candle. One day, she grew so weak, she was unable to talk at all.

Leaving the cellar, I made my way to Borysław and consulted a doctor after acquainting him with the woman's complaints. There was no hope for recovery, he said. I came back and told my landlords, who said it was time to think about digging a grave in which to bury her. But where? To dig a grave was not a simple matter. Neighbors would ask, Who died? The police and the Germans would be roused to suspicion. Yet a corpse had to be got rid of somehow; she could not be kept in the cellar or anywhere in the house. In the meantime, this woman, not yet thirty, whose husband had been killed in one of the actions, was running down like one of our candles.

Then a strange thing happened. She asked for milk. There being no milk, we gave her more carrot juice. Soon she wanted more. In the evening, when Nendza lifted a plank and looked down into the cellar to inquire how the poor woman was faring, we asked for a little milk. After it was brought and she drank it, she began to talk, saying that after this war was over and the enemy of mankind was defeated, we would all be welcome to come live in her great house in Drohobycz. Two weeks later, she was able to wash herself without Esther Backenroth's assistance, whose ministrations had made it possible for her to survive.

There are periods of brief respite. During one such period not long ago, we caught up on the reading of newspapers—the war news, in particular— over which the Germans are becoming less and less exultant; we played chess and cards, solved mathematical problems and crossword puzzles, and exercised. We've long ago given up the study of English.

A matter of some concern to us is that we are running out of money. Having given our landlord all our clothing except the frayed garments we are wearing, we are compelled to break the gold teeth and bridges in our mouths.

The respite was very brief. One morning recently, we heard screams and shots above our heads. Terror-stricken, we waited for the planks above us to be removed and guns pointed at us. Then it grew quiet, and Nendza finally came down to tell us what had happened.

A boy had arrived in Schodnica, a ten-year-old named Noah Feuerberg. With the sure instinct of a carrion bird, a *Volksdeutscher*, Beck, sensed the boy was Jewish and grabbed him. The boy defended himself, but Beck overcame him, dragged him to our landlord's house, and demanded that he be kept there until the police arrived. Normally, Nendza would have allowed the boy to escape, but he was afraid that if the area were searched, the Jews hiding in the cellar would be discovered. Nendza therefore said nothing. He fed the boy, who for a moment forgot he was in peril and sat back, relaxed. Beck, arriving with the police, charged the landlords with treating the Jewish child too well. The Germans shot and killed the boy behind our stable and ordered the landlords to dig his grave. Thus the boy became a silent neighbor, lying in the ground near his Jewish brothers who, for the moment, were still alive.

The Feuerberg boy's life story, brief though it was, had its own special interest. He was not the natural son of the shoemaker Don Feuerberg, for Feuerberg had no children. But years earlier, a poor wandering woman from Lublin had passed through the town with a small boy, and she had stopped at Feuerberg's and asked for permission to rest awhile. He granted her wish, and then suddenly the woman vanished, leaving the child behind. No one ever saw her again, and Feuerberg raised the boy, naming him Noah and teaching him that he was a Jew. The happy years of his childhood culminated in the Nazi terror, and all the Jews he knew were killed. He was driven from Schodnica to the ghetto of Borysław and managed to escape and drift back to Schodnica, where he met his fate. Thus our silent neighbor was one whose history we all knew, and we mourned his passing. Somehow, we felt that he had died on our behalf, and we could not banish the thought of him or drive the sound of his weeping from our minds.

A few days later, water from an overflowing river inundated the area. One morning, we woke up and saw water rising in our hideout. We began scooping it out, working hours on end, but the water continued rising, and in several days, the area was inundated. The bedstead on the floor was now useless, as even the upper section of the bed was wet.

Fortunately, the landlord, who lately had been running away to the woods at the slightest hint of trouble, was on hand to help us out; without him, we would have drowned. He opened the trap door. The water finally receded.

Now it is August 1944. There are no terrorists walking the streets any longer or combing the woods in search of Jews because there are none left. From time to time, trucks rumble through the streets above us in the direction of the Carpathian Mountains, but they are no longer loaded with Jews on the way to execution areas. At first, only a few trucks came by here in a westerly direction, but now there are large numbers of them—whole armies, it appears—full of retreating German soldiers. By day and night, artillery thunders deep in the Carpathians. Nendza knocked on the board yesterday and told us Brody has fallen, Tarnopol has been captured, and Lemberg has been taken, news that makes us rejoice. For the first time in the fifty-three weeks we've been entombed here, there are smiles on our faces.

The once-mighty German army is being beaten to its knees. Hitler's Thousand-Year Reich is falling apart. Will we live to see it? Millions of us have prayed for this day. They were, many of them, hoping to live long enough to see the end of Hitlerism.

Yet with all the mounting excitement, we realize how terribly alone we are: our dear ones dead, our towns destroyed, our homes burned, our way of life a heap of ashes.

Where do we belong? Where are we to go?

At one time, not long ago, before the German plague spread over our land, Jewish life flourished in Poland, with a culture and beauty all its own. We took inordinate pride in our Jewish communities, some of them dating back many centuries. But now only dust and rubble are left. Out of the cellars, there will emerge a small number of poor, half-starved, ragged, broken-down human beings, a wretched reminder of a once-proud people.

How terribly lonely we are! How ardently we prayed for this time of imminent victory! But now what?

The smoky ruins of the ghettos stand out against Europe's violated skies. The ruins look back at us, a reminder—as though we need one!— that our wives, children, mothers and fathers, friends and relatives are all gone. Judaism in Poland has been torn up by the roots; it ceases to exist.

We tell ourselves in this cellar that we are a miserable remnant. Vanish, we say to ourselves, disappear . . .

Tuesday morning, August 8, 1944, Janiewski's sixteen-year-old son, Benek, opened the trap door and cried down to us, "The Allied troops are marching in! You can come up now!"

I remained at my bedstead, holding on, my body trembling, my knees weak. For a year we've been waiting for this summons to go up, but now we hesitate, one waiting for the other to make the first move. Then we suddenly lunge for the ladder.

I climb up, emerge from the stable, where our landlords embrace us. Emerging in the open, I look up, blink at the sky, and start walking with uncertain steps, as though it is necessary, all over again, to learn how to walk.

Figure 1. The author's father (center, looking at camera), in Schodnica, undated pre-war image.

Figure 2. Leon Thorne, as a young man, pictured on far left in the second row.

Figure 3. Postcard depicting Schodnica and its oil wells.

Figure 4. Postcard depicting oil production in Schodnica.

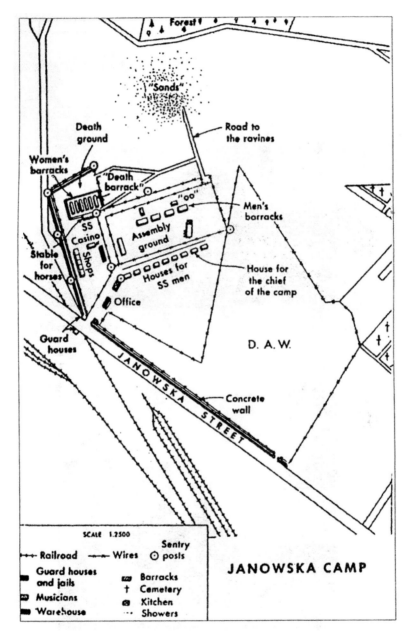

Figure 5. A map of the Janowska Labor Camp.

Figure 6. Backenroth Oil Wells. Thorne and his cellar-mates hid in the cellar of the shed at lower left for 53 weeks.

Figure 7. Jacob "Yankel" Prener, who fought in the Vilna partisans, is pictured standing, second from left in the rear row. Leader Abba Kovner is pictured standing, at center.

Figure 8.  A formal portrait of Leon Thorne in the uniform of the Polish army, 1945.

Figure 9. Leon Thorne, left, his wife Rachel, and his brother David in Kraków in late 1945.

Figure 10. Leon Thorne and his brother David in the late 1940s.

Figure 11. Stella Backenroth, one of the other four people who survived in the cellar, in Kraków in 1945.

Figure 12. Leon Thorne, author photo for *Out of the Ashes*, 1961.

Figure 13. The Thorne family in the United States, about 1960.

# PART II

CHAPTER 1

## AUGUST 1944

One after another, we crept out of the cellar that had been our hiding place for more than a year. We climbed the steps to the stable and slowly moved toward the stable door. There we stopped, for none of us dared to be the first to go out. This was no surprise, for after all that we had gone through, not only in that past year but in the years of ghettos and labor camps that had come before, we had come to view the world outside as a place of pain and suffering. How then could we have expected to go out of our hiding place with firm steps and heads raised high? We poked our heads through the cracks in the door just enough to catch a glimpse of what was beyond, as if we had never seen anything outside the walls of the farmhouse. After what seemed like hours of indecision, we finally crossed the threshold of the stable door.

It was a beautiful August day, as beautiful as a summer day can be in the Carpathian Mountains. It was still early in the morning, but the sun was already high above the hills on the horizon. How beautiful was this world of ours—how blue the sky! How fragrant the warm summer air! For more than a year, we had known only the stale drafts that had come in to us through the chimney, and now we could not get enough of the fresh breeze outside. We had never known that air, just plain air, could be so delicious.

We looked at each other. There were five of us, two women and three men: Mrs. Mahler, who already knew that her husband was dead; my young cousin Stella, whose parents had died in the Drohobycz ghetto; Dr. Friedman, the lawyer; my younger brother David, who had been only nineteen when the war had first broken out, and me. I had seen the white faces of many dead those last few years, but none had been as pale as those of the four with whom I had spent fifty-three weeks in the stable cellar. They looked like ghosts, ashen-faced and little more than skin and bones. Our clothes, which had not been impressive to begin with, hung from us in rags. There we stood, outside the stable, looking worse than the ancient, tattered beggars of old who used to go from house to house in search of a few pennies or a crust of bread.

In the distance, I could see stark, towerlike frames that pointed to the sky. These were the oil derricks that our family had owned before the outbreak of the war. I remembered how, as a child, I had watched the rich golden oil gush out through those derricks. Our family had discovered this wealth beneath the ground back in the 1860s and had owned the wells until the Russians came in 1939. Each well had been known either by a number or by a name—Arthur, Armand, Lina. There was even one named Xanthippe, the shrew.[1] I had always wondered how that well had received such an odd name. I was sure that the idea had not come from my grandparents; they had known of neither Xanthippe nor her husband, Socrates, the Greek philosopher. The only Greek they had ever heard of—except, perhaps, for Plato—was Aristotle, and they had known him only from the philosophic writings of Maimonides and other Jewish philosophers.[2] For all I knew, my grandfather might even have thought that Aristotle was not a Greek at all but a Jew, for why should the great Maimonides have taken the trouble to quote a mere Gentile? How, then, could Grandfather have known about Xanthippe?

But now my grandparents were gone, and so were my father and mother, and there we stood, out in the open air, looking about us and filling our

1. Xanthippe was the wife of the ancient Greek philosopher Socrates. Various writers in antiquity characterized her as nagging and abusive, and thus Xanthippe has come to symbolize a shrewish wife.

2. Rabbi Moshe ben Maimon (1135–1204), better known as Maimonides, is considered the most important Jewish philosopher of the Middle Ages. He is best known for authoring the Mishneh Torah, his codification of Jewish law, and for *Guide for the Perplexed*, a work that aims to reconcile the Hebrew Bible with the philosophy of Aristotle.

lungs with the cool, clean morning breeze. Suddenly, everything began to spin before my eyes, and I had to sit down on the fragrant green grass that spread out around the stable. I lay in the grass with my eyes closed, and a strange thought came to me: Perhaps all those months of hiding, of terror and anguish, had never happened at all. Perhaps it had only been a bad dream in which a demon had set a nightmarish stage with cardboard scenes of ghettos and death camps. My heart beat fast with joy and longing. *Soon, soon,* I told myself, *you will awaken from this nightmare, and when you open your eyes, you will be back at home again with your family and your friends. They will all smile at you, and you won't be sad and lonely anymore.*

But when I opened my eyes, I saw that it had not been a dream after all. Our home was gone, and so were our family and friends. In fact, there were no more Jews left anywhere. Our whole world had been slaughtered and our lives uprooted by an evil whirlwind. We, the five who still lived, lay in the grass, weak from our first breaths of fresh air after months in a damp cellar—not moving, not speaking, each lost in his own thoughts.

I closed my eyes again and relived all that had happened to me from the time the murderers had first come into my hometown. I wondered where I had gotten the strength and the willpower to remain alive after I had come face-to-face with death so many times. From where had I drawn the spark of faith that kept me wanting to live? Had it been mere instinct, a primitive urge to fight those who had sought not only to kill me but to erase the memory of my entire people from the face of the earth? Or was it a powerful, superhuman drive not to die so that I might tell the world of the unspeakable things that had been done to my brothers and sisters?

About noon, we finally rose from the ground and started slowly on our way to the little town of Schodnica. The Carpathian mountain roads were jammed with Russian soldiers, tanks, trucks, armored cars, horses, and even camels. Each vehicle was packed with men and guns. The first house we passed on the Borysław-Rybnik highway had been turned into a temporary hospital for the Russian soldiers. The building was already filled with the wounded; we could smell the antiseptic in the air as we went by. Soldiers who had been moved up to the battle lines only hours before were already back here, swathed in bloodstained bandages. The sky was dark with airplanes, and the ground shook beneath the roar of bombs and heavy artillery. The thought that we were practically on the battlefront came as a surprise. By a sheer miracle, we got through the mass of armor and humanity and finally reached the outskirts of our birthplace, Schodnica, which was about a quarter mile from our cellar hideout. The townspeople were not happy to see us. They had been sure that not one Jew was left alive, and now their faces reflected their terror that we had returned to bear witness to their crimes against our people.

Even the caretakers of our cellar hideout had their failings. They had agreed to give us shelter in the cellar of their farmhouse—at the risk of their lives. But they had tried to make us pay a peculiar price for our survival. A few days before Christmas Eve 1943, they announced that they would come to see us and make us a proposal of mutual advantage. We were, naturally, nervous about that. They had taken a risk to allow us to hide in their farmstead and were, without a doubt, under considerable tension. What would their proposal be?

On Christmas Eve, we had our answer. All four of them—two married couples—came down into the cellar in their holiday finery, their faces solemn. We held our breaths. One of the women was first to speak. Her voice was hoarse and nervous.

"Listen carefully, my dear friends," she said. "I don't have to tell you that outside there are no more Jews. They have all been killed, and we are the only friends you have left in this world. We have been hiding you from the Germans these last few months, and we can go on hiding you until this war is over. But we cannot hide you from our Lord Jesus. He knows you are here, and if it is His will to annihilate the Jews, He will find a way to have you discovered by the Germans. And if Jesus wishes that you should die, we will not be able to help you."[3]

---

3. After the Holocaust, antisemitism persisted in overwhelmingly Catholic Poland. One reason was that it was not until the Second Vatican Council (1962–1965) that the Catholic Church officially renounced the deicide, the accusation that the Jews had murdered Jesus.

How were we to escape the wrath of Jesus, who our Polish caretakers thought was using the German Gestapo as his agents? Simply by converting to Catholicism. If we just said the word, our landlords would bring some holy water, sprinkle it on us, and recite the appropriate prayers, and we would be spared all harm, safe under the wings of Jesus.

We looked at each other in amazement. We were certain that this could not have been our landlords' idea. They were simple, uneducated peasants. Surely, this little inquisition was authored by the village priest. We did not fear that our refusal would lead the priest to betray us to the Nazis. The priest was not a murderer. He was merely a dedicated prelate who was eager to prey on our fear of annihilation to "save" our souls. But we were afraid nonetheless. We could be reasonably sure that he would tell the story of our obstinacy to others in his parish, perhaps even to his bishop, and the more people who knew about us, the greater was the danger of our being found and put to death.

We said nothing; we only kept looking at each other and our friends who wanted to "save" us. They were visibly embarrassed. One of the men told us that if we really did not like the idea of being Christians, we could always go back to being Jews after the war. "Just try it, at least until the war is over," he said.

Such was the power of the zealots who had charge of the Catholic Church in Poland and, thus, of the lives of millions of simple, uneducated peasant folk. If only the bishops had preached to their flocks that Jesus would not mind their hiding Jews from the Nazis, that to save the life of a Jew was an act of great moral significance, countless lives could have been saved and our caretakers would not have felt compelled to make us this humiliating offer. But what could one expect if even the pope, the head of all Catholics, had remained silent while innocent Jews were slaughtered?[4]

---

4. Controversy still surrounds the legacy of Eugenio Pacelli (1876–1958), who served as Pope Pius XII between 1939 and 1958. Many historians believe that during World War II, Pius XII failed to speak out sufficiently on the crimes being perpetrated against Jews at the very moment when his moral authority might have saved lives.

Eight months passed, and our caretakers did not repeat the offer. Perhaps they understood that, under the circumstances, our conversion would have been nothing but an ungodly sham. They had left us alone, and we were still alive.

We went straight to our old House of Study.[5] Our caretakers had told us that the "Jewish temple" had been turned into a horse stable. The House of Study, our synagogue, which had been built in the late 1890s, stood in the center of town. It was a bright, spacious building divided into two sections, one for the men and one for the women, separated by a wall.[6] Each section had its own entrance. High above the wall between the two sections ran a row of windows. On special occasions, such as on Simchat Torah[7] (when the men circled the sanctuary seven times in a festive dance with the scrolls of the Torah), when a baby boy was initiated into the Covenant of Abraham,[8] or when a bridegroom was called to read from the Law on the Sabbath before his wedding,[9] the women would stand up on their benches and peer through the windows into the men's section. Each of the two sections could accommodate several hundred people. The synagogue was well attended even on ordinary Sabbaths, but on the holidays, the crowds were so large that the aisles were blocked and many worshippers had to stand in the vestibule and even in the street outside. To us, the House of Study had been not only a place of worship but also a center of communal and social life. It had been the place of family celebrations—weddings, circumcisions, and bar mitzvahs. If someone in town was seriously ill, his

---

5. A *beit midrash* (House of Study) is a dedicated space in a synagogue or yeshiva for Torah study. In small communities, the entire synagogue may serve this function.

6. A *mechitza* is a wall or screen in a synagogue that separates men and women.

7. *Simchat Torah* is a holiday that marks the completion of the annual cycle of Torah readings. Part of the celebration involves circling the synagogue with the Torah scrolls seven times.

8. The *brit milah* (known in Yiddish as a *bris*) is the ritual circumcision and naming ceremony of Jewish males eight days after birth. It fulfils God's command in Genesis for Abraham and his descendants to be circumcised as a sign of their membership in the covenant.

9. The *Shabbat Chatan* ("groom's Sabbath"), known in Yiddish as the *Aufruf* ("calling up"), is a Jewish marriage custom where the bridegroom is called on to read the blessing over the Torah on the Sabbath before his wedding. He thereby ceremonially announces the marriage to the community.

family would rush to the House of Study to "storm the heavens," weeping and wailing and praying before the open doors of the Holy Ark[10] for the recovery of their loved one.

Not everyone was able to come to the House of Study for the daily morning service. Workingmen and tradespeople could not spare the early weekday hours to pray with the congregation. They recited their morning prayers at home instead. But almost every Jewish man in town appeared for afternoon and evening prayers at the end of the day. If one of the men did not come, some of the other worshippers would inevitably go to his home after the service to inquire after his health. It was taken for granted that anyone who had not been at *shul*[11] for evening services must be ill.

Moreover, in the House of Study, we had a whole library of sacred books that the young students pored over all day long. Not only the students but also the householders and the elderly would come over to the House of Study whenever they could to devote a couple of hours to the wisdom of the sages.[12] Some of the men stayed after the evening service to study far into the night.

We knew the name of every man in our congregation—first, middle, and last. We knew where each man had his seat, what kind of person he was, what he did for a living, and whether he was rich or poor. We knew exactly who would weep during the sounding of the shofar on the New Year or during the solemn Kol Nidre service on Yom Kippur Eve.[13] We also knew who would be carried away with exultation on Simchat Torah and who would remain unmoved.

I would be hard pressed to remember when I was taken to the House of Study for the first time. Probably my mother brought me there as soon as I was old enough to be carried out of the house. It may have been on Simchat Torah, when Jews forget their daily cares and dance in honor of

10. The ark is the ceremonial receptacle in a synagogue in which Torah scrolls are stored.
11. *Shul* (Yiddish for "school") is a colloquial term for synagogue.
12. *Chazal*, a Hebrew acronym meaning "our sages of blessed memory," designates the collective consensus or authoritative wisdom on matters of Jewish law.
13. A shofar is a bugle-like instrument made from a ram's horn that is blown during Rosh Hashanah services. For more on Kol Nidre, see part I, chapter 7, note 6.

the Law that God gave to His people. Or perhaps it was on Yom Kippur Eve, when the congregation stood huddled together in fear and trembling before the divine judgment.

And now I was there again, standing on a mound of horse manure in this house of prayer and study, which the Germans and their henchmen had turned into a stable. The sanctuary had been cleared out, except for the benches at the eastern wall, the seats of honor, which the Germans had used as feeding troughs for their horses. The Holy Ark was still there, standing against the eastern wall, but there were no scrolls inside and the doors were broken. The floor was covered from wall to wall with horse manure and other refuse; it had obviously not been cleaned in many weeks. But the murals on the walls looked as fresh as if they had been completed only the day before. The scenes of the Wailing Wall, the Holy Temple in flames, and the Tomb of Rachel were still there, unchanged.[14]

As I stood in the empty hall, immobile, I saw the faces of the men and women who had prayed there in the old days. I saw them all; not one of them was missing. I could not believe that all these people were really dead. There was my father, wrapped in his long, heavy woolen prayer shawl. I could see him quite clearly, with his patriarchal beard and his high scholarly brow, absorbed in a complicated Talmudic passage that he was studying when the service began. Why had I survived when he and all the others had gone to their deaths? Had I been condemned to remain alive only to bear witness to the tragic end of the Jewish people after four thousand years of history?

I quickly walked out of the House of Study into the courtyard. Before the war, there had been some trees in the little open space. They were not there anymore; only the stumps were left. But as I turned to go away, I saw that on the very spot where one of the old trees had been cut down, a new young sapling was striving for life. The roots of the lost tree had given birth to a young sprout. Perhaps we Jews too were not lost after all. This

14. The Wailing Wall, the Holy Temple, and the Tomb of Rachel are Judaism's holiest sites.

young tree rising from the remains of the old became a symbol of hope to me; the ancient roots of Israel were still alive and would someday bring forth a new Jewish nation.

Suddenly I heard my name called. I turned in the direction of the voices. Beyond the courtyard fence, I saw my four comrades. They had left me in the House of Study and had gone to the house of a Polish Gentile they had known before the war to ask him for some clothes. Now they were shouting and gesticulating wildly. I could not hear what they were shouting, but I immediately sensed that something was amiss.

They rushed over to me and told me that we would have to leave Schodnica at once. They had just learned from their Polish friend that the Germans had launched a counterattack and had broken through the lines and forced the Russians to retreat. We knew only too well what would be in store for us if the Germans were to return.

We spent the next few hours frantically looking for a way to escape. We could not walk in our condition. But we could not even find a horse cart to take us out of Schodnica to a place of relative safety. We resigned ourselves to the thought that fate was about to catch up with us after all. But then word came that the Russians had managed to stop the Germans just a few miles from Schodnica. Obviously, we were not meant to die just yet. Nevertheless, one thing was sure. We had to leave Schodnica, for we could tell from the ugly, sullen faces of the townsmen that even if the Germans did not return to kill us, the Poles would do so with pleasure. But would we be better off anywhere else in Poland?

Meanwhile, it had become dark, and we did not have a place to spend the night. We did not want to go back to the cellar, for the Gentiles knew all about us now, so that place was no longer safe. Then we saw some Russian soldiers coming toward us. They turned out to be Jews. "You can go and sleep in the stable," they said. "We'll watch that nothing happens to you."

They even sent a medic to examine our swollen legs and ankles, and then they took up positions outside the stable, guns ready, to make sure that no one would disturb our rest. But our hearts were heavy. All the joy of our first moment of freedom was gone.

# CHAPTER 2

# CAN THESE BONES LIVE?

The day after our liberation, we made our first contact with the world outside—in the town of Drohobycz, about thirty kilometers from Schodnica. We found the journey to Drohobycz easier than we had expected. For safety's sake, our group had decided to split up; Mrs. Mahler and I started out several hours earlier than the three others. Mrs. Mahler had a special reason to get to Drohobycz as soon as possible; she was sure she would be able to reclaim the house that her family had built there before the war. If she got the house back, all five of us would be able to live there, she said, at least for the time being.

We stood at the edge of the highway that led to Drohobycz and signaled passing Russian army trucks, the only means of transportation available. We were lucky; one of the very first trucks stopped. The driver invited us to join him and helped us climb aboard.

The truck tooled swiftly over the winding Carpathian mountain road. We could not get enough of the fragrant mountain air, and it made us lightheaded. After what seemed only minutes, the first rooftops and steeples of Drohobycz came into view. When we reached the center of the town, the driver slowed down, stopped his truck, and ordered us to get out. We had hardly set foot on the ground when the truck took off and disappeared around the corner.

We felt like wayfarers in a strange, new land. The streets were crowded with people—men, women and children, Poles and Ukrainians. Suddenly we realized we had become unaccustomed to the hustle and bustle of a busy town. We slowly started on our way to Mrs. Mahler's house, but we had hardly walked one block when we heard people shouting after us, "Jews! Jews! You're still alive? How come they didn't get you?"

At first, we pretended not to hear them; we kept on walking without looking back. But it was no use. Some of the people near us stopped, and we could feel a menacing ring of angry Poles tightening around us. We could not move any farther. Our first impulse was to turn around and dodge into the next side street, but it was too late. Every corner was blocked; we were surrounded by a circle of red and threatening faces, by eyes burning with pure hatred. We stared back at the mob in shocked amazement. What we saw in their faces was more than just the old Jew-hatred; it was sheer panic. Here were Jews, still alive, who probably would not keep their mouths shut.

We began shouting for help, hoping that some Russian soldier might hear us and come to our rescue. Luck was with us. A Russian officer, with a gun in his hand, pushed his way through the crowd and led us away. He marched behind us until we came to a little park on Mickiewicz Street. All this time, he did not speak a word. Only as he turned to leave us did he speak at last. He looked at Mrs. Mahler and me with eyes full of sadness and compassion and said, "Don't let this upset you too much. Someday the sun will shine again—even for us." He too was Jewish.

After our rescuer had gone, Mrs. Mahler and I sat down on a bench in the little park, not quite knowing what to do next. We were hungry, and our clothes were in shreds. A decent pair of shoes or a piece of bread cost money, and we didn't have a penny between us. It occurred to us to try to find work in town. But how could we look for a job if to merely walk through the streets could mean our deaths? Besides, who would be willing or able to give us work? We did not even know what currency they were using in Drohobycz now—was it Polish złotys, German marks, or Russian rubles?

We had spent the last of our money during our final weeks in the cellar. With no more money to give to our landlords, the five of us had found ourselves face-to-face with starvation. Then my brother had hit on

a happy solution: we could remove the gold crowns and bridgework from
our teeth and use them to pay for food. The first one to try was my brother
David himself. Without saying a word to anyone, he began to manipu-
late one of his gold teeth, pushing it to and fro, to work the jacket loose.
One morning, he triumphantly held up the extracted crown. This encouraged me to follow suit, and within two days, I had produced enough gold
from my mouth to send our landlords into Drohobycz on a shopping trip
for us.

But now here we were, Mrs. Mahler and I, with no gold left in our
mouths and terrified at the very idea of leaving the park. Once again, we
wondered what sense there was in our having survived. For four long
years, our only desire had been to survive. Now, on August 9, 1944, we were
free. But was it really freedom that we had gained? We found ourselves on
a park bench, afraid to stay and no less afraid to move on.

We finally got up and continued on our way to Mrs. Mahler's house.
This time, we walked quickly despite the pain in our legs; with lowered
heads, we tried to avoid the glances of passersby. When we reached the
house, the neighbors informed us that a Russian NKVD[1] officer was now
living there with his family. We went to the Russian headquarters, which
happened to be on the same street and, after some searching, located the
officer. After a lengthy discussion, the officer agreed to let us have the small
room directly under the roof. He explained that he needed all the other
rooms for himself and his family.

The little attic room was completely bare. Not a piece of furniture was
left. But there was a tiny niche in one of the corners with a sink and a small
gas stove, both in working order. We flung open the room's two tiny windows and sat down on the floor to wait for my brother David, my cousin
Stella (Esther) Backenroth, and Dr. Friedman, who were to meet us here.
After a while, they arrived. When we told them of our narrow escape, they

---

1. The NKVD, an acronym meaning "People's Commissariat for Internal Affairs," was
the Soviet secret police from 1934 to 1946 and a forerunner of the KGB ("Committee
for State Security").

seemed surprised; they had had no trouble at all on the way. No one had even turned to look at them.

Dr. Friedman looked around the room and made no attempt to hide his disappointment. "How are we supposed to live here?" he demanded. "Why, this place is cleaned out. No beds, no table, no chairs, not a dish to eat from, not even a nail in the wall, nothing at all." He was looking for an excuse to part company with us and go off somewhere on his own. He had been born in Drohobycz; his father had been a well-known lawyer, and before the war, he himself had started a law practice in the town. The Friedmans had plenty of Gentile friends in those days, and he was sure he would do better to look them up than to stay with us in the bare attic chamber where he would not even have a bed to sleep in. He left us without much ceremony. His departure only served to increase our feeling of blank despair.

After it had become dark, we went to the Russian officer downstairs and borrowed a bucket from him. Then the four of us went to a field on the edge of town and dug out some new potatoes with our bare hands. Back in our attic, Mrs. Mahler washed the potatoes and cooked them in the bucket, which the officer had been using to water his horses. When the potatoes were done, we sat down on the floor and began to peel and eat them with our fingers. As we sat on the cold, bare floor chewing the tasteless potatoes, the dam broke at last and our tears began to flow. We envied our dead loved ones who no longer had to cope with a world left cold and barren by war. I recalled the words uttered by the prophet Ezekiel when he found himself in the midst of the valley of dry bones: "And He said to me: 'Son of Man, can these bones live?' And I answered: 'O Lord, Thou knowest.'"[2]

2. The reference is to Ezekiel 37:3.

# A JEWISH CHAPLAIN
# IN THE POLISH ARMY

The next day we went into town and found a few more Jews who had survived the war.[1] Meeting them gave us new hope. These were weary, broken people, but they were our own, and being together made it easier for us to face whatever the future might bring. It also made it possible for us to earn a living. We began to earn a little money selling watches and whiskey to the Russian soldiers. The Russians, in turn, sold us heavy army boots, which could be dyed and were much in demand among the civilians. To save money on food, we lived mostly on potatoes that we would dig up in the fields.

On our very first Sabbath morning in Drohobycz, we held a service in the room of one of the survivors. It was a sad congregation; we had no Scroll of the Law,[2] not even a Bible or a prayer book. About fifteen of us stood around a rickety table and recited our prayers by heart. One of the men, who acted as our cantor,[3] wore the only prayer shawl we had. Together, we recited "El Malei Rachamim"[4] for our loved ones and begged God to grant them eternal rest.

By the time, a week had gone by, and it became obvious that Russia had no intention of returning to Poland all the Polish territory it had "liberated"

1. Jews displaced persons (DPs) who survived the war and the Holocaust are known collectively in Hebrew as the *she'erit ha-pletah* ("the surviving remnant").
2. A Scroll of the Law (*sefer torah*) is a scroll used in public synagogue readings that contains the Pentateuch (the first five books of the Hebrew testament).
3. Known in Hebrew as a *chazzan*, a cantor leads singing and prayer in a synagogue.
4. See part I, chapter 8, note 1.

from the Nazis. The Soviets had set up a border station at Przemyśl, a sure indication that Russia was not even planning to vacate the areas of Lwów, Tarnopol, and Stanisławów, which it had seized from Poland in 1939. The front line ended about forty kilometers beyond the town of Rzeszów, between Dębica and Tarnów. At the time, however, the borders between Russia and Poland were not too closely guarded. After we had been in Drohobycz three weeks, my brother, David, and I decided to take advantage of the situation and cross from Russian-occupied Drohobycz into the free part of Poland before the Russians sealed off the border.

After a whole day's journey, made mostly in army trucks, David and I arrived in Rzeszów. The town had been liberated from both Germans and Russians only three weeks before, but the forty-some survivors of the prewar Jewish community of ten thousand had already managed to create a semblance of organized Jewish life. They had even set up an official Jewish community council headed by Dr. Reich, a young lawyer. Religious services were held in one of the small prayer rooms that had not been destroyed. Thanks to the efforts of Hayim Moshe Halberstam, a grandson of the famous Hasidic rebbe of Sandz,[5] the group had been able to buy back a Scroll of the Law that the Nazis had taken away and that had found its way into the hands of a peasant. But they did not know where to put the precious scroll because the Nazis had completely cleaned out the prayer room. Halberstam did not want to place the sacred scroll on the floor, so he gave it to one of the men to hold while he ran off in search of a little cabinet to serve as a Holy Ark. By the time I arrived, the little synagogue already had a table that was used as a reading desk. But autumn, with its wind and rain, posed a problem: the windows of the room had been knocked out, and glass panes were still not available.

The Jews of the town eked out a living by traveling from place to place, buying and selling whatever merchandise they could lay their hands on. The war was still far from over, and the situation was still unsettled, to put

5. The famous Hasidic rebbe was Aryeh Leib Halberstam (1797/99–1876), founder of the Sandz Hasidic dynasty. See part I, chapter 7, note 8.

it mildly. It was dangerous, particularly for Jews, to travel on the highways. Gangs of Polish hooligans would stop cars, drag out the Jews, take them deep in the woods, and shoot them.

At the time, Poland was ruled by a provisional government led by Premier Osóbka-Morawski, with Lublin serving as the temporary capital.[6] One of the members of the provisional government was Dr. Emil Sommerstein, a Jew who had been a member of the Polish parliament before the war and had been active in the Zionist movement at the same time.[7] Officially, Sommerstein's position in the postwar Polish cabinet had no direct connection with Jewish affairs; he was minister of reparations, working on Polish demands for indemnities from Germany. Nevertheless, the Jews still regarded him as their own leader and frequently came to him with requests for official intervention. Although his health had been ruined by thirty months in Russian prison camps, he was glad to receive any Jew who sought him out. The Jews, in turn, drew hope and courage from the fact that their leader had been given a place in the new Polish government.

I first met Dr. Sommerstein in October 1944, after I had been named a representative from Rzeszów to the "Central Jewish Committee" he had set up. I had called on him at his office in Lublin to intervene on behalf of some thirty Jews who were being held behind the front lines as Russian prisoners. This is the story of these unfortunates: A group of about forty Jews had dug a primitive bunker in the woods between Dębica and Tarnów and had hidden out there for more than a year. But eventually, that area became a battlefield for the Germans and the Russians, and the

6. On July 22, 1944, the Polish Committee of National Liberation (also known as the Lublin Committee) formed a provisional, Soviet-backed communist puppet government in the territory reconquered from Nazi Germany. Edward Osóbka-Morawski (1909–1997) served as its head. The Soviets formed the Lublin Committee to keep noncommunist organizations out of power, specifically the Polish government in exile in London and the Armia Krajowa (Home Army) in Poland itself.

7. Emil Sommerstein (1883–1957) was a legal scholar, Zionist leader, and former deputy to the Sejm (Polish parliament) in the 1920s and 1930s. The Soviets imprisoned him in November 1939. From July 21, 1944, to December 31, 1944, he served in the provisional Lublin government, and in February 1945, he became the head of the Central Committee of Jews in Poland.

forty Jews in their bunker were caught in the middle of the fighting. It takes no great imagination to picture what these Jews endured: bullets and shrapnel flew over their heads day and night without cease. Of course, they could no longer venture out to get food and water. Soon, they felt they faced death no matter what they did. Therefore, they took a desperate step. One night, all of them—men, women, and children—crept out of their bunker together and dashed toward the Russian lines. About thirty of the group reached the Russian side. The Russians, who suspected they might be spies, questioned them in great detail and then locked them up in a little house just behind the battle line. One of the Jews managed to escape, got to Rzeszów, and told us what had happened to the others. That same day I went off to Lublin to see Sommerstein.

Seated behind his desk at the ministry, Sommerstein, with his long, white beard, looked more like a gentle patriarch than the high government official he was. As I talked, I could see tears rolling down his cheeks. After I had finished my report, he asked me to remain in my seat and write a memorandum of all the facts in the case. While I was writing, he telephoned Jakub Berman,[8] who, if I remember correctly, was then deputy minister of foreign affairs, and requested him to receive me at once. With the memorandum in my hand, I went to Berman, whose office was in the same building as Sommerstein's. Berman too was Jewish, but he was a fanatic Communist with little regard for Jewish interests. He impressed me as a quiet fellow, but I could tell from the look in his eyes that he did not like me and was eager to get rid of me. He did not even respond to my greeting; he only took the memorandum from my hand and looked through it. When he had finished, he dismissed me with a curt nod of his head. Needless to say, I was none too happy with the reception Berman had accorded me. But when, on my return to Rzeszów several days later, I learned that the entire group of Jewish prisoners had been released, I realized that beneath his quiet, Communist exterior, Berman was indeed a Jew.

8. Jakub Berman (1901–1984) was a member of the leadership cadre of Stalinist postwar Poland. He oversaw cultural policy and the Polish secret police.

Before going back to Rzeszów, I reported to Sommerstein again. There was something that he wanted to talk over with me, he said. It seemed that two Polish army divisions that had come into the Russian sector during the early days of the war had returned to Poland and were now fighting under a Polish commander, Marshal Rola-Żymierski.[9] Sommerstein had learned that there were several thousand Jews among these soldiers. He had just succeeded in getting the provisional Polish government to agree to appoint three Jewish chaplains to meet the religious needs of the Jewish men. He told me that he had already found one chaplain, Rabbi David Kahane, who had taught Hebrew in Lwów before the war.[10] Two more were still needed. Would I, he asked, be willing to accept a commission as a chaplain in the Polish army?

There was no doubt in my mind that, as an officer in the Polish army, I would be able to do much more for our fellow Jews—in and out of uniform—than I would as a mere civilian. The Poles were impressed by military men; my uniform would open the doors of many high places. Accordingly, I accepted Sommerstein's offer immediately. He shook my hand warmly and said that he was sure I would make an excellent coworker in our joint venture to rebuild Jewish life in Poland.

Several weeks later, after all the formalities had been completed, I received an official notice from Polish army headquarters, signed by Marshal Rola-Żymierski, stating that I had been appointed as a Jewish chaplain in the Polish army with the rank of captain. I was also directed to get my uniform.

9. As marshal, Michał Rola-Żymierski (1890–1989) was the highest-ranking officer of the Polish Army established by Soviet forces.
10. David Kahane (1903–1998) was a rabbi and member of the Lwów (Lemberg) *Judenrat* who, like Leon Thorne, escaped the Janowska labor camp (which Thorne calls "Janover") and survived the ghetto. Kahane survived thanks to Andrey Sheptytsky, the metropolitan archbishop of the Ukrainian Greek Catholic Church, who hid hundreds of Jews in monasteries and in his own home (See part I, chapter 10, note 5). Between 1945 and 1949, Kahane was the chief rabbi of the Polish armed forces before eventually immigrating to Israel. His Holocaust memoir, one of the few to come from the Lwów ghetto, appeared in Hebrew in 1978 and in English in 1990.

I stared at my uniform for a long time before I could make myself put it on. When I had finally donned all the army regalia, I was almost ashamed to go out into the street. I remembered the ditty I had learned as a little boy: "I've got boots and a uniform too, oh my! Just like a regular soldier boy!" It all seemed un-Jewish to me somehow.

But in fact, my induction into the Polish army was the beginning of a period of fruitful and rewarding work. Rabbi Kahane and I conceived of our task as a twofold one. We would work with the Jewish soldiers in the Polish army, raising their morale, teaching them about Jewish history and tradition, and helping them observe as many of our religious customs and ceremonies as possible. At the same time, we would endeavor to seek out and serve all the Jews who had survived the war in Poland, even in the remotest corners of the country.

Our aim was to convince the Jews that we were not lost, that the Germans had not succeeded in destroying us or in breaking our spirits. We had lost six million of our people, but we were still alive and so were millions of Jews in other parts of the world—in America, England, South Africa, and Palestine. Once the war was over, we said, we would establish contact with the Jews in all those countries; they certainly would not abandon us. And although, as Polish officers, we had no right to do so, Kahane and I intimated that the Jews of Poland would eventually have to consider joining a larger Jewish community somewhere else. The "larger community," of course, was Palestine. We knew that there was no future for us in Poland. The country's soil was saturated with Jewish blood; every step recalled our tragedy to us. Moreover, for centuries the Jews of Poland had been accustomed to living in large, close-knit Jewish communities and in the midst of a rich Jewish culture—not in scattered handfuls under the constant threat of hostile neighbors.

David Kahane and I did not have trouble finding audiences as we traveled the length and breadth of Poland. All we needed to do was to locate one single Jew in a town, and within half an hour, the entire Jewish population of the locality would have gathered around us to hear our message, devouring every word we spoke. We might be eager to move on because we had other Jewish communities to visit that day, but invariably our audiences would beg us to stay with them for just a little bit longer.

I started the practice of wearing a prayer shawl on my "pastoral tours." It was the first tallit[11] I owned after the war, and a very special tallit it was. It had been given to me in Lublin by Leib Sztekacz, a leader of the Orthodox Agudath Israel movement.[12]

"I have a gift for you which I am sure you will cherish," he said. "It is a prayer shawl from Treblinka."

That was how I came to hold in my hands this, the last possession of an unknown Jew who had gone to his death in Hitler's gas chambers. In addition to wearing it, I used it in place of a marriage canopy at weddings that I was called on to perform. Four men would grasp it by its corners and hold it over the heads of the bride and groom. Almost all the wedding guests would run to touch the prayer shawl. Fathers and mothers would hold up their little children so they could touch it. Some guests, chiefly women, would rush up to kiss it.

Before long, my activities were to take me beyond the borders of Poland. On January 17, 1945, the Russian army launched an offensive that freed the last of Poland from German rule. Then the Soviet forces crossed the German frontier, and as Jewish chaplains, Rabbi Kahane and I went with our troops into the heartland of Hitler's Germany.

11. A tallit (Yiddish: *talles*) is a fringed prayer shawl worn by religious Jews.
12. On Agudath Israel, see part I, chapter 10, note 4.

# CHAPTER 4

# BRESLAU REVISITED

As the little army truck in which I traveled sped over the wide, smooth Silesian Autobahn from Łódź to Breslau, I tried hard to restrain my excitement.[1] In a matter of hours, I would see my alma mater, the Jewish Theological Seminary of Breslau, where I had studied ten years before. I hardly expected to find any of my old professors or their families, but I was hoping against hope that at least some part of the seminary's huge library had survived.

The Breslau seminary was founded in 1854 by Zacharias Frankel in a move to counter the growing challenge of Reform Judaism, which had officially denied the validity of the rabbinic tradition for modern, nineteenth-century Jews. Frankel's seminary had been the first institution of Jewish higher learning to apply the scientific methods of critical scholarship to Jewish studies, but at the same time, it honored the rabbinic tradition as a basic component of Judaism.[2] From Breslau, Frankel's "positive historical"

---

1. After World War II, the German city of Breslau became the Polish city of Wrocław as part of the Allies' postwar redrawing of Europe's national boundaries. The German population was expelled and replaced with Poles from Eastern territories annexed by the Soviet Union.
2. Zacharias Frankel (1801–1875) is considered the intellectual founder of Conservative Judaism, a major Jewish denomination that emerged in the mid-nineteenth century in response to both Reform Judaism's attempts to adapt the faith to modern life and Orthodoxy's adherence to traditional religious law. Frankel believed in the need to adapt Judaism to the times but also to maintain what he called a "positive historical Judaism." The Jewish Theological Seminary of Breslau was the first modern rabbinical seminary. It was closed by the Nazis in 1938, and much of its library was lost in the *Kristallnacht* pogrom.

approach to Judaism had gone forth out into the world; on the American continent, it found expression in the Jewish Theological Seminary of America in New York.[3]

Now, on May 11, 1945, I was returning to the seminary and to Breslau for the first time since 1935. Three days before, what had remained of Germany's leadership had surrendered to the Allies; the war in Europe was over. Breslau, once the proud capital of Silesia, was almost completely in ruins. The bombings and artillery shelling had left fires flickering here and there, and the air was heavy with smoke. Drunken Russian soldiers caroused through the ruins.

Surprisingly, the Wallstrasse, where the seminary had been, had suffered little damage. The large Orthodox "Storch" Synagogue too stood almost untouched.[4] I walked up to number fourteen, the seminary building. The metal letters above the main entrance had been torn out, but they left traces on the wall clear enough to read: "Jüdisch-Theologisches Seminar—Hochschule für Jüdische Theologie" (Jewish Theological Seminary—College of Jewish Theology).

I knocked several times at the yellow gate, but no one answered. Then I began to shout in German so that whoever was inside would know I was not a Russian soldier. Several minutes later, I heard footsteps inside and a key turned in the lock. The door opened, and I went in.

The corridor of what had once been the seminary was crowded with people, mostly old men, women, and small children. They stood before me in a semicircle, staring in silence at the man in the Polish army uniform who, like them, found himself at a loss for words.

For a moment, I thought that I was in the wrong building. The entire floor that had once housed the lecture halls, the boardroom, and the

3. Founded in 1886, the Jewish Theological Seminary of New York remains a major intellectual and spiritual center of Conservative Judaism.
4. Named after an inn that once occupied its site, the *Synagoge zum Weißen Storch* (White Stork Synagogue) held its first service in 1829. It was one of Breslau's two main synagogues, and it survived the war largely unscathed.

faculty and student lounges had been altered beyond recognition. Some of the walls had been broken through and others built in their place. Several doors had been walled up and new ones put in elsewhere. The seminary building had been converted into a public shelter for bombed-out families.

"Is Hütter, the custodian, here?" I asked. Hütter had been a German and a Gentile. I felt that he might still be there. A woman quickly pushed through the group that stood facing me.

"I'm his wife," she said. "I'm Mrs. Hütter."

I recognized her immediately. Every morning after the first Talmud class, she had come into the students' lounge with a pitcher of warm milk and a bag of fresh rolls. Every student who sat down at the table was served a cup of milk and two rolls, paid for by the students' society.

I told her my name, but she did not remember me. She said that her husband and her son had both been killed during the Russian siege of the city.

I wanted to know what had become of the lecture halls. Mrs. Hütter asked me to follow her. We entered a large room. In one corner, I saw a kitchen range and several beds on which little children were playing. From there, we passed through a door, directly into the main auditorium. The door had been put in at the very spot where the lectern had once stood. Now this hall was almost completely filled with beds.

I stopped at the threshold and looked from the one room to the other. For more than eight decades, those walls had gathered the words of the brilliant men who lectured there and had shared their thoughts with hundreds of disciples: Zacharias Frankel, the founder and first dean of the seminary; Heinrich Graetz,[5] author of the classic history of the Jewish people; Michael Guttmann,[6] dean of the seminary and author of a

---

5. See part I, chapter 4, note 4.
6. The Hungarian scholar and rabbi Michael Guttmann (1872–1942) was a professor and dean at the Breslau seminary between 1921 and 1938. At his death, he was still working on his projected twelve-volume work *Mafte'ah ha-Talmud / Clavis Talmudi* (*Key to the Talmud*), first published in 1906.

monumental Talmudic compendium; Isaac Heinemann,[7] the philosopher and classical philologist who eventually settled in Israel; Israel Rabin,[8] the noted Bible scholar; and H. J. Zimmels,[9] later to become principal of Jews' College in London.

I thought of the countless students who had gone forth from these halls to become eminent scholars and teachers: Adolf Schwarz,[10] dean of the Jewish Theological Seminary in Vienna; Hermann Cohen,[11] the philosopher; Alexander Kohut,[12] remembered by Jewish scholars the world over for his *Aruch Completum*; David Kaufmann,[13] professor at the Rabbinical Seminar of Budapest; and Moritz Güdemann, who had been chief rabbi of Vienna when Theodor Herzl first set forth his idea of a reborn Jewish State.[14]

I turned and went on to the faculty lounge and the boardroom. Wherever I looked, there were beds and kitchen stoves.

Mrs. Hütter followed me without a word.

"And what became of the library?" I asked her.

7. A philologist and expert in relationships between Hellenistic and Jewish philosophy, Isaac Heinemann (1876–1957) taught at the Breslau seminary from 1919 to 1938, when he immigrated to Palestine.

8. Between 1926 and 1933, Israel Rabin (1882–1951) lectured on postbiblical literature at the Breslau seminary.

9. The historian Hirsch Jacob Zimmels (1900–1975) worked as an historian at the Breslau seminary from 1929 to 1933. He left Germany in 1939 and, from 1942 to 1969, was a lecturer at and later director of Jews' College in London, known today as the London School of Jewish Studies.

10. Adolf Schwarz (1846–1931) was the first head of Vienna's Israelitisch-Theologische Lehranstalt (Israelite-Theological Seminary) upon its founding in 1893.

11. Born into a devout family, Hermann Cohen (1842–1918) first studied to become a rabbi at the Breslau seminary but opted instead to become a philosopher. He is known today as a cofounder of the Marburg School of philosophy, which interpreted and built on the work of the German idealist philosopher Immanuel Kant.

12. Alexander Kohut's (1842–1894) magnum opus, the eight-volume *Arukh ha-Shalem* (published between 1878 and 1892), was an edition of a massive eleventh-century dictionary of the Talmud.

13. David Kaufmann (1852–1899) was a prolific scholar of the philosophy of religion, genealogy, history, and art. An avid collector, he also amassed an important collection of Hebrew manuscripts.

14. Moritz Güdemann (1835–1918) was the chief rabbi of Vienna, a historian of Jewish education, and an opponent of Theodor Herzl (1860–1904), the founder of modern Zionism. Güdemann spoke out publically against the proposal for the independent Jewish state in Palestine that Herzl outlined in his 1896 work *The Jewish State*.

The library had numbered some forty thousand books, along with hundreds of documents and scores of priceless manuscripts, some of them unpublished.

Mrs. Hütter said she did not know. One day, back in 1938, shortly after the Nazis had closed the seminary, several trucks had pulled up in front of the building. Nazi stormtroopers leaped from the trucks, rushed inside, took all the books they could find, and threw them in the trucks. Then they had driven off full speed, and that was the last that Mrs. Hütter had seen of the library.

All that remained of the seminary I had known was the old, tall grandfather clock at the main entrance. We students had always liked that clock because it stood at a spot everyone passed at least twice a day and because it had always run on time, to the second.

Now the clock was still there, ticking away just as it had been when I had left it ten years before.

—≺—

# CHAPTER 5

# FISHKE, MY RESCUER

One day late in May 1945, I happened to be standing in front of the building of Kraków's Jewish Committee on Długa Street. There were always crowds of Jews milling around that place. Some would come to the committee for funds or clothes, which had begun to arrive in Poland from America and Palestine. Others came to get their documents put in order or to locate relatives abroad. And then, of course, there were those who came simply to meet and talk to other Jews or hear what was going on in the world. I went there myself almost every week. On that particular day, as I stood talking with some people I knew, I saw a man on the other side of the street whose face looked familiar. But at the moment, I was unable to place him. Where and when had I seen him before? I kept looking at him and finally began to walk toward him. But when he noticed me, he deliberately turned away and walked off in another direction, as if he wanted to avoid me by disappearing into the crowd. My curiosity got the better of me.

"Say, aren't you Fishke from Drohobycz?" I called after him. "Don't mind my uniform. Tell me, aren't you Fishke?"

The man was obviously frightened. "What do you want of me?" he stammered. "I don't know you. I've never seen you in my life."

"Don't be afraid," I said. "I'm the man whom you saved from the police, back in Drohobycz in 1943. They were going to shoot me at sunrise. Remember?"

I told him my name. Only then did Fishke—for it was indeed he—look me in the eye. He even gave me a broad smile.

"Sure, sure," he said. "Now I remember. You're Mrs. Backenroth's cousin. Sure, you were in trouble that time. Something about a woman's fur coat."

He seemed to take a new lease on life.

"Why were you so afraid when you first saw me?" I asked him. "Have you done something wrong? Are you in trouble?"

"God forbid!" he replied. "I've got nothing on my conscience. It's just that there are some people who don't especially like me. During the war, I got to know a couple of German policemen and Ukrainian militia boys, and I used my connections to help as many of our Jews as I could, in any number of ways. You, of all people, should certainly know what I'm talking about. But in some cases, it didn't work out, and I couldn't do anything. So there are some Jews who hate me and wouldn't mind seeing me dead."

I looked at him. His clothes were torn, his shoes were badly misshapen, and his face was pale and drawn. He obviously had not had a shave or a haircut in some time. I remembered what he had looked like when I had seen him for the first time at the police headquarters in Drohobycz, and it was hard for me to believe that this was the same man.

I have never before told anyone the story of Fishke. Why not? Because I was ashamed. Even now, almost thirty years later, I am embarrassed to remember what chances we took with our lives in the ghettos and in the concentration camps. Although our lives always hung by a thread, we were willing to tempt fate even further and risk death just to earn a few złotys.

The story I am about to tell took place sometime in April 1943. I was in the Hyrawka labor camp just outside Drohobycz. We were sleeping in bunks, one on top of the other, about seventy men to a barrack. The bunk beside me was occupied by David Lefkowitz, the husband of my cousin Recha Gertner. Recha and her daughter were in the ghetto in Drohobycz. Lefkowitz did not work with the rest of us. He was a male chamberlain of sorts and kept the barracks in order. Since he did not have to travel to his work assignment, he generally had some time to talk to people during the day and even to read newspapers. At night, before "lights out," he would tell me whatever he had heard during the day, mostly about the war. But one night, he leaned over his bunk and asked me to come closer. He had a piece of news that no one else was supposed to hear. He had received word that day from Recha that a friend of hers, a Polish Gentile woman from Görlitz, had come to Drohobycz to do some business. The lady in question made a good living buying various items from Jews and selling them at a handsome profit. At this particular time, the lady was in the market for a woman's Persian lamb coat. She had told Recha that she was prepared to pay good money for a nice fur coat. In those days, fur coats were quite expensive.

As mentioned before, as early as the winter of 1941–1942, all the Jews in our area had been ordered to give up their fur coats to the German authorities. Any Jew caught with a fur coat in his—or her—possession would be summarily executed.

Now as Lefkowitz talked, I remembered that only a few days before, a friend of mine by the name of Lindenbaum, who was in my labor detail, had told me a secret: he had a woman's fur coat in the camp with him. He had kept it carefully hidden, but he was looking for a way to get rid of the coat because he was afraid of being caught with it.

I had been amazed. What was Lindenbaum doing with a woman's fur coat? The Germans were killing Jews anyway—why give them a special invitation? Seeing my surprise, Lindenbaum had explained the situation. It was a beautiful fur coat, practically new, which he had ordered for his wife about a year before the outbreak of the war. He hadn't had the heart to give it to the Nazi gangsters, and he had not been able to persuade his wife to destroy it. But in the meantime, Mrs. Lindenbaum had died in the ghetto, and Lindenbaum had realized that he would have to dispose of the coat somehow. He knew that if he were caught with it, he would bring disaster not only on himself but on all the other Jews in the labor camp as well.

Now my cousin's proposition would afford Lindenbaum a chance to get rid of the coat. It also occurred to me that I might benefit from the deal myself; it could bring me a few złotys. This was not an unimportant consideration, because it looked as if I would be left without a penny to my name. When the war began, my family and I had buried our money and valuables in three different places. Two had already been discovered and looted by the Ukrainians and the Poles. The third was in another city, in Sambor, and I had no way of finding out whether it was still undisturbed.

At any rate, here was my golden opportunity to earn a little badly needed cash. All that I had to do was tell Lindenbaum of the deal, get the coat from him, and take it from the camp to my cousin in the ghetto. I did not give too much thought to the dangerous part of the undertaking: the trip from the camp to the ghetto with the fur coat.

At work, the very next morning, I asked Lindenbaum whether he still had the coat. He did.

That evening, I brought him and Lefkowitz together. The two men discussed the transaction and came to an agreement on every aspect of it except one: Which of the three of us would risk his life to take the coat to the ghetto? Even though we had agreed that the one who acted as courier would receive half of the money for the coat, the decision to volunteer for the job was not an easy one.

To this day, I cannot quite explain why I should have been so eager to offer my services for the errand. Was I just being cavalier about my life? Was it childish bravado? Was I so anxious to make some money that I was willing to risk death for it? Or was it blind faith, the firm conviction that God, who had saved me so many times before, would not permit me to die now because of a fur coat? I do not know.

At any rate, I told myself that my mission would not be particularly difficult. I believed I would be able to make the trip to the ghetto and back within one hour.

The next day, Lefkowitz told me when and where I was to meet his wife and her Polish friend. In the evening, after work, Lefkowitz, Lindenbaum, and I stole into the attic of one of the camp buildings. There, they helped me put on the fur coat and, on top of it, my own winter overcoat. The fur coat was very tight, and with two heavy coats, one on top of the other, I was not exactly comfortable. But I told myself, in twenty minutes' time, I would be in the ghetto and able to rid myself of my burden. Lindenbaum and Lefkowitz assured me that the fur coat didn't show at all.

I got out of the camp without any trouble. We had agreed that I should walk through the fields rather than use the highway that led directly into the ghetto. On the highway, I might be stopped by the Jewish ghetto police, and that would mean trouble, because I did not have the pass required to enter the ghetto. The two Jewish foremen at the labor camp who issued these passes were such unpleasant characters that I did not want to include them in this business.

The first hint of trouble came just after I had left the camp. I saw two Ukrainian policemen coming across the field, straight toward me. I made a sharp turn to the left and stepped onto the highway. Better, I thought, to be caught by the Jewish ghetto police than, heaven forbid, the Ukrainians. I was lucky; the Ukrainians paid no attention to me. The rest of my journey on the highway went smoothly. But when I reached the entrance of the Drohobycz ghetto, two Jews from the ghetto police force suddenly appeared and barred my way.

"Your pass! Show me your pass!" one of them barked.

"I left it at the camp," I replied. "When I come back here tomorrow, I'll bring the pass with me."

Unfortunately, the two men were not willing to listen to my excuses. My argument that Jews should have compassion and understanding for one another instead of placing obstacles in each other's way left them unmoved. The policemen seized me by the arms and took me to the headquarters of the Jewish ghetto police. I did not even attempt to wrench myself loose; I could not afford to let the fur coat show.

At headquarters, I was led to a desk where the deputy police chief was busily at work. The two policemen came to attention and reported in Polish that they had caught me *bez przepustki,* "without a pass."

When I saw the deputy police chief, I was relieved, for I knew him well. His name was Weinberger, and he had lived with my family for years in Schodnica, where he had been working for an oil refinery owned by another Jew named Birenbaum. Weinberger had always impressed me as a soft-spoken, refined young man. I was sure that once he looked up from his papers and recognized me, he would let me go at once.

Finally, Weinberger raised his head. I greeted him and even managed a smile. But he did not respond. Perhaps, I told myself, he did not want to let his two subordinates see that he knew me, but once they were gone, everything would be all right.

In the meantime, fatigue, excitement, and the weight of the two coats had brought me close to suffocation. At that point, I would gladly have thrown off the two coats and forgotten about the money, but of course this was impossible now.

Weinberger slowly took a new sheet of paper and began to write down a number and some words I was unable to distinguish. Then he turned to me.

"Your last name?" he asked.

Now, at last, I understood. Weinberger had no intention of showing that he had ever known me. Still, I tried one more time.

"Mr. Weinberger," I said, "you know my name. Don't you recognize me?"

Weinberger banged on the table. "Your last name!" he shouted. "Tell me your last name!"

I gave the proper reply.

"Now your first name!"

I told him that too.

He wanted to know why I had come to the ghetto without a pass. I told him that I had left my pass at the camp by mistake. He then asked what business I had in the ghetto. I made up some innocuous reason. Weinberger took careful notes of everything I said. When he was done, he filed away the paper and shouted, "Three days in jail!"

I did not say a word. I didn't even look at Weinberger anymore. The two policemen who had brought me in and stood there the whole time seized me by the arms and led me away again.

(Incidentally, Weinberger survived the war and the Nazis, but he was not so lucky when he met up with the Russians. They arrested him and gave him fifteen years in prison. But back to my story.)

As I was taken from the police building, I saw some friends of mine outside. They had seen me brought in by the two policemen and were waiting to learn what would happen to me. As I passed them, I was able to tell them that I was on my way to the ghetto prison. They rushed into the building. I do not know what happened inside; all I know is that I had hardly settled down in my prison cell, with its barred window and steel door, when a policeman came in and told me that I was free and could leave on the condition that I would never again try to enter the ghetto without a pass.

I was delighted with my escape. Little did I know what still lay in store for me.

After I left the prison, I hurried to the place where I was supposed to meet my cousin and her Polish friend; it was the house of a barber named Scheiber, where I had often stopped for a haircut in the days before the war.

Scheiber lived with his wife and his mother-in-law in a small apartment where he also had his barber shop. When I arrived there, I found the door unlocked, but no one was inside. First, I shed my two coats. It was a tremendous relief; at last, I was able to breathe again. A few minutes later, my cousin Recha Lefkowitz and her Polish friend tiptoed into the apartment. Recha told me that when I had not turned up at the appointed time, she had gotten worried. Afraid to stay in the apartment, she had gone out into the street again, kept an eye on the house from there, and returned as soon as she had seen me enter.

The fur coat business took less than five minutes. The Polish lady was apparently an expert on furs, for after only one glance at the coat—it was broadtail[1]—she accepted it and paid me twenty thousand złotys in five hundred złoty bills. In addition, she paid two thousand złotys to the barber for permitting us the use of his place. I was to take all the money, including Lefkowitz's share, back with me to the camp because Recha considered the camp safer than the ghetto.

I did not want to leave with the two women because I did not think it wise to be seen with them in the street. After they had gone, I lay down to

---

1. Broadtail fur is a prized luxury item harvested from a fetal or infant karakul lamb.

rest on a small sofa that probably served as the barber's bed at night. But I did not intend to stay long because I wanted to be back at the camp before dark.

Suddenly, I heard some excited voices outside. I sat up on the sofa and listened. The voices became louder, and I was able to make out Recha's voice. She was shouting something in German.

I quickly drew the twenty thousand złotys from my pocket and shoved the bills into a corner of the sofa. I did not want to be caught with the money.

The door was flung open, and my cousin and her friend came in, both with their hands up. Behind them was a German policeman with a machine gun.

"Stay where you are!" the policeman bellowed at me.

The worst that could possibly befall us had come to pass: the two women had been caught with the fur coat by the German police.

The policeman pointed his machine gun at me.

"To whom does this fur coat belong?" he demanded.

Recha, afraid that my story might be different from the one she had just told the policeman, in Polish shouted something to her friend.

The policeman did not wait for my answer. He ordered us to march ahead of him, out of the building. In the street, he hit me on the shoulder with his machine gun and gave me a rough shove.

My cousin was the first of us to regain her composure. From the insignia on the policeman's tunic and from the direction in which he was taking us, she understood that we had not been arrested by the dreaded Gestapo but by a regular German policeman. There was a big difference between the two. The regular police never shot anyone at night; they waited until the next morning. Sometimes, they did not do it themselves at all but turned their victims over to the Gestapo. At any rate, we still had at least a few hours to live. During the fifteen minutes or so that it took us to walk to the German police headquarters, Recha, the Polish woman, and I agreed on the story we would tell there. I was going to take the blame for the "crime." The fur coat belonged to a Polish man who lived somewhere in the suburbs—exactly where, we did not know. I had only acted as an intermediary to show the coat. It had not yet been sold; no money had changed hands. My cousin Recha had nothing to do with the entire transaction; she had met the Polish woman by pure chance. We hoped that the police would believe our story and let Recha and her friend go. Once the two women were free, they would manage to get me out also.

At police headquarters, we were taken to a desk, behind which sat a man who was obviously a high official. The Polish woman took off her raincoat and then the fur coat that had caused all the trouble. The police official examined the coat carefully and began to question us. We told him the story we had agreed on on the way to headquarters.

With his watery, colorless eyes, the officer reminded me of a fish. He made short work of us. Together with the policeman who had brought us in, he searched us for money and then dismissed the two women. After that, he pointed his finger at me.

"This bastard will be shot at six fifteen tomorrow morning," he said.

No one asked me my name, my occupation, or where I lived. I was ordered to sit down on the floor in the corner of the room and warned that if I made so much as one move or tried to look out the window, I should be shot at once.

Recha and her friend quickly ran out of the room.

I sat down on the floor as I was told; it was a spot where all the policemen in the room were able to see me.

I leaned my head against the wall and tried not to think. This was not the first time I had been in trouble with the Germans, and so I knew from past experience that the best course to follow was to let one's mind go blank. But thoughts have a habit of forcing themselves into one's head, and there is no driving them away. This time, I told myself, the angel of death had really caught me, and I had to admit that I had made it quite easy for him.

I noticed a large clock on the wall. It was only a few minutes before seven. Not quite an hour had passed since I had left the labor camp.

I tried to look out the nearest window, but I could not see much because it was covered with thick, strong bars. Outside, policemen on guard duty were marching back and forth. I could hear the heavy tramp, tramp, tramp of their boots.

The hours passed. Ten o'clock. Eleven. Midnight. German policemen and Ukrainian militiamen entered the room, said a few words to the official, and left again. From time to time, the telephone rang.

Shortly after one o'clock, the door opened and in came two Ukrainian militiamen, along with a man who wore a "Jewish armband" with the Star of David on his left arm. This man was dressed in dark, elegant clothes and had on a pair of shiny boots. He looked and acted like a very important man. My heart began to beat faster. This man was a Jew—could he have come to the police to help me?

He looked around the room, saw me in my corner, and walked over to me.

"What's your name?" he asked.

I told him.

"Are you the fellow who got in trouble on account of a fur coat?"

I nodded.

"Wait a minute," he said. He called over an officer who was sitting at a desk in the next room and held a brief conference with another policeman. Finally, I was called in. The man with the Star of David began to talk to me in broken German. He said that the entire story about the fur coat must be kept quiet. I readily agreed.

"And now—come along." He motioned to me, and we left the building, escorted by the two Ukrainian policemen who had come in with him. Later, I learned that the two Ukrainians had been in his pay.

Once in the street, I asked my rescuer who he was and why he had been interested in my release. He told me his name and seemed surprised that I had never heard of him before.

"You mean to say you've never heard of Fishke?" he kept asking me. "How come? Have you been living on the moon?"

Embarrassed, I muttered sheepishly that, come to think of it, I had heard his name mentioned, but in all the confusion and excitement of my arrest, I had momentarily forgotten about it. It turned out that my cousin Recha Lefkowitz was a good friend of his wife's. Immediately after her own release, Recha had hurried to Fishke's house and begged him to save me. He said he would have come sooner but had had to wait for the two Ukrainian policemen who served as his escorts, because it was dangerous for a Jew to be seen out in the street after curfew—"Even for me," said Fishke.

"Did you see the respect they gave me at police headquarters?" he asked with a touch of pride in his voice. "I want you to tell your cousin about it. She'll tell my wife. But you mustn't think that I got all this free of charge. I wish that you and I together could earn all the money this little episode cost me."

I assured him that I did not want favors free of charge and that I would pay him handsomely for his troubles the next day. Fishke did not respond.

When we got to the ghetto, I told him that it would be best for me to spend the rest of the night in a doorway and to move on in the morning. But Fishke would not hear of it; he insisted that I come home with him.

Fishke lived in a house at the other end of the ghetto. At his door, he said good-bye to our escorts and slipped something into their hands as they departed.

The one room he and his wife occupied served as a combination bedroom and kitchen. It was clean and neat. When Fishke turned on the light, his wife awoke, leapt from the couch, and gave me a hearty welcome. He sat down at the table and told his wife how hard it had been to get me out and what clever tricks he had used to obtain my release. Then he and his wife invited me to sit down with them.

"And now, Tillenka," he said to his wife in Polish, rubbing his hands like someone who had good cause to be proud of himself, "make us some scrambled eggs with six eggs and lots of butter."

His wife, a quiet, attractive young woman, threw a robe over her shoulders and turned on the oven. She began to crack some eggs, and soon the room was filled with the pleasant aroma of eggs frying in fresh butter.

When she served the scrambled eggs, she turned to me and said in Polish, "With six eggs—see?"

I had never known that people could use so many eggs for one dish. Eggs were expensive and practically unobtainable for Jews. To tell the truth, I did not feel like eating scrambled eggs just then, but my protests did not help. I had to join them in their festive meal.

When we had finished eating, I recited the "Grace after Meals."[2] I thanked God for having saved my life once again. I did not know how much longer my luck would hold out, but for the present, I was still in one piece, and for this I was grateful. After every few words of prayer I recited, Fishke covered his bare head with his hand—he probably did not own a yarmulke—and bellowed, "Amen!" His wife, who had gone back to bed in the meantime, also joined in lustily, "Amen! Amen!"

Later, Fishke went to sleep, and I also went to bed on a cot that his wife had prepared for me.

At the crack of dawn, I got up quietly, stole out of the room, and went to Scheiber's place, where I had left the twenty thousand złotys. I found the money inside the couch, where I had hidden it, and took it to my cousin Recha. We divided the money. Half of it was to go in equal shares to her husband, Lindenbaum, and Scheiber; the other half was mine. I took my ten thousand złotys and hurried back to Fishke's house.

I found Fishke and his wife awake in bed; they had been unable to sleep. I went over to Fishke's bed and held out the ten thousand złotys to him.

"This is for you, Fishke, because you saved my life," I said. Only then did I tell him how I earned the money and how I had managed to hide it just before my arrest.

Fishke took the money in his hands. He looked at it, then at me, and then again at the wad of bank notes.

"No! No!" he shouted, and it seemed to me that he was shouting down his own impulse to accept the offered gift. "No! I don't want to take

---

2. *Birkat Hamazon*, known in English as "Grace after Meals," is a blessing recited after any meal with bread, as eating bread officially counts as a meal in Jewish law.

anything from you! If you were willing to risk your life to get this money and went through so much trouble for it, you must need it much more than I do. Thank you very much, but no, I can't take this from you."

His wife, who had been listening quietly, gave her husband an admiring look. "Fishke, I'm proud of you," she said.

I thanked my two new friends for everything they had done for me and bade them farewell. Then I left them and went back to the labor camp.

Now two years later, in front of Kraków's Jewish Committee building, I saw Fishke again. Judging from the way he looked, he had probably come to get a meal from the public soup kitchen the committee had set up.

He stared at me in surprise.

"Ah, so you've become a big shot. A captain in the Polish army, no less! You've got it made! Who would have imagined it back there at the police station, when I came just in time to save your head? I didn't take a penny from you then, not a penny. Remember? Or would you rather not be reminded, eh?"

"Of course, I remember, Fishke," I replied. "If I had not wanted to be reminded, do you think I'd have taken the trouble to run after you here? Why, I even remember what your wife said when you refused the money. I want to make it up to you."

When I mentioned his wife, Fishke gave a deep sigh. They had been hiding in the forest with a whole group of other Jews, he told me. One day, about two months before the liberation, he had gone off to find some food. While he was away, a band of Ukrainian Fascists had discovered the hideout and murdered all the Jews there, including Fishke's wife.

I bought Fishke a suit and a pair of fine boots. When he put on the new clothes, he seemed to come to life again. Then I took him to a restaurant. When the waiter came to take my order, I pointed grandly to where Fishke was sitting and said, "Please make this gentleman a dish of scrambled eggs—with six eggs and lots of butter."

# CHAPTER 6

# A RABBI AT WORK

Rzeszów, September 1944.

When I first arrived in Rzeszów from Drohobycz, there were only four hundred Jews in the town, but they had already organized a religious community. They wanted me to become their rabbi.

"What do you need a rabbi for?" I asked them. "Isn't there anything else you need before you hire a rabbi—like money for a good meal or decent clothes in place of your rags?"

But the Jews of Rzeszów would not listen to my arguments. Without a rabbi, they said, they would not have a religious community. Once they had a rabbi, everything else would fit into place before long. There would be kosher meat because a rabbi would not allow the town to remain without a *shochet*[1] to slaughter animals in accordance with Jewish law. Even more important, they needed a rabbi to perform marriages. During all the dark years in the ghettos, concentration camps, and underground hideouts, Jewish boys and girls had lived together without a religious ceremony. Now that the war was over and they were free, these couples wanted to be married properly as soon as possible. Finally, as the Jews would begin to do business with one another, there were bound to be disputes, and Jews did not sue each other in Gentile courts of law; they wanted a rabbi whom they could respect and whom they could rely on as a fair arbiter to settle disputes in conformity with Jewish tradition.

---

1. A *shochet* is a kosher slaughterer.

These arguments were compelling, but after all that I had gone through, I wondered whether I was physically and emotionally capable of assuming the responsibilities of a full-time rabbi. Besides, the Rzeszów community would hardly be able to pay me a living wage. And so, I told the Jews of Rzeszów that I would be glad to help them whenever and wherever I could but that I did not want to commit myself to them officially. Yet in the end, I agreed to become their rabbi because I saw how anxious these people were to build up a traditional Jewish community.

One of the first tasks I set for myself in my position as rabbi of Rzeszów was to find sustenance for my flock. As soon as it became known that the town had a rabbi, I was besieged by Jews from the entire area. To my dismay, I found that their plight was even worse than I had been led to believe. Some of the people who came to me had had nothing to eat in days and were literally dying for a piece of bread. A committee of women was organized to raise money for those who had none. We contacted Jews who had already begun to make some money and asked them to give a part of their earnings to those who were destitute. Thanks to the devoted efforts of the women on the committee, headed by Mrs. Nathanson, we were able to accomplish a great deal. My work gave me much satisfaction; I felt that by becoming their rabbi, I had been able to bring the remnants of the Rzeszów Jewish community back to life.

On Yom Kippur Eve 1944, the Jewish community in Rzeszów celebrated the first High Holiday services since the liberation. How well I remember the services and especially the two Russian girl soldiers who came to them. The services were held in the old synagogue, which had been used before the war. The room was packed with solemn-faced men and weeping women. In front of the congregation, close to the eastern wall, the man who had volunteered to act as our cantor began chanting the Kol Nidre service.[2] He was wrapped in the only prayer shawl that could be found in town and was reading from the only Holiday Prayer Book we had managed to find after much searching.

2. See part I, chapter 7, note 6.

Suddenly, the door opened, and two young Soviet girl soldiers in uniform, rifles slung casually over their shoulders, entered the room. Despite their guns and uniforms, they looked more like children than fighters. They remained standing in the doorway as if afraid to come in. Alerted by furtive looks and whispers, I went to the back of the room and asked the two girls if they were Jewish.

"I am Jewish," one of them said. Then pointing at her companion, she continued, "And her father is Jewish too." They had known, she explained, that this was a Jewish holiday. By chance, they happened to pass by and saw us at prayer. Could they join us for a little while? I invited them in, and they moved to the part of the room where the women stood, apart from the men.

We had no prayer books for them, not even chairs or benches where they might sit down, yet the two girls not only remained with us the entire evening but also returned the next morning and stayed the whole day, their eyes fixed on our cantor until the very end of the concluding service. They did not speak a word, not even to each other, until they saw that the prayers had ended and everyone was exchanging wishes for a happy New Year. Then at last, they came up to me and said in Russian, "A happy New Year to you and to Jews everywhere."[3] Several women invited them to their homes to break the fast, but the girls did not accept any of the invitations, explaining that they were due back at their barracks. They excused themselves, thanked everyone, and vanished from sight.

The next day, a third Russian girl, also a soldier, appeared at my apartment. She told me that she had been aware there was a Jewish holiday but had not known about our services. Had she known, she said, she would have come to our place of worship along with the other two soldiers. But she had missed the chance. What was she to do now? Yom Kippur 1945 was still a long way off, and she did not want to wait that long. So she asked me for a favor. Her entire family had been killed during the Nazi occupation

3. The Jewish New Year (Rosh Hashanah) had just happened on September 18, 1944. The Day of Atonement (Yom Kippur) was on September 27, 1944.

of Zhytomyr, her hometown in Ukraine, and she did not know where they were buried. Could I get permission for her to visit our Jewish cemetery here in Rzeszów? She thought that, perhaps, amid the graves of her fellow Jews, she might not feel that her parents, and her brothers and sisters, were so far away.

She burst into bitter sobs.

When she had recovered her composure, she opened her army kit and took out half a loaf of bread. She wanted to leave it with me for the poor Jews. At first, I refused to take it because I knew that the Russian soldiers lived on meager rations, but she insisted.

"Look, I won't be needing it for myself," she explained. "I'll be fasting all day tomorrow anyway because I'll go to the cemetery."[4]

I accepted the bread.

That first Yom Kippur at the Rzeszów synagogue, I rose, as I still do each year to this day in my synagogue on Yom Kippur, and recited the mourner's kaddish[5] in memory of a man whom I saw only twice in my life. I do not know much about him; I never even learned his name, but I came to consider the story that he told me, and the request he made of me only hours before his death, as a last will and testament that he desperately wanted me to carry out.

I met him in the fall of 1942 at the Janover labor camp, where more than three hundred thousand Jews would perish before the war was over.[6] When I was there, the camp had twelve thousand inmates, whereas the accommodations had been designed for barely five thousand. The barracks were so jammed with humanity that there was no room to sit, much less to stretch

4. Jews traditionally visit the graves of loved ones around the time of the High Holidays (Rosh Hashanah and Yom Kippur).
5. See part I, chapter 8, note 1.
6. Thorne's claim of 300,000 killed reiterates statistics generated by the Extraordinary State Commission, the Soviet agency tasked with documenting Nazi crimes. The commission often exaggerated numbers for propaganda purposes. Current scholarship estimates between 100,000 and 120,000 deaths at Janowska. See Evelyn Zegenhagen, "Lemberg (aka Lemberg [West-Strasse]), Lemberg (Janowska)," in *The United States Holocaust Memorial Museum Encyclopedia of Camps and Ghettos* (Bloomington: Indiana University Press, 2009), 1:884–885.

out on the floor. As a result, many of the inmates, including myself, preferred to spend the nights outdoors, even when the weather was cold, as it was on that damp and chilly night, three days after Rosh Hashanah. I felt one of my fellow inmates huddle close to me in the dark for whatever heat my emaciated body had to offer. Each person has his own way of reacting when he feels he has reached the end of the road. I wanted nothing more than to be left alone, to sit without moving and to let my mind go blank. But the man beside me appeared to be driven by a compulsion to talk, regardless of whether or not anyone else would listen. Speaking in flawless German with the merest trace of a Czech accent, he told me his story.

Before the war, he had lived in Brünn, a large city in Czechoslovakia, where he had owned a bank and much real estate. Along with countless other Jews, he had been deported by the Nazis to Poland. It had all seemed very strange to him, for until that time, he had not been much of a Jew at all. In fact, he had despised his Judaism and had been convinced that the sooner the Jews forgot their Jewishness, the better it would be for everyone. Accordingly, he had had his two daughters baptized in the Catholic faith when they were born. For some reason that he never explained to me, he and his wife had not formally converted, but they had accompanied their children to church every Sunday and stayed with them throughout the service.

I must say that, at first, I scarcely listened to the man's recital. I did not even turn my head in his direction. What was the sense of this confession? What was there to talk about? By this time, I told myself, not only his wife but even his children, little Jews whom all the baptismal water in the world could never have turned into Aryans, had probably been killed. Before long, he too would be dead. And how much time did I have left myself? Surely, there was never a time when talking made less sense than on that cold autumn night, when everything seemed about to come to an end.

But then, as if he had been able to read my thoughts, the former banker from Brünn began to explain why he felt the need to tell me—to tell someone—the story of his life. He was aware of the fate that lay in store for him. Now before he was killed by the Nazi murderers, he wanted to atone for the sins he felt he had committed against his religion and his people. How could he do that in this place and at this time? Why, it was all very simple. He would draw up a last will and testament. He had graduated from law school, he told me, so he should certainly know how to do that properly.

Since he had no one left in the world, his will would leave his entire estate to the Jewish community in Palestine. True, the Nazis had taken his property, but he was convinced that eventually they would lose the war, and the money that could be realized from his houses and chateaus in Czechoslovakia would come in very handy when the war survivors rebuilt the homeland of the Jewish people in Palestine. In this way, he would atone for his past indifference to the fate of his people and for his former violent opposition to Zionism. Then too, his will would include a clause to the effect that, on one day each year, someone should stand up in the synagogue and recite the mourner's kaddish for him and for his wife and his two children. The fact that his children had been baptized at birth made no difference, he said. In his will, he would declare them posthumous converts to the Jewish faith. Surely such an act would be in accordance with Jewish law; after all, despite their baptism, his two daughters had been murdered because they had been Jews.

He fell silent for a few minutes. It seemed to me that he was weeping quietly. Then he began to speak again, with increased intensity. In order to make his will, he said, he needed only two things: first, a piece of paper on which to write it, and second, a person to whom he could entrust the document. He already had a pencil, he told me, holding up a stub so tiny that I could hardly see it between his thumb and index finger.

He proposed to name the World Zionist Organization as his executor.[7] They would surely know how to dispose of his assets in the best interests of the Jewish people.

"But to whom can you give your will to keep until the war is over and it can be sent to them?" I asked. "How do you know that any Jew in this place will still be alive then?"

---

7. Theodor Herzl established the World Zionist Organization in 1897 during the First Zionist Congress to pursue the goal of establishing a Jewish state in Palestine.

"I will give it to you for safekeeping," the banker replied without another moment's thought. "If and when the time comes that you are about to die, you will turn it over to someone else whom you consider honest and reliable, with instructions that when he feels that his time has come, he too will turn it over to someone who is likely to outlive him. Look, I know that I can't last much longer. Even if they don't kill me, I will die in a few days. I am at the end of my strength. Now if I could find some paper, write out my will, and hand it over to you, I would be able to die in peace."

I turned toward him and, for the first time, saw his face by the light of a weak bulb outside the barracks. He looked not much older than forty, but his long, thin face was a mask of agony. Despite his filthy prisoner's rags, his matted hair, and the stubble that grew thick on his hollow cheeks, one could see that this man had come from better stock.

I promised to do as he wished. He asked me my name. I told him and at the same time assured him that he was not necessarily at the end of his endurance, that within ourselves we have secret reservoirs of strength that we are not even aware of until we need to draw on them. Nevertheless, I said I would do my best to find a scrap of paper for his last will and testament when I went out on my labor detail the next morning.

When we parted before dawn to return for roll call, we agreed to meet again at that same place. I would surely have the paper for him.

As fate willed it, we were not able to keep our rendezvous. Several days later, early in the morning, our battalion passed through the gate of the camp on the way to an "outside" work assignment. Suddenly, I heard a voice calling my name. I turned around; it came from somewhere behind the fence near the gate, the place where they kept the inmates who were to be shot that morning, after the others had gone out on their labor details. There I saw him again, the banker from Brünn. Our eyes met, and he gestured with his hand as if he wanted to write.

"Remember?" he shouted to me through the fence. "Paper! Paper for the will!" The guard beside me shoved me forward. As I moved away, I could still hear the banker behind me, crying mournfully, "Kaddish! Kaddish! Remember, Thorne! Say kaddish for my children!"

CHAPTER 7

# NO. 6 TANNENBAUM STREET[1]

I must add that my new position as rabbi also brought me at least one tangible reward: an apartment of my own—no small thing in those days, when most Jews in Poland did not even have a place to sleep. The homes and apartments where the Jews lived before the war had been taken by Poles who not only refused to move out but threatened to shoot any Jew who dared claim his old apartment. Eventually, our committee managed to obtain two buildings to shelter the homeless, but there was not enough space to allow any one person to have a room to himself. I was more fortunate. At first, the community got me two rooms. Later, I was given a four-room apartment at No. 6 Tannenbaum Street, opposite the building that had housed the town's Yiddish theater before the war.

My apartment became the center for the Jews not only of our town but of the surrounding smaller Jewish communities as well. It also served as a transit shelter for the Bricha refugees.[2] Bricha—the Hebrew word means,

---

1. In this chapter, Thorne offers an account of the June 12, 1945, pogrom in Rzeszów that began with the false accusation that the Jews murdered Bronisława Mendoń, a nine-year-old Polish girl. For more extensive scholarly histories of this episode, see Jan T. Gross, *Fear: Anti-Semitism in Poland after Auschwitz: An Essay in Historical Interpretation* (New York: Random House, 2006), 73–80; see also Marcin Zaremba, "The Myth of Ritual Murder in Post-War Poland: Pathology and Hypotheses," *Jews in Kraków*, Polin: Studies in Polish Jewry 23 (Oxford, U.K.: Littman Library of Jewish Civilization, 2011), 465–506.

2. Between 1945 and 1946, the clandestine network known as Bricha helped approximately 110, 000 Jews leave Poland. For more on the history of this movement, see Avinoam J. Patt, *Finding Home and Homeland: Jewish Youth and Zionism in the Aftermath of the Holocaust* (Detroit: Wayne State University Press, 2009), 68–83.

literally, "flight"—was the underground network of dedicated young Zionist leaders who, aided by Jews sent from Palestine for that purpose, guided survivors of the Holocaust across Europe to seaports where they could set sail for a new life in the Jewish homeland. Both the refugees and their Bricha escorts constantly imperiled their lives because the British authorities sealed Palestine's borders to Jewish refugees and also pressured European governments not to permit Palestine-bound Jews to cross their frontiers. Nevertheless, Jews by the tens of thousands, escorted by Bricha guides, streamed out of Poland into the world beyond the fast-descending Iron Curtain.[3] In the displaced persons' camps of Austria and West Germany, Bricha had set up clandestine reception centers to accommodate the refugees until they could safely begin the next lap of their journey at the Mediterranean seaports. To the survivors of the death camps, Poland could never be more than a giant graveyard where everything reminded them of their lost loved ones and where Gentile former neighbors bluntly asked them how it was that Hitler had not finished them off. As a consequence, my apartment in Rzeszów was never without a group of Bricha refugees. They would spend the night there before they continued on their westward trek the next day. In one of these Bricha transports was the young lady who is now my wife.

Rachel Rosenthal, daughter of David and Gennia Rosenthal, had been born and raised in Lithuania, in the great Jewish community of Kovno. She had completed her high school studies at the Jewish gymnasium[4] there and had intended to go on to university. But she was unable to carry out her plans, for in the summer following her graduation, Germany attacked Russia and overran Lithuania. Late in 1943, Rachel's mother, grandmother, and two younger teenage sisters were murdered by the Nazis. Her father had died earlier, during the Russian occupation. Through an accident of fate, Rachel survived. Thanks to Dr. Kissin, a Jewish pediatrician, and

---

3. On March 5, 1946, British prime minister Winston Churchill used the term *Iron Curtain* to describe the Soviet domination of Eastern Europe.

4. In its European usage, a *gymnasium* refers to a high school designed to prepare students for study at a university, as opposed to a vocational high school.

Father Paukštys,[5] a kindly Lithuanian priest, she was taken into the home of a peasant family in a village not far from Kovno. Only the peasant and his wife knew that Rachel was Jewish; the children, the farmhands, and the neighbors thought her an ordinary Lithuanian girl who had been hired to tend the cows and the pigs.

Rachel remained with this family for eight months. All that time, she lived in constant fear that someone in the village might discover her secret and turn her over to the Germans. Thus on Christmas Eve 1943, she went to Midnight Mass with her employers. As she sat through the long service in the crowded church, she envied her parents and sisters for having passed beyond the pain and anguish that filled her own heart. Then her eyes fell on the crucifix above the altar, and she felt an odd sense of relief.

"I'm not entirely alone among strangers," she told herself. "There is one other Jew suffering beside me here in this church!"

She was comforted and did not take her eyes from the figure of Rabbi Joshua ben Joseph of Nazareth[6] until the services were over.

In August 1944, Rachel was liberated by the advancing Russian armies. Returning to Kovno, she found other Jewish girls who, like herself, had lost their families and were eager to start life anew. Together, the girls made their way to Poland and contacted the Bricha organization. That is how Rachel and her friends came to my home in Rzeszów.

It took Rachel and me only a few days to decide to spend the rest of our lives together. We both wanted to put an end to our loneliness and build a new family. Eventually, we were to have four children—two sons and two daughters: Emanuel David, Irving Daniel, Risa Gail, and Ziva Pearl.

Following our marriage, Rachel and I set up housekeeping together at No. 6 Tannenbaum Street. We had to share our home with one permanent roomer—Reb Yudel, a *shochet* who hailed from Tarnów and was among a group of thirty Jews who had made their way through the battle lines into

---

5. The Jesuit priest Father Bronislovas Paukštys (1897–1966) and his brother, Juozas Paukštys, were honored with the title of Righteous Among the Nations in 1977 for their efforts save Jews in Kovno, including the referenced pediatrician Dr. Pesya Kissin.
6. That is, Jesus Christ.

the "liberated" sector of Poland. Since he had been unable to find a place to live, I had invited him to share my apartment. He established himself in the kitchen, which was the least-used room because we did not have gas or wood to fuel the oven. At any rate, Reb Yudel had set up a cot for himself in the kitchen, where he was able to say his prayers, chant his psalms, and pour out his bitter heart before God in complete privacy.

As soon as the word spread that a *shochet* had come to town, a never-ending stream of visitors bearing chickens they wanted killed in accordance with the kosher laws converged on my home. Reb Yudel told me rather diffidently that he had a problem: he did not know where to set up shop. To go to the local slaughterhouse, he said, would be to take his life into his hands—the Gentile butchers would probably kill him. He had thought of using the courtyard of our apartment building, but the janitor had threatened to call the police if Reb Yudel killed chickens there. What was he to do? Should he turn away all the housewives who, after so many years, wanted to have kosher meat again?

Of course, I agreed that he could not fail our good Jewish housewives. Reb Yudel then confessed that he had already begun to work in his room—my kitchen. So as not to ruin my floor, he drained the bird's blood into a tin bucket. At the end of each day, before going to sleep, he emptied the contents of the bucket outdoors and scrubbed it until it was spotless, ready for the next day's batch of chickens.

I told Reb Yudel that he could keep using my kitchen until he was able to find a place better suited for his work. Little did I know then that Reb Yudel's presence in my home would soon bring disaster on the entire Jewish community of Rzeszów. Who could have imagined that the Gentiles of the town would use the presence of a "chicken killer" in my house as a pretext to revive the hoary, barbaric ritual murder accusation and take action to "punish the Jewish murderers of innocent Christian children"?

To someone unfamiliar with the history of Polish antisemitism, it seems strange that a country so recently liberated from Nazi rule should continue to follow in Hitler's footsteps. But pogroms had not been a rarity in modern Poland even before the advent of the Third Reich. Two decades earlier, when Poland reemerged as an independent state after World War I, the mobs perpetrated bloody outrages against Jews. Jews were thrown from moving trains, and the aged rabbi from Płock was shot on a fabricated charge of espionage.[7] What happened in Rzeszów on June 12, 1945, should have come as no surprise to us.

My wife and I were out of town at the time. About six hours before, we had left for Lublin and Warsaw on community business. Only days later did I learn what had happened. At one o'clock that morning, a band of armed policemen broke into our home. The police herded together the Bricha refugees along with some other homeless Jews who had been staying with us temporarily and ordered them to get dressed. While our lodgers were in the kitchen scrambling into their clothes, the policemen searched the house, turning everything upside down. Then they marched all the people in the apartment into the cellar and, there, by the dim light of an electric light, led them to a box in which a dead child lay. The child, a little girl of about six or seven, was covered with bruises; she had obviously been cruelly beaten before she died. She had also been virtually scalped; the bare bone of her skull could be seen in spots. The police ordered the terror-stricken Jews to confess that they had killed the little Christian girl and then hidden the body in the dark cellar.

The Jews understood at once that the dead child had been placed in our cellar by some local Poles who wanted to blame the murder on the Jews and to use the occasion as an excuse for a pogrom. The policemen did not even wait for the Jews to "confess"; they chased them up the steps and out into the street and marched them off to the police station. At first, the Jews refused to move, but a few minutes later, a second group

7. Between February 1919 and March 1921, Poland was at war with the Soviet Union, and on August 18, 1920, during the Soviet invasion, the Hasidic rabbi Chaim Shapiro was seen swaying back and forth on his house's balcony in the central Polish town of Płock. Although such swaying is common in Hasidic prayer (see part I, chapter 10, note 7), Shapiro was accused of provoking Soviet gunfire through his movements and of remaining on the balcony during the gunfire. A Polish military court convicted Shapiro on trumped-up charges of espionage and executed him by firing squad. For more on the case, see "Seek to Clear Name of Polish Rabbi Shot by Military Tribunal," *Jewish Daily Bulletin*, December 10, 1933.

of policemen arrived on the scene, armed with knouts.[8] My lodgers had no choice but to obey orders. They were sure that once they got to police headquarters, the whole misunderstanding would be cleared up. Unfortunately, they were never given a chance to protest their innocence. As soon as they arrived at the police station, they were locked up in a room with barred windows.

During the hours that followed, hundreds of policemen scoured the town, rounding up Jews. By the time they reached the police station, some of the new victims had been beaten beyond recognition. Other policemen were busy at the railroad station, dragging Jewish passengers from incoming trains and placing them under arrest.

By midmorning, everyone in town knew that the police had raided the rabbi's house and found the body of a little Christian girl who had suffered unspeakable tortures before she died. The streets of the town were soon alive with hordes of Poles, some armed with clubs and hatchets, screaming curses at the "Jewish child killers" and ready to murder any Jew who crossed their path.

Then about noontime, an unexpected visitor arrived at the police station. He was a Russian army officer and seemed to be especially interested in the Jewish prisoners at the jail. He briskly walked past the cells, going from one floor to the next. Some of the Jews recognized him, for they had seen his picture in the newspapers. He was Itzik Feffer, the well-known Russian-Yiddish poet.[9]

"Friend Feffer! Friend Feffer!" the Jews shouted in Yiddish from the cells. "Look what they've done to us! The damned Poles want to kill us all."

8. A knout is a whiplike weapon that was used extensively in the czarist Russian penal system.
9. During World War II, the prolific Yiddish poet Itzik Feffer (1900–1952) was a Red Army colonel, a military reporter, the vice chairman of the Jewish Anti-Fascist Committee, and an informant for the Soviet secret police (NKVD). Later, he was one of at least thirteen Jewish cultural figures whom Joseph Stalin had executed during the August 12, 1952, purge known as the "Night of the Murdered Poets."

Feffer shouted back, first in Yiddish and then in Russian, "Moscow is going to hear about this! Comrade Stalin will be told! I'll telephone Stalin this minute!"

Feffer, then in his middle forties, had attained a high officer rank in the Red Army. Who would have thought that only a few years later, he would be arrested in Stalin's anti-Jewish purges and murdered by those same Russians?

Itzik Feffer did not wait until he could send a report to Moscow. He rushed out of the police station, rounded up all the other Jewish officers in the local Russian occupation forces, and brought them back with him to police headquarters. While the Polish police officials stood by in stunned disbelief, the Russian Jewish officers stormed the jail and freed the Jews.

One look at the scene in the street told the Russians that it would not be safe for the Jews to remain in Rzeszów. A hysterical Polish mob was waiting to hurl itself on the released prisoners. But even if the mob could be dispersed, what guarantee was there that the Polish police, apt pupils of Hitler's Gestapo, would not arrest the Jews again the next day? Knowing that the Jews were in dire peril, the Russian officers did not permit them to return to their homes but escorted them directly to the railroad station. They ordered the stationmaster to prepare a special train to take the Jews to Kraków, some one hundred miles to the west. The train was ready in short order, and the Jews, grateful to escape with their lives, climbed aboard. As the train pulled out of the station, they shouted their farewells to the Russians on the platform: "Jews! Brothers! Dear Jews from Russia! *L'Shana Haba'ah B'Yerushalayim*."[10]

Until then the Russian officers had been grinning broadly. But now the smiles left their faces, and some of the Jews, looking out of the train windows, believed they saw tears in the eyes of their rescuers.

I did not hear what happened in Rzeszów until three days later. I had left my wife in Lublin with some friends and set out alone for Warsaw. I

---

10. *L'Shana Haba'ah B'Yerushalayim* ("Next year in Jerusalem") is the phrase sung at the end of a Passover seder.

made the journey to Warsaw in a crowded freight train. The passengers sat on their bags, on their suitcases, or on the hard floor. Because it was night and there were no lights in the car, we sat in total darkness. Traveling by train was an ordeal in those days. Our train, with its two puffing engines—one in front pulling the cars, the other pushing from behind—came to a screeching halt at every whistle stop, jostling passengers against each other. Our trip took three or four times as many hours as it would have under normal conditions. To pass the time, the travelers began to exchange news.

Suddenly, out of the darkness, came a strident voice of a man, warning all those who might have to go to Rzeszów not to take any children with them. The Jews in that town, he declared with an air of authority, had set up an organization for the purpose of killing Christian children. Everyone else in the car stopped talking to hear what this man had to tell. He said that only a couple of days before, the police had raided the home of the rabbi of Rzeszów and had found the bodies of no less than fourteen Christian children, all brutally massacred in his cellar. Their throats had been slashed, their eyes gouged out, and their fingers and toes chopped off.

At first, I barely listened to the man's story, even though it had to do with Rzeszów. I had already heard so many antisemitic atrocity tales that I had become inured to them. But his next words made me pay attention. "It so happens," he was saying, "that this Jew rabbi in Rzeszów, in whose basement the police found these fourteen murdered children, is a chaplain in the Polish army. This makes him an army officer, and so he has a gun. When the police came to arrest him in the middle of the night, he shot at them. Naturally, the policemen shot back, and in the ruckus that followed, the rabbi jumped out of the window into the pitch darkness, and that was the last that the police saw of him."

"The rabbi . . . a chaplain in the Polish army . . . an army officer . . ." My heart began to beat wildly, and I broke into a cold sweat. Now I understood that this story was about me and my community. Clearly, something terrible had happened in Rzeszów. The passengers were already in an uproar, cursing the Jewish "child killers." It seemed that almost everybody in the car had his or her own tale of horrors to tell about the Jews.

I wanted to see who had told the story. In a voice so choked with dread that I could hardly recognize it as my own, I asked the passenger nearest me for a flashlight. One woman lit a candle. I glanced in the direction from which the man's voice had come. By the dim candlelight, I was able to discern the figure of a stout, elderly man who sat on a piece of luggage, clad in a cassock—a Catholic priest.

I asked the priest whether he was the one who had been talking about the murders in Rzeszów.

"Yes, I was the one," he calmly replied.

"And from whom did you hear the story?" I asked him.

"Why, everybody knows about it," said the priest in pious tones. "By this time, probably everyone in Poland must know the story. The funeral was held right after the autopsies. The coffins of the little ones were carried to the cemetery by the schoolchildren of the town."

"Were you at the funeral yourself?" I asked him.

"No, I wasn't there myself," the priest answered, "but I have talked to people who were."

I was still trying to tell myself that the story of the fourteen children had merely been a rumor the priest had heard somewhere. I was eager to get to Warsaw; there, I was sure, the Jewish Committee would be able to tell me exactly what had happened in Rzeszów during the short time my wife and I had been away.

Two of the passengers near me began to discuss the priest's story. From what they said, it was obvious that they were Jews. I called them closer and began to talk with them in Yiddish. I told them that I was the rabbi of Rzeszów who, according to the priest, had eluded arrest by opening fire on the police and escaped through the window—but the priest had lied. I had not even been in town at the time of the supposed police raid. My new friends tried to allay my fears. Since the priest's account of my "escape" had been made up out of whole cloth, they said, his report of the police raid might well be false.

For a moment, I felt tempted to get up and tell all the passengers who I was, but then I decided this would serve no useful purpose. If all the people in the freight car could believe that the Jews were child murderers, then no argument on earth, no matter how logical, would convince them otherwise. If I revealed my identity, I would only bring trouble on myself and the other Jews on the train.

At noon the next day—it was Friday—our train finally pulled into the station at Warsaw. I took a taxi to the headquarters of the Jewish Committee, the official community center for the Jews of the entire country. The committee had already been informed of what had happened in Rzeszów. They did not yet have all the details. But the officials were able to assure me that, thanks to Itzik Feffer and his fellow officers, all the Jews had escaped with their lives. The committee described the "evidence" the police had found in my home. There had been one child, not fourteen. Also, there had been balls of human hair in the oven and traces of blood in a bucket in our kitchen. Evidence, indeed! The hair? Probably from the Bricha refugee girls, who had been temporarily staying with us; they invariably used our oven as a receptacle for the hair they cleaned from their brushes and combs. The blood? In all likelihood, blood from the chickens killed in our kitchen by Reb Yudel, the *shochet*. However, just then the police were not interested in facts that did not serve their purposes.

The Jewish Committee, of course, had immediately suspected the truth. Their only concern was how the dead child was smuggled into the cellar while no one in the house heard or saw anything unusual. I could not offer any explanation. In all the months I had lived there, I had never once had occasion to go to the cellar; as far as I knew, the cellar could only be reached by way of the apartment of the janitor, a Pole.

As soon as the Sabbath was over, I took the first train out of Warsaw to Rzeszów. I arrived in Rzeszów at about ten o'clock the next evening and went straight to our house on Tannenbaum Street. The door had already been locked for the night. I rang the bell. A few minutes later, the janitor appeared, holding a lighted candle in his hand.

"Something awful happened while you and the lady were out of town," he told us excitedly. "The police found a dead child in our cellar, and all the Jews ran away. There isn't one Jew left in the city."

"How did the child get into our cellar?" I asked him.

It seemed that neither the janitor nor his wife knew.

"How could you not know?" I demanded. "You are here all day long, either in your apartment or in front of the house. And you know very well that the only way to the cellar is through your apartment."

Again, the janitor had nothing to say.

"But you did see that the child was murdered in my apartment. Right?" I persisted.

He had seen no such thing, he protested.

"Is that what you told the police and the magistrate when they questioned you?"

"No one ever questioned me about anything," the janitor replied.

"Well, then, how did the police get the idea to look for the dead child in our cellar of all places?"

The janitor could not answer the question either. But his averted eyes and the ugly sneer on his face told me everything I wanted to know. There was nothing to be gained from questioning him any further. The damage had been done.

He told me the police had sent a truck to take away everything the Jews had left behind. Among the articles the police had removed were sixteen Scrolls of the Law, which we had bought back from peasants who had stolen them during the war. The janitor had no idea where the police might have taken them. All he knew was that my apartment had been taken over by the Polish army.

I climbed the steps to my apartment. The janitor followed with his candles close behind. Two soldiers stood in front of the door, barring my way. They were sorry, they said, but they had orders not to let me in. However, they assured me that they had found nothing of mine in the apartment; it had been cleaned out completely by the time they had arrived.

CHAPTER 8

───≺

# THE ŻYDOWICA'S STORY

I went out of the house into the street. People had gathered there in little knots; apparently word had spread that the rabbi had come back. The talk was all about the child who had been murdered in the building. I asked one woman whether any Jews remained in town.

"No," she answered. "They're all gone. Cleared out last Tuesday, the whole lot of them. All on the same train too."

I was ready to return to the station and take the next train to Kraków, where the Jews had been sent by their Russian rescuers. But just then, a husky man stepped out of the crowd. He knew one Jewish woman, he said, who had stayed behind. If I wanted to see her, he would take me to her house. It wasn't far away. I agreed, and we set out, the young Pole leading the way through a maze of dark alleys. Finally, he stopped in front of a dilapidated old house and pointed to the gateway.

"There," he said, "that's where the *żydowica* lives."[1]

I passed through the gateway into a dark, narrow corridor. By the dim light of the street lamp, I was able to see that there were two doors, one on the right, the other on the left. From the left, I could hear loud shouting and singing. It did not sound like the place I was looking for. I knocked on the door at my right, but there was no answer. After a while, I decided to try the left-hand door; perhaps the people there would be able to tell me where the woman next door had gone. I knocked, but the noise inside

1. *Żydowica* is a pejorative Polish term for a female Jew.

was so loud that no one heard me. I tried to turn the door handle, and to my surprise, the door opened.

The odor that assailed me was overpowering. It was a mixture of liquor, salami, cigarette smoke, and cheap perfume. I found myself in a long, low-ceilinged room lit by a weak electric bulb. Some young men and women sat around a table in the center of the room, drinking, shouting, and belting out vulgar songs in Polish. Others were disporting themselves on beds arranged along the walls. I remained standing at the door, wondering who in that crowd would possibly know the whereabouts of the Jewish woman I was looking for. When the people in the room noticed me, they stopped singing, but only for a second. Then all hell broke loose. I was nearly mobbed by the guests of the establishment, who pulled me inside, bellowing, "Come on, Captain! Come inside! We'll give you a good time!"

I had hardly managed to extricate myself from the pushing, shoving company when a woman broke through the crowd, headed straight for me, and began to shout at the others in Polish, "Let this man go! Don't touch this man! Don't touch him!" Apparently surprised by the woman's outburst, my pursuers drew back and stood aside. I looked at the woman who had rescued me. I could have sworn that she was Jewish, but I dismissed the notion. What was a Jewish girl doing in a place like this? Could she be the *żydowica* who was supposed to be living in this house?

I was eager to get away and moved toward the door of the apartment. But the woman followed me out into the street. We stopped underneath one of the street lamps.

I asked her whether she was Jewish.

"Yes, Rabbi," she replied. "I'm Jewish."

I looked at her in amazement.

"Is there any other Jewish woman in this house besides you?" I inquired.

"No, Rabbi, I'm the only Jewish woman in this house. As a matter of fact, I'm the only Jewish person that's left in town now," she answered, and she launched into the story of the police raid, the pogrom, and the dramatic rescue of the intended victims by Itzik Feffer and his Russian comrades.

I listened intently without interrupting her, although I could hardly wait to ask her more questions. Everything about her was strange and bewildering. She had told her friends to keep away from me. I could not recall ever seeing her before. Yet she called me "Rabbi." How had she known I was a rabbi? Unlike the uniform of American chaplains, my officer's tunic bore neither the Ten Commandments nor the Star of David. And finally, why had she insisted on following me when I left her apartment? Was she trying to get my advice on some personal problem?

At last, the woman stopped talking, and I was able to ask her what I wanted to know. To my surprise, she told me that she had seen me several times at the religious services our community had been conducting in the old synagogue almost ever since the Germans had left the town. She said she had come there to the first High Holiday service in order to recite memorial prayers for her family, all of whom had been killed by the Nazis. She had come from a strictly Orthodox home. Back in Łódź, where she had been born and raised, her father had been a Hasid, the disciple of a well-known rebbe[2] who had been a spiritual leader to thousands of adherents throughout Poland before the war.

When she told me the rebbe's name, I shuddered inwardly at the thought of how her pious father would have felt if he knew what had become of his daughter. Apparently, the girl took my shocked silence for disbelief, for she hastened to reassure me that she had indeed been to services on that Yom Kippur. "Remember the two Russian girl soldiers?" she asked. "I was standing right next to them."

Now I was sure she had told me the truth, for I certainly remembered the sudden appearance of the two Russian girls in uniform at services on Yom Kippur Eve 1944.

Those young Russian women had known nothing of their Jewish heritage, but on the holiest day of the year, they had felt drawn to it and, acting on impulse, had come to a synagogue to pray. And here I stood, face-to-face with the girl who had stood beside them on that Yom Kippur, a girl

2. Hasidic Jews use the word *rebbe* (a Yiddish word derived from the Hebrew "rabbi") to refer to leaders of their movement. See, for instance, part I, chapter 10, note 3 and part I, chapter 13, note 4.

who had received a good, traditional Jewish upbringing but had lost her bearings and gone astray.

"Now do you believe me, Rabbi, that I really was at services on Yom Kippur?" the girl asked me, with an almost triumphant note in her voice. "And I wasn't there only on Yom Kippur; I came also on Rosh Hashanah, and this year I was even there on Passover."

I looked at the girl before me. Her features were typically Jewish—big, dark eyes and a slightly bent nose. Her mother and grandmother had probably looked a great deal like her. I could picture them, the two women sitting on a Sabbath afternoon bent over their Psalms or the Jewish Woman's Book of Prayers.[3] What, I wondered, would they have thought of their daughter, their granddaughter, who now stood facing me beneath the street lamp in Rzeszów?

"Of course, I believe you," I assured her. "I'd have believed you even if you hadn't told me the story about the two girl soldiers. Besides, what's so unusual about a Jewish girl going to the synagogue on Yom Kippur?"

I was eager to end our conversation, as it was already late. The streets were quiet and deserted. But I felt genuinely sorry for this girl. Here was the daughter of a fine Hasidic family turned into a common prostitute by the human urge for self-preservation. Left alone in the world, she had escaped death by descending to the dregs of human society. Yet there was a calm dignity about her that was oddly at variance with her present way of life. She spoke softly, addressed me in the respectful third person, never looked into my eyes, her head bowed, as though my presence filled her with shame.

I tried to talk to her, to restore her self-respect. I told her that the war was over, and she was free to come out of hiding and return to the Jewish community. Now that Jews everywhere were joining together to build new lives, why should she continue to live apart, among the Gentiles?

The girl was silent for a long time. Then she asked me what she was to do. She had no other place to go. Her family had been killed, and all

3. *Tkhines* (from Hebrew for "supplications") are prayers in Yiddish recited primarily by women.

the friends of her childhood were gone. The only friends she had were the men and women I had seen in her apartment. They liked her and had been good to her. They were the ones who had saved her life when she had first come to Rzeszów's ghetto from Łódź. Why should she force herself to leave them and start life all over again among strangers?

With all my might, I tried to persuade her to change her mind.

"You mustn't believe that if you return to our people, you'll be among strangers," I told her. "We're all in the same position. We've lost our families and our friends. But we don't consider any fellow Jew a stranger. We try to help each other as best as we can to rebuild our lives, as Jews and as individuals too. I'm sure that if you were to move away from this place and settle among Jews, you would soon get married to a nice young man and you would set up a Jewish home, the kind you knew in Łódź, with your father and mother."

As I spoke of her parents, she covered her face with her hands and began to weep softly, but then she shook her head and said quietly, "I can't . . . I can't go back . . . it's too late for me."

When I saw that I could not change her mind, I bade her farewell and suggested only that she reconsider her decision. It was never too late to start life anew, I reminded her. I gave her the address of the Bricha organization in Lublin. If she ever decided to make a break with her recent past, they would help her get to Palestine. All she needed to tell them was that I had sent her.

I walked toward the railroad station to catch the next train for Kraków. When I got to the end of the street, I looked about me in the darkness to see which way I would have to turn to reach the station. I happened to turn in the direction from which I had come. I saw the girl, still standing under the street lamp where I had left her, looking after me.

Several weeks later, one of the Bricha leaders from Lublin told me that sometime before, a girl had come to him and asked him to help her get to Palestine. She told him that she had been born and raised in Łódź and gave him my name as a reference. He had placed her in the very next transport. I would like to think that she was the girl from Łódź, the last *żydowica* to leave the town of Rzeszów.

# CHAPTER 9

# MY FAREWELL
# TO POLAND

During the long train trip to Kraków, I had plenty of time to ponder the fate of Rzeszów's Jews. During the year that had passed since the Germans left the city, most of the Jews had been able to rebuild their lives after a fashion. They had found places to live and managed to obtain the basic articles they needed to set up housekeeping: tables, benches, a few pots and pans, some plates, cups, and spoons. Admittedly, these items were not luxuries, but the Jews had become very modest in their wants and were content with the knowledge that after years in flight and in hiding, they had possessions to call their own. And now, suddenly, they had had to leave everything behind and start life in Kraków all over again. They were back where they had been a year before, when they had first emerged from the forests, bunkers, and basement hideouts.

Indeed, what sort of life could they build in Kraków? Kraków, like Rzeszów, had recently experienced a pogrom—an even more devastating one.[1] It occurred during the High Holiday season, the first pogrom since the end of the war. Kraków's Miodowa Street Synagogue was located near a marketplace where peasants came from the countryside to sell their produce. On the second day of Rosh Hashanah, the Jewish New Year, some

1. The 1945 pogrom at the Kupa Synagogue on Miodowa Street in Kraków occurred on August 11, 1945, not on the second day of Rosh Hashanah, which in 1945 took place on September 9. For a scholarly account of this episode, see Jan T. Gross, *Fear: Anti-Semitism in Poland after Auschwitz: An Essay in Historical Interpretation* (New York: Random House, 2006), 81–82.

Polish hooligans paid a young Gentile to enter the synagogue while the services were in progress and then rush out of the building into the marketplace, shouting that the Jews inside were killing a Christian child. The ruse worked. When the peasants heard the young man's shouts, they left the market stalls and burst into the synagogue. The Jews tried to fight off the invading mob but to no avail.

Within hours, Kraków's entire populace was up in arms against the Jews and the incident had blossomed into a full-blown pogrom. The Poles ran through the streets and fell on every Jew who happened to pass their way. Some broke into homes where Jews were known to live. The police, instead of protecting the Jews, joined the attackers. Many Jews, mainly women, were injured and had to be hospitalized. One of the women, who had suffered a broken skull, died.

But unlike Rzeszów, Kraków was a large city; the news of the pogrom could not be stifled. When it reached the rest of the world, it prompted an influential American Jew to publicly censure Poland and withhold badly needed funds from the Polish government. The American Jew was Herbert H. Lehman, former governor of New York, who was director of the United Nations Relief and Rehabilitation Administration (UNRRA), the then newly organized relief agency of the United Nations.[2] As soon as the war ended, officials of UNRRA traveled extensively through the ravaged countries of Europe to see where help was most urgently needed. In September 1945, it was announced that Lehman would personally visit Poland.

The Poles at once organized a gala reception for the American visitors, including a tour of the districts that bore the most striking scars of war. They particularly hoped that Lehman would be duly impressed by Warsaw, which had been pounded into rubble by the Nazis. This had been the German Army's revenge for the uprising that General Bór-Komorowski had organized in Warsaw late in 1944, when the Russians were practically

2. UNRRA provided economic aid to European countries after World War II and assisted refugees as well. Herbert H. Lehman (1878–1963) served as general director of UNRRA from 1943 to 1946.

at the gates of the city.[3] The Polish leader had been sure that the Russian armies would come to his aid. Unfortunately, his hopes were not fulfilled; the Russians, unwilling to support an independent Polish effort at liberation, remained at their nearest outpost in the suburbs of Praga, only a few miles away, and calmly watched the Germans crush the revolt. While the Russians prepared to move in and "liberate" the Polish capital in their own good time, German battalions of hand-grenade throwers crisscrossed the city, systematically pulverizing every street and house. Indeed, Warsaw was so badly battered that after the war the new Polish government considered abandoning it and situating a new capital elsewhere.

Now that the Americans had announced their intention to pour vast funds into the rebuilding of Europe, the Poles were eager to show the ex-governor of New York and his entourage a sight calculated to arouse their compassion. But after the news of the pogrom reached Lehman, he announced that he would not come to Poland. Taken aback by the adverse effect of the pogrom on world opinion—and also on the help they might be able to expect from UNRRA—the Poles became thoroughly upset. For the first time, the Polish press felt it necessary to come out in open condemnation of the pogroms and the rabble-rousers who had instigated them.

We Jews derived a measure of grim satisfaction from Governor Lehman's decision to cancel his visit. This gesture from a high American official, who had never personally experienced antisemitism, gave us renewed courage, for it made us understand that we were not alone and that there were other Jews throughout the world who were actively concerned with our welfare.

But in spite of Kraków's high visibility among the world's Jewry, there had still been a pogrom and a Jew clubbed to death in the street only a

3. On August 1, 1944, General Tadeusz Bór-Komorowski (1895–1966) commanded forces of the Armia Krajowa (Home Army) to reclaim control of Warsaw from the Germans, who by that point were in rapid retreat. Soviet forces were nearby—just across the Vistula River in the Warsaw suburb of Praga—but on Joseph Stalin's orders, they did not assist Bór-Komorowski's insurgents in their uprising because doing so would have complicated Stalin's aim to install a Soviet-friendly government.

few months ago. I was uneasy, to put it mildly, about what lay in store for Rzeszów's Jewish community in Kraków.

It was early morning when I arrived in Kraków. I immediately went to the headquarters of the Jewish Committee on Długa Street, certain that I would meet most of my people from Rzeszów there. After all, this was the one place where homeless Jews could be sure of finding temporary lodging and a few free meals from the soup kitchen. To my dismay, I found the building empty. The fact that no one was there, even at this early hour, filled me with alarm. If the Jews from Rzeszów were not here, where else could they possibly be? What if they had never reached Kraków at all?

Much to my relief, I came upon a night watchman, who informed me that the Jewish refugees from Rzeszów had reported to the committee at the time of their arrival but that after only two or three days, they had dispersed and settled in various parts of the city. I went out of the building and headed for the marketplace near the city's business and trade exchange. There, at last, I found them: dozens, even hundreds, of Jews from Rzeszów, who crowded around me so eagerly that the police appeared, sure that someone was about to start a revolt against the "Polish People's Republic."[4]

To my pleasant surprise, I learned that my little community had already gained a firm foothold in Kraków. They had made useful contacts and were doing business from dawn to sunset. The faces I saw around me showed no trace of despair or depression. I stood in awe of this new proof of Jewish courage, of Jewish determination to survive against incredible odds, a precious heritage preserved over countless generations of exile and persecution.

I was to return to Rzeszów only once. About three months after Rzeszów's pogrom, I was informed by some Jews in Kraków that one of the pogrom victims, Jonah Landesmann, was still in jail at Rzeszów police

4. The Polish People's Republic (Polska Rzeczpospolita Ludowa) was the name of Communist postwar Poland, although it did not formally adopt this name until 1952.

headquarters.[5] At the time of the mass arrests, poor Landesmann had somehow become separated from the other Jews and had been placed in a solitary confinement cell. As a result, he had been left behind when all the other Jews had gone free, and now, three months later, he was still in jail, almost dead from starvation.

I decided to go to Rzeszów myself to obtain his release. Immediately on my arrival, I called on the man who had informed my friends in Kraków of Landesmann's plight. He was Dr. W., a dentist, who had been a Jew but had converted to Christianity after the war when he learned that his entire family had been exterminated by the Nazis. He had married a non-Jewish woman and set up a prosperous practice in Rzeszów, but as he told me, the knowledge that a Jew was being kept in jail and cruelly mistreated left him no peace. Hence he had contacted his erstwhile coreligionists in Kraków and insisted that they do something about Landesmann. He was able to give me all the information I needed, including the name of the public prosecutor who was keeping Jonah behind bars without trial.

Half an hour later, I was in the public prosecutor's office at the courthouse. After I had identified myself and told him the purpose of my visit, the prosecutor sent his secretary for a file of documents, which he proceeded to study while I talked with him. He seemed to relish what he was reading. While he was talking to his secretary, I had an opportunity to glance at the title of the file. It was "The Ritual Murder Incident."

Finally, the prosecutor put aside his file and informed me he had definite proof that the Jews had been guilty of the murder of a little Christian girl three months before. He said that he had managed to obtain not only the tin can into which the Jews had poured the child's blood but also some of the hair pulled from the child's body.

5. Jonah (also Jonas) Landesmann lived in Thorne's apartment with the *shochet* (kosher butcher) after Thorne left. Landesmann had been arrested and accused of killing Bronisława Mendoń, the girl whose murder became the excuse for the Rzeszów pogrom described in part II, chapter 7.

"Corpus delicti, my dear rabbi! Corpus delicti!" he repeated several times. "I have all the evidence needed to convict the Jews."[6]

I looked straight into the man's eyes and asked him, "Do you, sir, really believe that this child was murdered by Jews?"

"Certainly, I do," the public prosecutor replied. "I know, and I am sure you know also, that there are perverts in this world who derive pleasure from the act of killing, particularly the killing of children. And no less a scholar than Professor Krzyżanowski of Warsaw University believes that, even in this day and age, there are humans who, in a manner of speaking, may be classed as cannibals."[7]

Professor Krzyżanowski may have been an acknowledged authority in his field, which was economics, but I had never heard him hold forth on cannibalism.

I calmly faced the public prosecutor. "I suppose this means you think that we Jews are cannibals. Right?"

The prosecutor did not reply, but he looked at me with a leer as if to say, "I didn't say it—you did."

At this point, I could no longer control myself. I leaped from my chair and told the prosecutor that I had not come to him to listen to his discourses on criminology but solely to obtain the release of the prisoner Jonah Landesmann. "If Landesmann isn't released immediately," I shouted, "I will make a personal appeal to the prime minister in Warsaw, and we'll see what will happen then."

Suddenly, the prosecutor's face took on a somber look. He reminded me that I was subject to prosecution myself as an accomplice in the murder of the child. As a matter of fact, he said, there was yet another serious charge against me. He had clear proof that during the past year, I had been engaged in smuggling Jews out of Poland. Under cover of my position as

6. Corpus delicti (Latin for "body of the crime") is the legal principle that, for someone to be convicted of a crime, the crime must be proven to have happened.
7. The prosecutor may have been referring to Adam Krzyżanowski (1873–1963), who was a leading economist in Kraków, not Warsaw.

a military chaplain, I had used my apartment as a meeting place for an underground organization that manufactured forged passports, visas, and other documents not only for Polish Jews but also for Jews who had come to Poland from other East European countries. The prosecutor told me that he had enough evidence against me to report me to the High Command of the Polish army. "I can have you arrested at any time I choose!" he shouted.

"You can do whatever you want with me," I firmly replied, "but you will have Landesmann released at once—or else!" With that, I turned my back on the public prosecutor and marched out of his office.

I left Rzeszów the same day and returned to Kraków. The very next morning, Jonah Landesmann arrived in Kraków too. He was so badly bruised and emaciated that I hardly recognized him, but he was a free man.

The public prosecutor's assertion that he could have me arrested at any time was not an idle threat. Within days of our meeting in Rzeszów, he sent a request to the High Command of the Polish army for my immediate arrest on charges of smuggling and complicity in the murder of a child. Fortunately for me, the High Command was not keen on ruining the international image of Poland by publicizing the ritual murder incident. However, it was made clear to me that I should resign from the army, and I knew that I would have to leave the country as soon as possible.

My work in Bricha was not my only crime in the eyes of the Polish government; my main sin, as far as the Communist regime of Poland was concerned, was my active interest in Zionism. About nine months before, in January 1945, two close friends of mine—the lexicographer Reuven Feldschuh,[8] a member of the Central Jewish Committee, and Mordecai Kosover,[9] president of the Zionist Organization of Poland—had asked

---

8. Reuven (also Reuben or Rubin) Feldschuh, also known as Reuven Ben-Shem (1900–1980) was a well-known figure in Zionist circles in interwar Poland. He published a lexicon about Jewish community life in Warsaw in 1939 and, during the war, wrote a massive eight-hundred-page Hebrew-language diary. He left Poland in 1945 for Palestine.
9. Aside from his active work for Zionist organizations, Mordecai Kosover (1908–1969) was also a linguist and professor at Brooklyn College.

me to cosign applications from two Jewish families for financial subsidies from the Central Jewish Committee. The committee had been receiving funds periodically from the Polish government for the rehabilitation of the Jews who were expected to remain in Poland. Each application for such funds had to be endorsed by two permanent members of the Central Jewish Committee. The two applications I had cosigned were approved, but the amount of money given to the applicants was much too small to enable them to reestablish themselves in Poland. As a result, the two families, along with a group of other Jews, left the country—without exit permits, of course.

By that time, the Central Jewish Committee had come under the control of Communists. They made it their task to ferret out Jews who were helping other Jews leave the country or, even worse, were involved in Zionist activities, which were strictly illegal under the new Polish regime. The Communists had long suspected both Feldschuh and me of Zionist proclivities and had been waiting for an opportunity to prove us "guilty." When it became known that the two families for whom Feldschuh and I had cosigned applications for financial support had left the country, the Communists in the committee's leadership decided to use these applications, which bore our signatures, to discredit us in the eyes of the government. But by the time they were ready to act, Feldschuh was no longer within their reach. Realizing that the Jewish Communists had set out to expose him, he too fled Poland. As a consequence, the investigation centered on me. They hoped that I could be made to "sing" and lead the authorities straight to the "hotbed" of illegal activity. I was called to Central Jewish Committee headquarters to explain my involvement with the two families. My explanation was not satisfactory. I offered to reimburse the committee from my own pocket for the money that the families had received (it had been a very small amount). But the Central Jewish Committee was not interested in the money; they wanted me to help them expose Bricha as an underground nest of "Zionist swindlers and smugglers." Like the Gentile public prosecutor, these Jewish officials too threatened to report me to the High Command of the Polish Army.

I was eager to leave Poland as soon as possible, but my wife and I had not been able to make any preparations for our departure. I therefore decided to buy some time. I requested that the committee give me a week in which to find out what had in fact become of the two families. When that week was over, I asked for an additional week. I explained that I had learned that the families had not, in fact, left Poland but were on a farm in some remote region of the country.

I called on Dr. Sommerstein,[10] who was still officially the president of the Central Jewish Committee. He listened to me and was visibly upset by my plight. But there was nothing he could do to help me; he was a prisoner in the hands of the Communist clique that had taken over Poland's Jewish community.

I resigned my commission in the Polish army the next day, and the day after that, my wife, my brother, and I left the country.

10. See part II, chapter 3, note 7.

# CHAPTER 10

# ARREST IN DRESDEN

When we decided to leave Poland, our aim had been to reach Germany's American zone[1] and to decide from there where to go next. Unfortunately, in our hurry to leave Poland, we did not have the time to plan our escape properly and to consult with the people who could have given us the best advice—the Bricha organization, which every day engineered such illegal journeys to the free West for refugees on the way to Palestine. In retrospect, we would probably have been better off if we had made our journey to West Germany by way of Czechoslovakia. But because we were eager to put Poland behind us as quickly as possible, we chose the route through East Germany instead, crossing at the Silesian border town of Görlitz. Our plan was to spend one night in Dresden, then the capital of Germany's Russian zone. We intended to proceed into the American zone by way of Leipzig the next morning.

Winter 1945 came early; the weather was cold, and a moist snow had been falling for days. My wife was eight months pregnant with our first child, and my brother and I had been concerned that the journey might be too much for her, but she gamely reassured us that if we two men were

---

1. At the Potsdam Conference from July 17 to August 2, 1945, the Americans, British, French, and Soviets divided both Germany as a whole and the city of Berlin into four occupation zones. As neither the Federal Republic of Germany (West Germany) nor the German Democratic Republic (East Germany) was established until 1949, Thorne's subsequent use of "West Germany" refers to the American, British, and French sectors and "East Germany" to the Soviet sector.

ready to brave the weather and all the other hardships of the illegal crossing, so was she.

We crossed the border safely, arrived in Dresden toward evening, and
settled down for the night in temporary lodgings. But before long, our
troubles began. In her eagerness not to hold us back, my wife had overes-
timated her strength. In the middle of the night, she went into labor and
had to be taken by ambulance to the hospital. An hour later, she gave birth
to our son.

Naturally, the unexpected arrival of our baby forced us to change our
plans. It would have been insane to attempt our next illegal border crossing—
into the West—with a newborn infant. Dresden had been almost totally leveled by Allied bombings,[2] but we managed to find a room at the home of
a German family, and the four of us settled down there to wait until the
spring, when the baby would be older, the weather warmer, and accordingly,
our chances for reaching West Germany much better.

To my pleasant surprise, I found that about one hundred Jews—mostly
of German origin—had survived the war and were living in Dresden. They
had already organized themselves into a community of sorts, complete
with an administrative staff headed by a man named Löwenkopf.[3] Most of
these survivors were on hand when we celebrated the circumcision of our
baby who, despite his premature birth, turned out to be a sturdy young fellow. We gave him the name Emanuel David; Emanuel means "God is with
us." It seemed a good omen for the future.

One afternoon, the doorbell rang. We heard our landlady open the door
downstairs. Someone asked her whether this was the home of the Thorne
family. We ran to the door and found two young men. I recognized one of
them immediately; I had met him in Lublin. Both our visitors were members of Bricha and had just arrived in Dresden from Poland.

2. Between February 13 and 15, 1945, Allied bombing raids leveled Dresden and resulted
in upward of twenty-five thousand deaths. Whether the raids were strategically necessary remains highly controversial.
3. Leon Löwenkopf (1892–1966) was a concentration camp survivor and the first head
of the postwar Jewish community in Dresden.

We embraced our guests as long-lost brothers, for they were our first contact with the outside world in many weeks. Because we lived in Germany's Russian zone illegally with no residence permit, we were forced to keep a low profile. We received no visitors and left our room only when absolutely necessary. In addition, the mail was not yet functioning regularly. Hence we had been unable to communicate with our friends in Poland.

We plied the two men with questions, but they insisted that they could not stay long; they were on the way to Leipzig, about fifty miles to the west. They told us why they had taken the time to seek us out. The Bricha route from Poland into West Germany through Czechoslovakia, which we had originally wanted to take, had been spoiled. It could no longer be safely used by refugees because one Bricha transport had been caught there and the travelers placed under arrest by the authorities. As a result, Bricha was now forced to move its refugees from Poland into West Germany over the same route that we had planned to use: from Görlitz to Dresden and then into the western zone by way of Leipzig. Thus Bricha wanted to set up an assembly point in Dresden, where refugees could spend the night before moving on. On their arrival in Dresden, the two Bricha men had called on Löwenkopf, the head of the Jewish community, who told them that we too were in the city. They considered this a godsend; they decided at once that my wife, my brother, and I would act as a reception committee to direct the refugees to temporary lodgings and obtain railroad tickets for their journey to Leipzig.

I waited for my visitors to finish. Then I informed them that they had better forget about a Bricha assembly point in Dresden. The city lay in ruins; the housing shortage was so acute that in many instances one single room was shared by several families. Where, then, should we be able to find a shelter to accommodate whole groups of refugees overnight? Besides, such conspicuous movements would draw the attention of the occupation authorities; the city was swarming with Soviet troops and secret police. It would be a miracle if the very first group of Jews to arrive in the city were not arrested immediately.

The two young men put their heads together and began to talk rapidly between themselves. They produced a large map of Central Europe, spread it out on our table and traced lines across it with their fingers. They were looking for safe alternative routes through East Germany that would bypass Dresden. Finally, they found what they had been looking for and said they would leave at once to explore personally the route for safety and negotiability. However, they told us that they had already arranged for one small group of refugees to be directed to our address. Would we be able to find them a place to spend the night? Once these people had moved on, our visitors assured us, they would send no more Bricha refugees to Dresden. We agreed to do our best, and the two men left.

Two days passed without word from Bricha. On the third evening, we heard a knock at the door downstairs. Moments later, our landlady burst into our room with a look of panic on her face. There were some strangers outside, she said, odd-looking people who apparently had come from a trip, and they wanted to see us. We went to the front window, looked down into the street, and saw about a dozen people standing there. We understood at once that these were our guests, the first—and, we hoped, last—Bricha transport to pass through Dresden.

We assured our landlady that there was no cause for alarm and promised to pay her handsomely if she would agree to let these people stay in her house overnight. She nodded, relieved, and we called out to the travelers to come in. The group consisted of fifteen refugees, including several small children who had made the long journey in their parents' arms.

They told us that they had crossed the Polish border the night before. All were soaking wet and chilled to the bone. The terror of the previous night still showed in their eyes. They dumped their knapsacks, took off their sopping coats and jackets, and dropped to the floor, exhausted.

We—my wife, my brother, and I—sympathized with them. We had been through the same experience not too long ago. Perhaps we had an even worse time of it, in view of my wife's condition and the fact that we had not had anyone to turn to for shelter. We quickly prepared hot coffee for our overnight guests, offered them all the food we had in the house, and found some blankets and pillows to make them more comfortable. Early the next morning, we escorted them to the railroad station—not all together but one by one, so as not to attract attention—bought them train tickets, and put them on the next train to Leipzig. When they had gone, we heaved a sigh of relief. It had been a dangerous business for both the refugees and ourselves, and we were glad that it was over.

To our consternation, however, our work had not yet come to an end. That very evening, we again heard a knock at the door downstairs. Again, we looked out the window into the street below. This time, the group we saw waiting for us was even larger than the one the night before. We did exactly as we had done the previous evening: we brought the travelers into the house, put them up for the night, and the next morning took them to the station.

The next evening, a third group turned up in front of our house, and the night thereafter, a fourth. In each instance, the refugees had come straight from the border, with no instructions from the Bricha center in Poland except to report to my address for shelter and further directions when they got to Dresden.

It was not a happy situation. We were afraid that if the steady stream of refugees passing through Dresden continued, it would end in catastrophe. But there was nothing we could do to stop them. There were no regular channels of communication between East Germany and Poland through which anyone could have passed word to the Bricha center in Poland that Dresden was not a safe assembly point. As for the two young men whom I had advised to find an alternate route, I did not know where they were, nor could they contact the nerve center in Poland that kept sending the transports to Dresden.

I must confess that we were a little afraid for ourselves too. What would happen to us, and to our baby, if the authorities were to find out that we were sheltering illegal transients? At one point, my wife and I seriously considered leaving our lodgings and moving into another neighborhood so that the refugees would not find us, but the thought of the frozen unfortunate Jews with their snow-covered knapsacks on their backs and their tiny babies in their arms, knocking on our door for shelter and not finding us, was too much for us. We could not abandon these poor people to their fate just because we wanted to keep out of danger. And so, we continued receiving new transports night after night, wondering when the authorities would finally catch up with them—or with us.

On the ninth day, the catastrophe came. We had seen our eighth transport off at the station that morning. It was late in the afternoon, and we were sitting in our room, wondering what to do if another transport arrived. Suddenly, the door opened without a sound and two men in civilian clothes entered. They announced that they were looking for a man named Thorne and identified themselves as officers of the Russian secret police. They searched my brother and me and then ordered us to come with them. They also wanted to take my wife, but when they saw our baby, they agreed that she would not be arrested as long as she did not attempt to leave the city.

Without a word, my brother and I preceded the two plainclothesmen out of the house. We were taken to the police station, where our neckties, belts, and shoelaces were taken away and we were searched once again. This time, even our socks were turned inside out, and we were not allowed to keep so much as a pin. Afterward, we were escorted to the prison, where my brother and I were placed in separate cells on different floors.

We remained in that prison for four weeks. During all that time, I had no news whatsoever from my wife. I also knew nothing of my brother. I had no idea whether he was still in the same prison or if he had been moved somewhere else. On one occasion, I overheard a prison employee who made the rounds of cells twice each day with buckets full of bread. He said there were many other Jews in the prison. I was never called for questioning; it seemed as if my captors had forgotten about me. My brother, as I later learned, had not been as fortunate. He was interrogated and ordered to sign a confession that he had smuggled Jews into and out of East Germany and that he had planted a bomb to blow up one of Dresden's bridges. When he insisted that he knew nothing about the bomb plot, he was brutally beaten and then dragged back into his prison cell, where he lay on the cold stone floor for days, unable to get up. He felt as if every bone in his body had been broken.

Then one day at noon, without warning, my cell door was opened, and I was ordered to go out. After four weeks of confinement, I was taken into the prison yard. There I found hundreds of other inmates—and my brother. The four weeks in prison had changed him almost beyond recognition. He was thin and pale as a ghost. I recognized some of the others; among them were refugees who had been sent to me by Bricha. They had been caught attempting to cross into West Germany and were brought back to Dresden and put into prison. There had been no way of informing the Bricha people that this particular route had become unsafe, and as a result, by now the prison held hundreds of innocent people whose only crime was that they wanted to rebuild their lives in the one place that was waiting to welcome them—Eretz Yisrael.[4]

4. Eretz Israel ("Land of Israel") is the traditional Jewish name for the Holy Land.

—∕—

# CHAPTER 11

# OUR RETURN TO POLAND

After all the Bricha refugees had been assembled in the prison yard, we were herded into trucks and driven under heavy armed guard to the Polish border town of Görlitz—the place from which my brother, my wife, and I had originally crossed into East Germany. In Görlitz, we were taken directly to prison. There, we found hundreds of Jews who had been caught attempting to leave Poland, some of them only the day before. There too I found my wife and baby son. The police had picked them up at our room in Dresden and brought them to Görlitz with the others.

We were kept in this prison for eight days. On the ninth day, all of us—men and women except for mothers with small children—were herded together, lined up five abreast, and escorted to the bridge of the River Neisse, which divided Germany's Russian zone from Poland. My wife and child remained behind in the Görlitz prison. We were told that they would follow us the next day.

Then on the other side of the Neisse bridge, the Russian occupation authorities turned us over to the Polish military border police. We were 305 people in all—men, women, and children between the ages of eight and ten.

We soon realized that the Polish border police had no idea what we had been doing in Germany's Russian zone and why the Russians were escorting us back across the border under police guard. Apparently, the documents that the Russian police handed over to the Polish officials did not help explain the situation. But one thing the Poles realized at once without needing to be told: we were all Jews.

The Poles demanded that we explain how we had gotten to Germany from Poland and what we had done to make the Russians send us back. Our group chose a committee of three to act as its spokesmen. I was one of the three. We tried to concoct a story least likely to cause trouble for either Bricha or ourselves. We told the Polish officials that some of us had been working in German labor camps during the war (this was true) and that others had gone to Germany to look for relatives who had been deported (this was also not entirely false) but that we were now ready to return to Poland.

The Polish officials went into a huddle. Finally, they reached a decision. Four police officers informed us that they would escort us, on foot, to Liegnitz, the nearest large city. Our march took fifteen hours. It was a wet, cold winter day. Because of the women and children, we had to walk very slowly and make frequent rest stops in the wet fields on either side of the highway.

I think we could have scattered on the highway and escaped without our police escorts stopping us. In fact, the four unfortunate Poles would probably have been relieved, for they certainly could not have relished the task of shepherding some three hundred people along the highway in the miserable winter weather for a whole day. But it did not occur to any of us to run away. We had no place to go, and none of us had any money. So we felt that we would be better off if we remained together as a group than if we dispersed.

It was midnight when we finally arrived in Liegnitz. We stopped in front of the city's police headquarters. Our escorts showed some kind of paper to the bewildered officer at the gate, who did not quite know what to do with three hundred unexpected guests. The policemen went into the building and left us standing outside.

After about an hour, we began to get impatient and started shouting and knocking at the windows. One of the Liegnitz policemen came

out and told us that we would have to remain outside until morning, when
the police chief would arrive and find a place for us. But we did not take
kindly to the prospect of being left to wait out in the cold after our fifteen-
hour march.

Suddenly, one of the men shouted, "Why don't you put us up in the
jail?" We all agreed with the suggestion; at the moment, all we wanted was
a roof over our heads. The night sergeant struck his forehead with his palm
as if to say, "A brilliant idea! Why couldn't I have thought of this myself?"

We were led into the prison. It was nice and warm inside. The men
rushed into the cells, and the turnkey did not lock the doors behind them.
The women and children were told to lie down on the cots; the men sat
on the floor of the cells or in the corridor. At last, we were able to shed our
outer clothes and shoes, which were soaking wet. No one had the heart to
think of what the next day might bring. The future seemed too dismal
to contemplate. What would become of my wife and baby back in Görlitz?
Had the police told me the truth when they said that I would see them
again the next day?

At six in the morning, all prisoners had to be out of their cells for roll
call, so we too could not remain in our cells. We put on our clothes, wet
though they still were, and (again under heavy police guard) marched out
of the prison back to the police station. At long last, the police chief arrived
in a jeep, accompanied by a girl who, we were told, was his secretary. He
stared at us in complete surprise. Obviously, he had not been told of our
arrival. His face bore a look of genuine bewilderment, even alarm.

"What the devil are you doing here?" he shouted at us in a hoarse, tense
voice. "Who brought you here? And why?"

We three elected "spokesmen" stepped out of line, went up to him, and
told him our story. After we finished, the police chief turned and, without
another word, went inside the station house. He motioned to the three of
us to follow him. The others remained outside.

He led us into his office, where his secretary handed him a sheet of
paper. It was the document that our escorts from Görlitz had handed to
the Liegnitz police sergeant on our arrival. As the police chief sat down at

his desk to study the paper, he could hear our friends coughing and sneez-
ing outside. He got up, looked out the window, and shook his head in
dismay at the sight of three hundred men, women, and children shivering
in wet rags. He began to question us in detail, all the while staring at our
friends outside. His secretary was writing down our story. Suddenly, we
saw that she was crying bitterly. When the police chief turned around and
noticed the girl weeping, he flew into a rage, pounded his desk with his fist,
and shouted that all our troubles were the fault of the bloodsuckers—the
bourgeoisie and the imperialists of the West. As long as those monsters
remained alive and in power, he declared, there would be no end to injus-
tice, poverty, misery, racial hatred, and war. Then he turned to the three of
us and looked us straight in the eye.

"You too," he said, "are in the imperialist camp, despite the fact that you
are the victims of imperialism."

If our situation had not been so desperate, I think we would simply
have laughed in his face. Bourgeois, imperialists, and capitalists, indeed!
Among the 305 of us, we did not have so much as one penny. The Germans
and Russians had been so thorough in their body searches that none of us
had as much as a pin left of his belongings. The linings of our outer garments had been torn out, and our shoelaces, neckties, and handkerchiefs
had been taken away. I do not think that anyone else in the world could
possibly have been so utterly without possessions as we, whom the Polish
police chief had just called bourgeois capitalists. But we felt too bitter just
then to appreciate the irony of it all.

After a while, the police chief calmed down somewhat. "Look," he said,
a little more gently. "What else can I call you but partners of the capitalists
and imperialists if you insist on sneaking across the border to the West
instead of helping rebuild your fatherland, the Polish Socialist People's
Republic? Why do you want to run away? You people have been living in
Poland for generations. Why can't you take your proper places in the new
society we have established here?"

All through this tirade, the three of us said not a word. We felt that if
the police chief did not understand why we and the others were so eager

to "run away," no amount of argument or explanation would do any good. Finally, the police chief ended his lecture, got up from his chair, and with our paper in his hand, went into another room. A few minutes later, he reappeared and announced to us that we were all free to go wherever we pleased except back to the border. We rushed out to tell the others that we were no longer criminals but free. Our friends went wild at the news. They danced with joy, hugged and kissed each other, and shouted in Polish over and over again, "Long live the police chief!"

We, the "committee of three," went back to the police chief to thank him on behalf of the entire group. We also told his secretary how much we appreciated her sympathy. Later, we found out that she was the police chief's wife and that she was Jewish. Now that we were no longer under arrest but ordinary transients, we felt that we were entitled to ask the police chief for help. We had heard, we told him, that in Liegnitz there was a municipal agency that assisted Poles who had returned from Germany. We asked him to give us a letter of introduction to that agency. We wanted food because we had not eaten in more than twenty-four hours and railroad tickets to Breslau, the Silesian metropolis. Once we arrived there, we would be able to make plans for our future. The police chief immediately telephoned the agency and asked his secretary to write the letter we needed.

Before leaving, we told the police chief that, within a day or two, another transport of returnees, some thirty women and small children who could not make the journey on foot, was due to arrive by truck from Görlitz. We hoped that he would accord them the same kindness and sympathy he had shown us and send them on to Breslau. The police chief promised to do his best for them, and we bade him and his secretary a cordial farewell.

Outside, we reported to the others that we would proceed at once to the relief agency, which would give us food and pay our train fare to Breslau. We pleaded with them not to disperse. As a group, we were in a position to request, and receive, help from various authorities and official agencies. Those who went off on their own would probably never have a chance. Apparently, our arguments—particularly the prospect of having our way paid to Breslau—were persuasive, because no one left the group. We formed a long column five abreast and set out in an orderly march to the headquarters of the relief agency, this time without a police escort.

The relief organization gave us a generous reception. We were led into a dining hall and invited to sit down on benches beside long tables. We were all in a good mood, happy to be free after weeks of imprisonment and police surveillance. Soon, the kitchen door opened and steaming kettles of pork stew were brought in. The pork smell, especially on an empty stomach, was overpowering. It made us sick. I noticed some of the faces near me turn green.

We begged the kitchen attendants to take the food back. They were not sure they understood us correctly. The head cook, perspiring in his white uniform, rushed into the dining hall to find out what was wrong. We assured him that we had no fault to find with the food, but that after our long fast, our stomachs could not stand this heavy, fatty meat.[1] We asked him whether we could have some plain, dry bread and hot water instead of the pork stew. The cook protested he had no sugar, but we said we did not mind that, as long as the water was good and hot. The cook went back into the kitchen, shaking his head and muttering to himself, "What a shame! Such fine, good stew!"

A few minutes later, the attendants were back with long loaves of black bread and coffee pots filled with hot water. The noise in the dining hall stopped abruptly as we began to chew the bread and drink the hot water. Now and then, we could hear a mother telling her child not to eat too quickly and to be careful of the hot water; otherwise, no one spoke. The bread was pasty and probably at least partly ersatz, but it was fresh, and it was a godsend for empty stomachs; the hot water made us feel pleasantly warm in the bare, cold room. As I ate, I looked at the others around me. From the expressions on their faces, I could tell that their minds were not on the food they were chewing and swallowing. They seemed deep in

---

1. Presumably, the real reason for the request to take back the food was that the stew was not kosher because of the pork.

thought, particularly the men who were wondering whether, where, and how they would be able to settle down with their families and resume a normal life.

After we had finished our meal, an agency official handed me a railroad pass for the entire group. Then we lined up once more and marched in semimilitary columns to the railroad station. We presented our pass to the stationmaster, who informed us that the next train to Breslau was leaving that evening and that it would have special coaches to accommodate us.

It was still dark when our train pulled into Breslau the next morning. We decided to stay together at the station until dawn. Then our group broke up. Each one went his own way except for those whose wives and children were due to arrive from Görlitz; we agreed on a time and place where we would meet to keep each other informed of arrangements to receive our families.

# CHAPTER 12

# BRESLAU AGAIN

After all the others had left, my brother and I remained in front of the station building, not knowing where to go next. It was a cold winter morning, and the city was enveloped in a dense fog. Only a few months before, I had visited Breslau in an official military truck and worn the uniform of a Polish army officer. Now I was in Breslau again, but this time I was merely a refugee, belonging nowhere. I tried to think of anyone I might know in the city. I vaguely recalled that some time before, in Kraków, Chaim Z., a young man who had come from my birthplace, in Schodnica, had told me he was going to Breslau to try to start a business there. But I did not know whether he had ever managed to get to Breslau, and even if he had, how would I ever find him?

I could not bear to think of my wife and baby, who were still in East Germany at the mercy of the Russian and East German police. What guarantee did I have that they would really be released from prison and brought to Breslau? When would I see them again? I had only myself to blame for our plight. Why had I agreed to take the refugees into our room in Dresden? And when they kept coming, why did I not simply disappear with my family and keep out of trouble? On the other hand, could I really have told these unfortunate people to go elsewhere and not to bother me? No, I could not have been so heartless, not even if I had known the full extent of the calamity that would befall us.

"Don't you two have any place to go?" someone asked us. I looked up and saw two young men. At first, I did not recognize them, but my brother reminded me that they had been in our group, among the 305. Before we could answer, the two suggested that we go with them to the Mizrachi house to wash ourselves and rest awhile.[1] They explained to us that the Mizrachi organization—religious Zionists—had acquired a permanent clubhouse in Breslau, where refugees and transients could rest, eat, and even stay as long as necessary. The clubhouse had served as a gathering point for Bricha refugees on their way West, and the two young men had stayed there for some time before moving on to Germany, where, of course, they had had the bad luck to be caught and imprisoned.

My brother and I gratefully accepted our two new friends' invitation. We asked them about Chaim Z., but they did not know him. As we began to walk with them, I found myself staring at every passerby to see whether he might be our friend Chaim Z. But none of the people was Chaim.

At the Mizrachi house, our two escorts led us into a long narrow dormitory with about a dozen primitive cots of raw logs, each covered with straw and nothing else. I remembered the *hekdeshim*,[2] the shelters for transient beggars, which almost every Jewish community in Poland had before the war and were generally known to be filthy, squalid places. But I had to admit that any *hekdesh* was a palace compared to this bare room with the cots that lined its walls. However, such extrinsic considerations did not matter very much just then. Our accommodations in prison had certainly not been better, and we had not had a chance to sleep at all the last few nights. We were hardly able to stand. My brother and I each staggered to a cot and fell asleep almost instantly.

When I regained consciousness, someone was shaking my arm. Standing before my bed were the two young men and—to my utter amazement— my friend Chaim Z. While I had been dead to the world, our two young

1. Founded in 1902, Mizrachi (an acronym created from *Merkaz Ruhani* [religious center]) is a religious and political organization committed to political Zionism as a means to realize religious goals.
2. *Hekdeshim* (singular: *hekdesh*) refers in general to property set aside for charitable purposes, but the word has come to designate the huts for the indigent that Thorne describes.

guides had gone to the headquarters of the Jewish community to track Chaim down, and when they found him, they had taken him to the Mizrachi clubhouse at once.

Chaim appeared thunderstruck; he seemed terrified at our appearance. Dazed, I sat on my cot and told him our story. Chaim listened with a sad expression on his face and then asked me whether I had any plans for the future. I told him that my most immediate plan was to sleep as long as I could and then wash myself. The next point on the agenda, of course, was to find my wife and son. I expected Chaim to offer to lend me some money, and when he made no such suggestion, I asked him outright for a loan of a couple of hundred złotys. Chaim was visibly embarrassed. He rooted through his pants pockets and mumbled something about having no cash just now. He explained that he was in a tight spot because he had invested all his cash in the bakery he had opened and business was not good. In fact, he said he might have to give up the bakery altogether. He was clearly not willing to help me out. Perhaps he did not consider my brother and me, filthy and in tatters as we were, particularly good credit risks. From his furtive glances at his wristwatch, I could see that was eager to get away. I must have looked very downcast, sitting there in front of Chaim, a man I had known since childhood, who had known my family and was now afraid to lend me a couple hundred złotys. I looked at the two young men, who had been listening to our conversation, and sensed that if they had been able to push Chaim out of the window, they would have done so with pleasure.

I don't know how it came about, but at just that moment, one of my fingers happened to wander into the little front pocket of my pants, where my pocket watch had once been. I felt a hard object there, and when I pulled it out, I saw that it was the gold chain from my pocket watch, which had been taken from me along with all my other possessions at the time of my arrest in Dresden. I do not know how the Russian and German policemen who had searched me so thoroughly in Dresden and then again in Görlitz had missed the little gold chain, but there it was, a miraculous find in this hour of need.

The two young men snatched the chain from my hands and ran out of the room, shouting excitedly. Minutes later, they returned with a third man, who turned out to be an expert on gold, ready to do business. He pulled out a little scale and weighed my chain. The two young men indicated to me that this was an honest, reliable man. Chaim seemed to have developed a new interest in me. He begged me not to sell the watch chain because if I did, I would only be cheated. He, Chaim, was ready to lend me all the money I wanted, and to prove it, he produced a wallet stuffed with bills. Perhaps, he said, he would buy the chain himself. But I did not react. The expert with the little scale did some fast figuring and bought the chain from me for 12,500 złotys. The whole transaction, from the moment I had found the chain until the money was in my hands, had taken exactly ten minutes.

Meanwhile, my brother had been awakened by the commotion. Seeing Chaim and the money in my hand, he at once concluded that Chaim had come to help us out. He jumped from his cot, threw his arms around Chaim, and began to thank him profusely for all his kindness. When he saw that Chaim was not particularly responsive, my brother hastened to reassure him that he would have his money back in a few weeks' time with interest.

Chaim mumbled a quick good-bye and left. When my brother learned the truth about the money, he burst into such loud laughter that everyone came running to see what was so funny. A little later, my brother and I went out into the street. Almost at once, we ran into a man we had known from Poland. This man told us that three friends of ours, a Mrs. Lena Gartenberg and her sisters, Risa and Golda Silberberg, were living in Breslau. We had not even known that the three women had survived the war. We went at once to see them and received a warm welcome. They refused to let us leave their home; they offered us a clean, comfortable room and gave us everything we needed to make ourselves look presentable again.

The next morning, we got in touch with some of the others in our group who had had to leave their wives and children behind in East Germany. We decided that if we received no news from our families by the next day, we would illegally cross the border back into East Germany that night to find out what happened to them.

As it turned out, we did not need to do that. The very next day, we received word from Liegnitz that our families had arrived there. However, they had not been taken there in trucks, as we had been promised; instead, they had been forced, like the men, to make the fifteen-hour march on foot with the babies in their arms. The police chief in Liegnitz had kept his promise; he had taken pity on the women and children and let them rest in the prison until we could arrange for their transfer to Breslau. One of the men in our group gave us the telephone number of a friend in Liegnitz. We called him at once and asked him to hire a truck to bring our women and children to Breslau. We agreed on the time and place of their arrival and added, of course, that we would be glad to pay all the expenses.

Several hours later, we gathered at the street corner where the truck was to arrive. Everything went according to schedule, and none of the women and children was missing. But they looked terrible; we were hardly able to recognize them. They had lived through three terrible days—first, the journey to Liegnitz on foot and then the truck ride to Breslau in the bitter cold.

My wife handed me a bundle wrapped in a brown army blanket and said, "Be careful, the baby's inside. I haven't heard a sound from him in hours. Who knows whether he's still alive?" I did not want to open the bundle in the street, out in the cold. So I grabbed it, and we ran all the way to our room at Mrs. Gartenberg's apartment. All the time, I strained to detect a sign of life inside the bundle, but I felt and heard none.

We were more dead than alive when we finally arrived in our room. I dumped the bundle on the bed and then stopped, unable to catch my breath. I could hardly make myself undo the bundle for fear of what I would find inside. After what seemed an eternity, I began to open the blanket. My wife could not bear to watch. She left the room, followed by Mrs. Gartenberg and her sisters. Finally, the bundle was undone. To our joy and relief, our three-month-old lay there, his eyes wide open and laughing, laughing at the stupid, wicked world. "Little one," I muttered to him, "what a time you chose to be born!"

After several days of rest in Breslau, my wife, my brother, and I decided to try to cross into Germany again—this time via Szczecin (known as Stettin before the war, when it had been part of Germany) and East Berlin, and from there into the American zone of West Berlin, where many Jewish refugees had found shelter in the Displaced Persons (DP) camp of Schlachtensee.[3]

However, the money I had received for my gold watch chain had almost run out. We therefore decided that I should go to Kraków to see some old friends who might be able to lend us some money. Meanwhile, my brother would go directly to Szczecin to make contact with smugglers who would guide us across the border. He would remain in Szczecin to wait for us and stay at the home of one of my friends from Schodnica, Shlomo Bleiberg, who lived at 22 Orlęta Street.

The night after my brother left Breslau, I boarded the train for Kraków, arriving there the next morning. I went directly from the station to the well-known textile center, where most of the city's Jewish merchants did their business. There, I had excited reunions with friends who had heard about my imprisonment and welcomed me as one who had returned from the dead. I was immediately taken to an apartment, where one hundred thousand złotys, about five hundred dollars, lay waiting for me on a table. The bills had been stuffed into a money belt of sorts, but when my friends began to arrange the heavy belt around my waist, I began to feel rather uncomfortable. I remembered my unfortunate experience with the fur coat that I had tried to smuggle from the Hyrawka labor camp into the ghetto of Drohobycz back in 1943.[4]

---

3. The Düppel Center was a DP camp in the American-occupied sector of Berlin. It was familiarly known as Schlachtensee because of its proximity to the lake in southwest Berlin of the same name.
4. See part II, chapter 5.

"No," I said to my friends. "This belt is too heavy and too tight. I won't be able to breathe. I can't carry the money on me that way."

In the end, we made the belt less cumbersome by removing from it a number of smaller bills totaling twenty thousand złotys. I did not need one hundred thousand złotys, I said; eighty thousand would be ample, at least for the time being. I thanked my friends, bade them farewell, and went to the station to catch the next train back to Breslau.

# CHAPTER 13

# THE STORY OF
# SIMON BECKER

On my way to the Kraków railroad station, I stopped at the house on 28 Starowiślna Street, where we had lived before our escape to Dresden. My former neighbors seemed glad to see me; they had heard of my arrest and said they were happy I was still alive. I asked them whether anyone had been looking for me or my wife.

"Yes, there was somebody," my next door neighbor replied. "A man named Hirsch. Said he came from Turka on the Stryj, where the Russians are now, and gave me a letter for you."

I looked at the envelope. The letter had been written by Simon Becker, a man some years older than I who had lived in my hometown, Schodnica. *What could Simon Becker, of all people, want from me?* I wondered. But I had no time to open the letter; I had to get back to Breslau as soon as possible.

I did not open the letter until I was settled in the train. "You remember, I suppose," Becker wrote, "that I married a Ukrainian woman, a Gentile.[1] Well, we have eight children. Three of them—two sons and a daughter—are already married and have children of their own. We feel there is no future for us here in Turka, and therefore we want to go to Palestine. This may surprise you, but we want to start a new life there, and we want to live in Palestine as Jews. In my case, that should be no problem.

---

1. Orthodox Jews in particular frown on intermarriage. See part I, chapter 15, note 4.

I never changed my religion. But my wife and children are Christians, of course, so they would have to convert to Judaism. You went to rabbinical school. Maybe you can help us out and get somebody to do whatever is necessary to have my family converted. It shouldn't be too difficult in the case of the children, should it? After all, they do have one Jewish parent." And so Becker continued, for page after page, reiterating his problem and the hope that I would help him.

My first impulse was to tear the letter into little pieces and throw it out of the window of the moving train. The Ukrainians had been Hitler's most enthusiastic collaborators. They had helped kill hundreds of thousands of Jews, and they had done it without many pangs of conscience because Jew-hatred had been a matter of ancient tradition with the Ukrainians, passed from generation to generation like a cherished heritage.

And yet I did not destroy Simon Becker's letter but put it back into my coat pocket. I looked out of the window. The train was rushing through a rapid succession of Silesian villages, formerly German but now occupied by Poland. The Poles had expelled the German population and replaced it with Polish refugees from territories that had been "liberated" by the Soviets. This wanton seizure of territory and the forced exchange of population had apparently been of no great concern to the great powers; they were too busy worrying about the "Palestine problem," about those Jew-ish troublemakers who kept insisting that, since no one else wanted them, they had a right to a home in Palestine. It certainly was a strange world, I thought to myself bitterly. And then, to top it all, I received this letter from a renegade Jew, asking me to help his Ukrainian family change their iden-tity and move to Palestine! I took out Simon Becker's letter again. It was written in Yiddish. He'd been living with the Ukrainians for a quarter of a century, but he had not forgotten his Yiddish.

I remembered the consternation Simon Becker had caused in our hometown back in 1918 when he left his family and married the Gentile woman. He had been drafted into the Austrian army at the age of only seventeen—it was the final year of the war and Austria's manpower reserve had been all but drained—and had come back only a few months later, badly wounded.[2] His right cheek had been torn by shrapnel. The wound had been clumsily sutured by a medic, and Becker had been left with an ugly scar. At an age when other young men went about town and flirted with girls, he sat at home, afraid to show his disfigured face in public. Sometimes he helped his father, who was a tinsmith, but he did it more to pass time than to learn a serious trade.

One of the Beckers' neighbors was a Jewish family named Gertner, who had a Ukrainian maidservant. This Gentile girl was intrigued by this odd, bashful, and lonely young Jew, and before Simon even realized what was happening, he was head over heels in love with the girl and began to follow her about, first secretly, but eventually openly so that everyone noticed and spread the word around town. His parents were mortified and ashamed to hold up their heads in the Jewish community. They begged Simon to have pity on them and stop seeing the girl. His mother took to her bed. At first, the family thought it was nothing more than emotional upset at her son's behavior, but the poor woman was seriously ill; in fact, she was dying. When she realized that she was close to death, she called her son to her. She told him that she would not be able to die in peace unless she was sure that he would not marry the girl after she was gone. The family called in the local rabbi—his name was Eichenstein[3]—and with two respected members of the community present as witnesses, Simon Becker shook the rabbi's hand, promising that he would terminate his relationship with the Gentile girl and marry a Jewish girl instead. A few days later, Simon's mother died.

Simon scrupulously observed the traditional week of mourning and went to the synagogue each day to recite the mourner's kaddish.[4] It seemed that he was going to keep the promise he had made at his mother's deathbed. But a few weeks later, rumors began that Simon was seeing the

2. Until the end of World War I, Galicia was still a province in the Austro-Hungarian Empire.
3. Moshe Eichenstein was the rabbi in Schodnica until 1939. He died in the Holocaust.
4. *Shiva* ("seven" in Hebrew) is the formal period of mourning, which lasts a week.

Ukrainian maidservant again. He was seen walking with her at night on the outskirts of town. His family and friends pleaded with him to stop the affair and settle down with a nice Jewish girl. Simon realized his conduct had become the talk of the town. One day, he suddenly disappeared from view and so did the girl. Almost a quarter of a century was to pass before I saw him again.

When Simon and I met again, it was not in Schodnica but in the Sambor ghetto, where the Nazis had gathered all the Jews of the neighboring towns and villages, the better to finish them off en masse. I remember that it was a Friday, and it was raining in torrents. My father and I had just arrived in the ghetto, and we were watching—our feelings numbed—as other Jews, their clothing drenched, were herded into the barracks that had been prepared for them. Most of them came on foot, but some of them arrived in style, crammed into Polish-style horse-drawn wagons.

Suddenly, one of the people from our hometown shouted, "Look! Just look who's coming there on that wagon! It's Becker! Simon Becker!"

Sure enough, it was Simon Becker, whom no one in Schodnica had seen in more than twenty years. Apparently, he heard the man shout his name, for he suddenly turned his head in our direction as if he had been pricked with a needle. But then we lost sight of him, for he was taken away and we could not see where.

The ghetto barracks were surrounded by armed Ukrainian militia who were under orders to shoot any Jew who dared leave the barracks. Nevertheless, one night, my father and I had managed to steal out of our barracks to find Simon Becker and bring him back to our quarters without being seen by the Ukrainians or their German taskmasters. We made him take off his wet rags and put on some of our own dry clothes. Then we asked him where he had been all these years and what had become of his Ukrainian sweetheart. Yes, Becker said, he had married her, and they had children. But having a Gentile wife had not helped him now; his wife and children had been permitted to stay at their home near Sambor, but he had been carted off to the ghetto along with all the other Jews.

"Tell me one thing, Simon," my father asked him. "How could you, a Jewish boy from a religious home, simply disappear among the Ukrainians? Did you never feel that you missed your family? Didn't you ever long to be back among Jews or the life in which you were brought up?"

"Well, it wasn't exactly easy," Simon confessed. "But after a while, I got used to it." One time in 1938, he said, he had felt an odd yearning to visit a synagogue. He had taken a trip to Sambor and seen all the Jews dressed in their holiday best, going to the synagogue. To his shame and consternation, he had not known it was a Jewish holiday. Finally, he stopped one of the Jews and asked him what holiday it was. He had been unable to recognize his own voice. He had not uttered a Yiddish word for twenty years, but now he had asked a stranger a question in Yiddish as if he spoke it all the time.

"Why, it's Passover, of course," the man answered, amazed that any Jew should ask such a question.

"Tell me," Simon persisted, "on what date does Yom Kippur come this year?"

But the Jew shrugged his shoulders in annoyance. "What do you want to know that for?" he demanded. "What kind of a Jew are you, anyway, if you don't even know that it's Passover now?" With that, the man turned and left Simon standing in the street. Simon went to the synagogue, repeated his question to the sexton and got the answer according to the Gentile calendar.

Simon had hardly been able to wait for Yom Kippur that year. Every couple of weeks, he had taken out the scrap of paper on which he had written the date of Yom Kippur. It was his only link to the Judaism he had abandoned so many years before.

"Well, finally the eve of Yom Kippur arrived," Simon told us. "That day, I left for Sambor, which was, of course, the largest Jewish community even then, before they put up the ghetto. I told my wife where I was going and why. She understood because she was still working for Orthodox Jews and knew what Yom Kippur was all about. So I went to Sambor, to the same synagogue where I had gone six months before to ask the date

of Yom Kippur. The sexton gave me a tallit and a holiday prayer book and
showed me to a seat. I stayed in the synagogue all night long and all the
following day until dark. Everybody else was going home; they were all
hungry after the long fast. But I wasn't hungry or even tired. Those twenty-
four hours at the synagogue gave me something—a sense of strength and
purpose I had all but forgotten. I was the last to leave the synagogue that
night. I didn't even feel like returning to the Gentile world into which I
had moved. I would have been happy if Yom Kippur had lasted one more
day—just so I could have stayed in that synagogue."

Simon had hoped to go back to Sambor on Yom Kippur the next
year; by that time, however, the war had broken out and Sambor was occupied by Russian troops. Then the Nazis had taken Sambor, and Simon had
been dragged from his home in a nearby village into the ghetto. The next
day, as we were marching through the ghetto street to our work assignment, Simon Becker saw his wife and eight children again. But he could
not go to them because they were standing on a pavement beyond the
barbed-wire fence that separated the ghetto from the rest of the city.
The children kept saying, "Daddy, Daddy," over and over again, but Simon
was afraid to stop and talk to them. His wife sat down on the pavement,
covered her face with her kerchief, and cried bitterly. At the sight of his
wife's despair, Simon stepped out of line, walked toward his family and
whispered a few words to them.

The next day, a wagon piled with hay stopped near the barracks where
Simon was quartered. We saw Simon climb into the wagon and disap-
pear beneath the hay. That was the last my father and I had seen of Simon
Becker.

Now four years later, I was holding Simon's letter in my hands. He had
been smuggled out of the Sambor ghetto in that hay wagon. The whole
plan had been cleverly engineered by his Ukrainian wife and children, who
had loved him and had wanted him back even though he was a Jew. So
Simon's wife was probably not a bad woman, but what kind of a Jew would
she make, with all the centuries of Jew-hatred in her blood? And what
about the children? Would having a Jewish father be enough to remake

them in an image resembling nothing they could ever have known? Regardless, I was in no position to act on Simon's request, even if I had been sure I wanted to help him. Here I was, with a wife and baby, a refugee seeking a way of fleeing to the West.

In the end, I decided that, once I arrived in Breslau, I should forward Simon's letter to my friend David Guzik, director of the American Jewish Joint Distribution Committee, which was then still active in Warsaw.[5] I figured that with all the rabbis returning to Poland from the Russian prison camps of Siberia, Guzik would find at least one who would investigate the merits of Simon Becker's case and determine whether anything could, or should, be done for him and his family.

I never heard from Guzik or Simon Becker again. Wherever Simon Becker is now, I wish him well.

---

5. David Guzik (1890–1946) had worked in Warsaw since 1918 for the American Joint Distribution Committee (the JDC or "Joint"), a New York–based Jewish aid organization. After surviving the war in hiding on the Aryan side, he continued his work for the JDC but died in a plane crash in Prague in 1946.

# CHAPTER 14

---

# A REUNION
# ABOARD A TRAIN

On the day I returned to Breslau, my wife and I had unexpected visitors—a delegation from the Breslau Jewish community council, led by two representatives of the "religious committee," Epstein and Asch. They had come to me with a request. Since the upheavals that followed the war, a whole string of Jewish communities had grown up in Silesia—enough, in fact, to require a chief rabbi. What was needed, Epstein and Asch told me, was an individual who not only would serve as a spiritual leader but also knew Polish well and would be able to deal effectively with the Polish authorities. Since they felt that I had all the necessary qualifications, they asked me to remain in Breslau and become chief rabbi of Silesia.

The offer came as such a surprise that I could scarcely catch my breath. My wife had tears in her eyes. Here were people who regarded us not as refugees but as full-fledged, respectable human beings. Here was a chance for us to resume a full and active life, to work for the welfare of the Jewish community.

But of course, I was in no position to accept the offer, because I was a persona non grata with the Polish authorities. I told my visitors about the tragic incident at Rzeszów and my run-in with the Communist-dominated Central Jewish Committee in Kraków. Apparently, they had not known of these events or they had not associated my name with them. They were disappointed but did not try to make me change my mind. Quiet and subdued, they left my room.

The next day, my wife, my baby, and I went to the station, where our friend Lena Gartenberg put us aboard the next train for Szczecin. We left Breslau with a light heart, confident that my brother had completed the arrangements to see us safely through to Berlin and freedom.

Since trains in Poland were slow and far between, we knew that the trip from Breslau to Szczecin would take at least a day and a night, so we provided ourselves with plenty of food to last through the journey. Unlike the coaches of most European trains, the coach in which we traveled had no compartments, and we could see who our fellow passengers were. Among them were a number of obviously Jewish men and women and a group of about twenty Jewish boys and girls who were going to Szczecin, escorted by two young men from Breslau.

These children were all war orphans. Their parents had been killed in the ghettos or concentration camps. The children had survived the war in hiding, either with Christian families or in convents. After the war, they left their hiding places, and some had found their way into orphanages established by the reorganized Jewish communities. Their two escorts were Bricha workers who were taking them to East Germany, from where they hoped to go on to West Germany and Palestine.

I was sitting at the other end of the coach with some Polish Jews who had just returned from Russia after five long years of "exile." Early in the war, they had fled from the German-occupied sector of Poland into the Russian zone and had eventually ended up in Siberia. Although they were spared the fate of those who had endured the Nazi ghettos and concentration camps, they had had their share of trouble. They had toiled from dawn to sunset in the dense northern forests, cutting down thick trees in subzero weather without any compensation except a primitive shelter and one meager meal each day. My wife and I listened quietly as they told us their stories.

Suddenly, we heard screams from the opposite end of the coach, where the Bricha children were sitting. One of the women had seized a little girl in her arms. The child was desperately trying to free herself from the woman's embrace. Some of the other women nearby were screaming;

others were sobbing quietly. We were witnessing the reunion of a mother and her child—that is, the woman seemed sure beyond a doubt that this little girl was her daughter—although the girl showed no sign that she recognized the woman. Later on, we heard the story of this mother and child, who had been separated for six years.

Before the war, the mother, her husband, and their little daughter had lived in Kraków. When the Germans invaded Poland in 1939, the little girl was only three years old. The family fled east to Lwów, in the Russian-occupied zone, where they found shelter with some other Jewish refugees. One night, early in 1940, they awoke to the sight of Russian police trucks pulling up at the front door of their hideout. Realizing that they would be taken to Siberia if the Russians caught them, the husband and wife tried to escape by jumping out a rear window into the backyard. They decided to leave the little girl inside since she was sound asleep on her cot. They were sure that the Russians would not take away a child without her parents; besides, if they woke her, she would only have cried and given them all away.

But when the parents landed in the backyard, they found policemen waiting there for them. The entire house had been surrounded by Russians, and all the refugees were taken to police headquarters. The young couple thought that they would be released at once if they told the police that they had left a child of three at home. But they were mistaken. The officer merely said that if indeed they still had a child at home, they could return the next morning under police escort to take the child with them.

But when the parents returned to their hideout the next morning, the little girl was gone. None of the neighbors seemed to know what had become of her. The distraught parents cried that they would not leave the house without their daughter, but their police escorts dragged them out of the house and back to police headquarters. A few hours later, they and the other Jewish refugees were herded into cattle cars bound for Siberia.

Incredibly, the journey took four months. When they were finally settled at a work camp in Siberia, the parents began to bombard their friends, the

police, and the local authorities in Lwów with letters and telegrams but to
no avail. No one was able to supply any information about their little girl.

Then in June 1941, war broke out between Russia and Germany, and
from that time on, the young couple was completely cut off from the rest
of the world. The husband was put to work in the forests, sawing trees for
lumber. One night, as the woman sat by the window of their cabin waiting
for her husband to come home, she saw a group of men carrying a lifeless
form on their shoulders by the light of the moon. It was her husband; he
had been crushed by a falling tree. He lived only a few days after that. His
wife was twenty-five years old at the time.

When the war ended, the young widow went back to Lwów, only to
find that none of her friends there had survived and that no one knew
anything about her daughter. After several weeks, she resigned herself to
the probability that her little girl had died and that she was now all alone
in the world. She did not want to remain in Lwów, which had become
part of the Soviet Union, and so she went west, back to the "liberated"
sector of Poland. At that time, the Polish authorities resettled all Jewish
returnees in Silesia, from which they had expelled the prewar German
population. Their plan was to firmly integrate Silesia into the new Poland
by populating it with Polish citizens, regardless of their religion.

The young widow remained in Silesia for some time, traveling from city
to city, hoping to find some relative or friend who had survived the war.
When she was finally able to accept the fact that her search was in vain, she
decided to leave Poland and cross into Germany by way of Szczecin. That
was how she had come to be on our train, the same train on which "her"
little girl was traveling to Germany on her way to Palestine.

It was clear to all of us that the little girl had to be her daughter, as
there was a striking resemblance between the woman and the child. Probably the only one who did not believe this and was not eager to believe it
was the terror-stricken little girl, who fought to extricate herself from the
hysterical woman's grasp.

We and the other Jewish passengers attempted to calm the mother, who
refused to let go of the child and tried to pull her away from the other

children in the Bricha transport. We explained to the woman that she would not help matters by trying to force herself on the child on the train. The Bricha escorts would certainly not permit the child to leave the transport because in Szczecin they would have to account for every child they had taken aboard the train. Once we arrived in Szczecin, we told her, she could go to the Bricha center and explain the situation. We were sure that the Bricha people would not attempt to keep the child from her because everyone could see that she was telling the truth—the family resemblance was unmistakable. Meanwhile, we assured her, she had no cause for alarm; the child was in good Jewish hands.

We gently asked the little girl whether she remembered anything of her early childhood, but she would not even look at us. To elude the woman's grasp, she had crept into a corner of the coach and hidden behind some of the other children in her group. The Bricha escorts only knew that the child spoke no Polish, just Russian.

Quite some time passed before the little girl was willing to talk to us. She said that she had come from Russia, in the Ural mountain region, where she had been living in a children's shelter. A few months before, she and a group of other children had been taken from the shelter to Przemyśl and from there to Łódź. She told us that she could not remember having lived anywhere but at the children's shelter.

At that point, her mother interrupted. She said that now, at last, she understood what had probably happened to her daughter. Sometime before she and her husband had returned from the police station in Lwów to fetch the child, other policemen had likely searched the house, found the little girl sleeping there alone, and taken her to a children's shelter, where she had been kept throughout the war.

Now as we sat in the coach, it became dark outside. The conductors lit the gas lamps in our car. The other passengers had gradually calmed down, returned to their seats, and dropped off to sleep. In the end, the only ones who remained wide awake were the two young Bricha men, who walked up and down the aisle to see to their little charges, and the mother, who never once took her eyes from her little girl.

When morning came, the little girl opened her eyes, looked around and, without saying a word, crept over to her mother's seat. She sat beside her mother and, still without a word, took the woman's hand. At first, her mother did not move, as if she were afraid that some hasty gesture might destroy her new great happiness. But after a while, she put her arms around her child, and tears began to flow down her cheeks. When we departed the train in Szczecin, we saw the mother and her child, hand in hand, follow the Bricha group through the station and out into the clear, bright winter morning.

—∕

# CHAPTER 15

# A NARROW ESCAPE

Szczecin's railway station looked just as it had before the war, down to the horse-drawn droshkies waiting for passengers in front of the building. I followed my wife and baby into a droshky and gave the driver the address of our friend Shlomo Bleiberg on Orlęta Street, where we expected to find my brother. We were eager to learn what arrangements David had been able to make to cross into Germany.

Fifteen minutes later, our droshky drew up to a tall building. The driver told us that this was 22 Orlęta Street, the address we wanted. I paid the driver, and we got off, entered the house, and climbed the steps to Bleiberg's apartment. It was very early, and Bleiberg and my brother were probably still asleep, but we did not want to wait outside with our baby. We knocked on the door, and moments later, the door opened. But the young man who received us was not Bleiberg.

"Doesn't Bleiberg live here?" I asked the young man.

"Yes, Bleiberg lives here," he replied, seeming still half asleep. "But he isn't here right now. He is away on a business trip."

"Where's my brother? Hasn't he been in this house?"

"Oh, so you're Dovke Thorne's brother!" the young man exclaimed. "Please come in."

He opened the door a little wider and, without another word, led us into the apartment, never even turning to see if we were following him. We trailed him down a long corridor and into a spacious, bright living room. Only then did the young man turn around to face us. He suddenly appeared uncomfortable and eager to have us leave.

"Your brother was arrested by the Russians yesterday morning," he said. "He's in jail."

I looked at the young man as if he had taken leave of his senses.

"My brother in jail? I don't understand."

"He and some other Jews tried to cross into Berlin last night," he said. "But the border police caught them and put them all into jail."

My legs could no longer hold me up, and I collapsed onto a sofa. I felt dizzy, and my head began to throb.

"But where?" I managed to stammer. "What jail are they in now?"

"Nobody knows," the young man replied. "You can never tell with the Russians. But when your brother left the house, he gave me a letter for you." He went to the desk, opened a drawer, and took out an envelope, which he handed to me.

I tore open the envelope and read my brother's letter. He told me that in order not to lose any time, he had decided to go straight to West Berlin to get things ready for us there. A few months before, he explained, it had been relatively easy to cross the border illegally, but of late, it had become much more difficult. There were a few Jews in Szczecin who were active in these "operations." He gave me the address of one of these individuals, who he said would guide us across the border and who was the most reliable man in this "business." He advised me to get in touch with this man as soon as I arrived in Szczecin. He ended his letter with the hope that we would soon meet in Berlin, where the road to freedom would lie before us.

By the time I finished reading my brother's letter, tears were streaming from my eyes. What was I to do now? To whom was I to turn? How would I get my brother out of the Russian prison? It seemed to me that fate had taken a perverse pleasure in singling us out for trouble. I already saw my brother and the others in his group shipped off to Siberia. Oh, I had prepared myself for the eventuality that things would not go smoothly, that my brother might greet me with the news that he had been unable to make the proper contacts, and that we might have to stay in Szczecin indefinitely.

But not an angel in heaven could have made me believe that he would be back in a Russian prison less than two weeks after he had been released from a Russian jail in Dresden. It was all too much to absorb at one time.

Suddenly I heard heavy, quick steps on the stairs outside. Someone was on the way to Bleiberg's apartment. The Russian police, I thought. When my brother had been arrested and interrogated, he had probably been forced to give the address where he had been staying, and now the police were coming to search Bleiberg's place. What if they searched me and found the eighty thousand złotys I had borrowed from my friends in Kraków in my belt? In addition to our other troubles, my wife and I would then be stranded in a strange city with a small boy and without a penny to our names.

There was a knock on the door of the apartment. The young man who had let us in motioned to me to open the door while he withdrew into another room. I got up from the sofa, and without even asking who was there, I opened the door. I blinked in utter disbelief. It was my brother.

"So you—you escaped from jail?" I stammered inanely.

"No," my brother said quietly. "We were released." He spoke in a low voice, afraid that others in the hallway might hear him.

My brother and the others who had attempted the border crossing with him had been under arrest for only thirty hours, but during that time, they had been in three different prisons. In the end, they had been released with the warning that if any of them were caught attempting to cross the border again, they would be sent to Siberia immediately. Everyone in the group had been photographed and fingerprinted.

My brother told me all this in the dim hallway. Then my wife, with the baby in her arms, came running out and led him into the living room. There, in the bright daylight, we saw what thirty hours in a Soviet jail could do to a man. David looked as if he had been in jail not thirty hours but thirty weeks. He was filthy, his hair was matted, the cuffs had been cut from his pants, and he had neither necktie nor shoelaces. It is customary for prisoners to be divested of ties, belts, and shoelaces at the time of their arrest to prevent them from attempting to hang themselves; however, it is also customary for them to get these articles back when they are released. But it never even occurs to inmates of a Soviet prison to ask for the return of their property; they are only too glad to escape with their lives.

We spent the rest of the day at Bleiberg's apartment recuperating—my wife and I from our long train trip and my brother from his harrowing thirty hours at the mercy of Stalin's police. The next day, we sought out an underground organization that smuggled Jewish refugees out of Poland, into occupied Germany, and from there to the free West. We could have made our arrangements with Bricha, which was active in Szczecin; unlike the smugglers with whom we negotiated, Bricha never took money from its refugees, for its mission objective was an idealistic one—not merely to smuggle refugees into the West but to bring them to Palestine. However, Bricha would have made us wait several weeks because, eager to reduce risks to a minimum, it was very circumspect in its operations. Our aim was to leave Poland as soon as possible. Accordingly, we had no alternative but to accept the terms of the smugglers, who charged exorbitant fees but promised fast action.

# CHAPTER 16

‿

# OUR SECOND EXODUS
# FROM POLAND

Eight days after our arrival in Szczecin, my wife, my brother, and I were sitting in the living room of Bleiberg's apartment waiting for nightfall. That night, under cover of darkness, we were to start out on our second exodus from Poland. Our destination was the Schlachtensee Displaced Persons (DP) Camp in the American zone of West Berlin. It was not going to be an easy journey. Berlin was a four-power enclave, totally surrounded by Russian-occupied territory. To get to West Berlin, we had to make two illegal border crossings—the first from Szczecin into the Russian zone of Germany and then from Russian East Berlin into the city's American zone. Both frontiers were heavily ringed by Soviet border patrols.

We packed two little suitcases and bundled our infant son in warm wraps for the journey through the night. We decided that my brother would not go with us this time but would wait in Szczecin for several weeks before attempting to cross the border again. His arrest was too recent, and the police were still likely to be looking for him. But we hoped that in a few weeks' time, the incident would be forgotten, my brother's photographs and fingerprints would be buried in some obscure police file, and it would be safe for David to follow us.

There was another consideration that made it seem wise for David to remain behind, at least until my wife, the baby, and I reached the West. If we were caught again and brought back to Szczecin, David would be there to receive us. We would leave part of our money with him so that we would not lose it all if we were stripped of our cash by the border police.

When it was totally dark, we quietly left Bleiberg's apartment on foot and went to the place where we were to meet our guides and the others who would make the crossing that night. My wife was carrying the baby while I carried one of our two suitcases and David, who was seeing us off, the other. David was naturally concerned for us, but he was acutely frustrated because, instead of leaving first, as he had planned, and making all the arrangements for our arrival in West Berlin, he would now be following us. My wife and I consoled him as best we could. In two or three weeks, we told him, we would all be together in the American zone, and from there, it would be an easy thing—or so we thought—to go either to Palestine or to the United States.

We did not want to think of the possibility that we might be caught, arrested, and put into prison. However, we were aware that it was much more difficult to cross borders now than it had been only a few months before. When we had made our first attempt from Silesia, shortly after the end of the war, international borders had not yet been firmly fixed and were therefore not too closely guarded. In those days, it had been possible to travel at night, by car or truck, to the river Neisse, a natural border between Poland and Germany's Russian zone, and it had been relatively simple to make the crossing from there. For only a few German marks, boatmen had been willing to ferry refugees across the river under cover of darkness. Sometimes, with luck, the refugees found the bridge across the river entirely unguarded and were able to make the crossing in comfort on foot. And even when Russian guards had been on hand, a small bribe had often done wonders. Once the refugees had passed into the Russian zone of Germany, they simply walked to the nearest railroad station and took the next train inland without ever being stopped for questioning.

But now, barely six months later, things had changed completely. The Neisse area was heavily guarded by Russian police day and night, and anyone caught near the border without legitimate papers was summarily arrested.

The Szczecin-Berlin route too was no longer as "easy" as it had been only a few weeks before. Since there were no railroad lines on the German side of that crossing point and Berlin was about one hundred miles to the southwest, the entire trip—from Szczecin, across the border, and then to Berlin—had to be made by truck. During the period immediately following V-E Day,[1] it had been easy for the drivers to find side roads where no border patrols ever passed. But now this sector too had come alive with Soviet border guards who stopped every passing car or truck and demanded to see the papers of all the passengers. No matter what out-of-the way-route he chose, no driver could be sure that trouble would not be waiting for him there.

However, we preferred not to think of these eventualities as we made our way through the dark streets to the gathering point from which we were to set out on our journey. Our meeting place was a large fenced-in vacant lot in front of a block of houses. Well inside the lot was the truck in which we were to travel. Around it stood a quiet, tense little group—our fellow passengers, men and women with all their possessions in knapsacks on their backs. Some were holding small children by the hand or in their arms. We tried to make small talk with them. We recognized some old acquaintances from our earlier crossing, men and women with whom we had been imprisoned in Dresden and who, like ourselves, had been sent back to Poland. They too had refused to give up and were now ready to try again to reach freedom on the other side of the Iron Curtain.

Our driver was walking up and down near his truck, a little apart from us. He was a Russian soldier who wanted to use his truck, which was the property of the Red Army, to make a little money on the side. He had been hired by the young men who had organized our crossing. If all went well, he would have his truck back at the army base by the next morning, and his superiors would never know about his lucrative sideline that enabled him to buy things in Poland—dresses, shoes, underwear, watches, and musical instruments—that were not readily available in Russia. Naturally, it was in the driver's own interest that we should not be caught, for if the Russians

---

1. On V-E Day (Victory in Europe Day, May 8, 1945), Germany surrendered unconditionally to the Allies, ending World War II in Europe.

caught him, he would be dismissed from the army immediately and sent off to Siberia. To be sure, there was an element of risk for him, but the financial rewards made it worthwhile, and it was known that many other Russian army drivers were engaged in the same "extracurricular" activity.

But the ones who made the real money were the smugglers who organized the crossings. They received twenty thousand złotys for each adult refugee and ten thousand złotys for each child. Only infants were entitled to a free ride. The money was required in advance; those who refused to pay at the time of their registration were not accepted. The departure point from which each transport left the city was a closely guarded secret, divulged only at the very last minute to those who had settled their accounts in full.

Before long, the three "directors" of our journey appeared, and by the dim light of a street lamp, they conducted a roll call from their "passenger list." After making sure that everyone on the list was present, they loaded us quickly into the waiting Red Army truck. We were fifty-six passengers, not including the babies and small children who were expected to sit on the grownups' laps. The trouble was that the truck only had seats for thirty persons. But to hire an additional truck would have meant less money for our smuggler friends, so we were shoved in pell-mell along with our baggage, which we had to cram into whatever space there was beneath our legs. Some of the passengers grumbled aloud about the lack of space in the truck, and young mothers wailed that their babies would never survive the journey in such cramped quarters. But the three organizers were not moved by the shouts and wails of their charges. They simply announced that anyone who was not satisfied with the accommodations could always get out and stay behind in Szczecin, though, of course, they could not expect to have their fares refunded. We knew that these hard-bitten characters meant what they said. These were men who had been made tough and ruthless by years in ghettos and concentration camps, where they survived by their shrewdness and tenacity. Such people could not be expected to turn into angels of mercy overnight. Besides, we were afraid that the commotion might draw the attention of the local police and our journey would end before it had begun. So we pleaded with the complainers to keep quiet, though what they said was true; we were pressed together so tightly that we could scarcely breathe, much less move an arm or a leg.

After everyone had come aboard, the three organizers raised the rear panel of the truck and flung a canvas cover over us. The canvas cover was meant to shield us from view, but it also deprived us of all light and air. We heard them order the driver to start the motor. A minute or two later, we were moving.

We settled wherever space permitted. Some had been lucky enough to find a seat. Others sat on the floor of the truck. Gradually, we adjusted to the darkness and the lack of air. Just a few hours, we told ourselves, and then we would be able to walk and breathe in the freedom of West Berlin.

As long as we were still traveling through the city, our progress was slow, but once we left the city behind us, the truck gathered speed. Under normal circumstances, the ride from Szczecin to Berlin should not have taken much more than two hours, but we had to figure at least double that amount of time. We knew that in order to avoid the border patrols, we would eventually have to leave the main highway and travel on side roads at a crawling tempo and with our headlights turned off. We left Szczecin at ten at night; accordingly, we could expect to be in Berlin at about two or three the next morning.

After driving along for some time at a fairly fast clip, the truck slowed down. We could not see outside, but we knew what the change in pace meant: we had turned off the main highway and were approaching the border. There was complete silence in the truck. No one spoke. Some of the cooler-headed passengers had dropped off to sleep. The only sound we could hear was the steady drone of the motor.

About half an hour went by. Suddenly, we heard shouts outside, followed by gunfire. During the first few moments, we were not even sure whose voices these were or in what language they were speaking, but after the second burst of gunfire, we were able to understand them only too well: "*Stoi, stoi! Ili strelyat v opony!*" ("Stop, stop or we'll shoot out your tires!").[2] Our truck shuddered to a stop. What we had tried not to think about had happened, after all. We had been caught by the Russian border police.

The driver got off the truck, and we could hear him and the police shouting at each other. The canvas cover was lifted, and the heads of two men appeared in the opening. A flashlight was turned on and beamed straight into our faces. Two pairs of steely cold eyes surveyed the scene inside the truck.

After what seemed like hours, the canvas cover was dropped, and we were in complete darkness once more. Outside, the policemen, cursing loudly, were ordering our driver to turn back and head for the border patrol station. The driver tried to argue with them. The people inside his truck were innocent human beings, he said, survivors of the Nazi massacre who meant no harm. But our captors remained unmoved. If our driver would not obey their orders at once, they shouted, he would be arrested and imprisoned as a counterrevolutionary. That threat finished our driver. He leapt back into his seat at the steering wheel, turned on the motor, and went into reverse gear.

At that moment, two youths who sat near the rear panel jumped off the truck and ran over to the policemen. They pleaded with the Russians to let us pass; if they would be accommodating, the youngsters said, they would be handsomely rewarded. A third boy jumped off to help the other two negotiate with the Russians. Meanwhile, some other passengers grabbed their wives and children and pulled them off the truck. They wanted to escape and hide in the woods rather than end up in a Soviet prison.

Moments later, one of the youths thrust his head under the canvas. Talking rapidly, scarcely able to catch his breath, he informed us that the Russian police would be willing to let us pass if we could give them twelve thousand złotys and four wristwatches—two for men and two for

2. The border police combine Russian and Polish in this sentence, *opony* being Polish for "tires."

ladies, no less. "We'd better give it to them fast too before they change their minds," he said. "Anybody who has a wristwatch, anyone who has any cash at all, give it to me. We'll settle accounts when we get to Berlin."

The money and watches materialized in no time at all. The young man took them and ran back to the Russians. We waited in the truck, a little more hope in our hearts. Several minutes later, all three youths were back and explained to us, half in Yiddish and half in Russian, what else the police wanted from us in return for our freedom: a promise, "on a Jew's word of honor," never to tell anyone about the incident, especially not if we were to be caught again by some other Russian officers. We were more than happy to promise them anything they wanted.

We knew that we had gotten off relatively cheaply this time. Divided into fifty-some parts, a total payment of twelve thousand złotys was quite inexpensive. Our driver started the motor again, but there was still one problem: we had to find those passengers who had run off into the woods. We could not leave without them. Some of us left the truck and began to shout after them, telling them that we were free and would be allowed to go on. The Russians, who were eager to have us get out of their sight, begged us not to make so much noise because there was another Russian sentry post less than a mile away. But we insisted that we could not leave these people in the woods to fend for themselves. It took us an hour to find them and persuade them to rejoin us, but we did, and at last we were ready to move on.

We resumed our journey along a narrow wooded path. The road was rough; the truck bounced and tilted from side to side. We felt as if we were riding not on a road but through a never-ending series of hurdles—ditches, logs, and rocks. We clutched our children closer in our arms to keep them from falling. We knew that the driver had no other choice, that it was only on paths such as these, unlikely to be used by cars, that we would have a chance to elude Russian border patrols. But before long, some of the passengers became ill and began to vomit. This set off a chain reaction. Within minutes, nearly everyone on the truck was sick. The canvas cover sealed us off from every breath of fresh air, and the stench became unbearable.

There were moments when it seemed to us as if the truck was about to turn over and spill us all onto the rocky road. We felt like so many pebbles, sealed inside a huge bottle that was shaken up and down, back and forth, without cease, by the hands of some unseen demon. Children were thrown from the laps of their mothers, the grown-ups tumbled against each other, hats and eyeglasses fell, and some passengers later said that their dentures had dropped out of their mouths. Not only the children but also the men and women could no longer control themselves and turned the truck into an inferno of screams and curses. We began to knock on the window of the driver's cabin and begged him to stop the truck for at least one minute so that we could restore a semblance of calm, but the truck plunged on through the woods as if driven by Satan himself. Later, we learned the cause of the physical agony we had to endure in that nightmarish ride through the woods. We had driven through a terrain where lumbermen had been at work only hours before; in the pitch darkness, without the benefit of headlights, the driver had not been able to see ahead and the truck had hurtled across fallen tree trunks and newly sawed logs.

Gradually, the road became less rough. Those of us who had managed not to lose our heads pleaded with the others to calm down. We were still in the danger zone, and if we did not maintain absolute quiet, we might be caught again. The very thought of that possibility accomplished miracles; the passengers fell silent. A moment later, the truck came to an abrupt halt. We held our breaths. Again, we heard voices outside but could not tell the language or what was being said. Was this the Russian border police all over again? Were we doomed to repeat the whole humiliating performance of pleading for mercy and offering bribes? We no longer felt strong enough to fight our fate. We were exhausted, physically and mentally. And so we did nothing except sit quietly and wait.

Then the sheet of canvas that had covered us throughout our journey was flung away by unseen hands. Our truck was standing in the center of a wide, brightly lit square surrounded by gray barracks-like buildings. We saw men in khaki uniforms with brass insignia that were unfamiliar to us. The insignia bore the letters "U.S." At first, we could think of nothing but that we had run afoul of a special division of Russian police. We looked at one another, uncertain and confused.

All at once, someone shouted, "They're Americans! Look, Jews—they're Americans! We're in the West! We're free, Jews! Free!"

At that, everyone in the truck burst into tears. One might have expected us to leap from our seats and jump from the truck, but we sat still, unable to move. The sudden shock of freedom had been too great, and we needed time to recover our senses.

⤙

# CHAPTER 17

# WE GO FREE

The Americans told us that we had arrived at our destination—Camp Schlachtensee, on the outskirts of West Berlin. It was three in the morning. Exactly five hours had passed since we had started out from the dark vacant lot in Szczecin. But we felt as if we had been traveling for an eternity. Slowly, we got up, collected our bundles, and climbed down from the truck. The American soldiers led us into a large, brightly lit hall. There we cleaned up a bit and stretched our cramped arms and legs. We were served hot milk and cookies, and the children were given chocolate bars. We could truly feel that we had arrived in a world of plenty. And of freedom.

As our group filed into the hall, I turned around for a moment to get a closer look at the driver who had brought us safely across the border. What kind of man was this who had risked his own life and security to smuggle some fifty people, whom he had never seen before, from captivity into freedom? I saw him standing near our truck, surveying the scene with an air of studied indifference. He looked about twenty or twenty-two. He was of medium height. His face was blank, revealing nothing of the vigor and daring he had shown during our nightmare journey. He was covered from head to toe with some kind of black grease. But his eyes showed the spirit of the man; they were burning like two gleaming coals. I was not the only one interested in our driver. I noticed several others in our group looking at him, and one of the women asked him whether he was single.

Each one of us was assigned a cot with two army blankets. Larger families got a room to themselves, while smaller families and individuals had to share a room with others. We took off our soiled clothes and stretched out on our cots with a warm, comfortable feeling of security. It was a sensation to which we had become unaccustomed—a sense of personal freedom and dignity.

The commotion we caused in the camp awakened dozens of other Jewish refugees who had arrived there before us. They came running, half-dressed, to see whether any of their relatives or friends had arrived in our transport. I saw more than one touching reunion as many of the "old timers" recognized one or the other of our group. We had met them before, either in Poland or in one of the prisons, and we were pleasantly surprised to see that they too had managed to get to Berlin.

One of the men who welcomed us to Schlachtensee was my old friend Yankel Prener.[1] He told us that, for weeks, he had been the first on the scene whenever a new transport of refugees arrived from Poland, no matter what the hour. He had known all along, deep in his heart, that we would be coming someday. Yankel and I had known each other for many years. We had been in the same Zionist group. He had always been a militant Zionist, a true disciple of Vladimir Jabotinsky and his activist Revisionist Party.[2]

Yankel had originally come from Vilna. His family had all been killed in the Vilna ghetto. When he had realized that he was all alone in the world, he'd escaped from the ghetto to the woods, where he'd become a leader of a band of partisans. His name had soon become a byword for fearlessness and valor. Yankel and his partisans had been a real thorn in the side of the Germans. After the liberation, Yankel had helped found Bricha in Poland, and now he had made his way to Berlin on Bricha business. Yankel sat down on my bed, and soon we were so deeply immersed in conversation that we did not even notice that it was already morning.

Three weeks later, my brother too arrived from Szczecin.

1. Yaacov Yankel Prener (1914–1999) was a partisan commander affiliated with the United Partisan Organization, a Jewish resistance group formed in the Vilna ghetto.
2. Vladimir "Ze'ev" Jabotinsky (1880–1940) was the founder of Revisionist Zionism, the right-wing faction of the Zionist movement formed in opposition to the dominant left-wing socialist Labor Zionism.

One of my first visitors at Schlachtensee was an American army chaplain, Rabbi Herbert Friedman,[3] who was stationed in Berlin. He had heard that there had been an ex-Polish army chaplain among the latest arrivals, and he had been eager to meet me. Rabbi Friedman was only in his twenties at the time, but he had an air of maturity about him and had formed his own well-thought-out views on the situation of postwar European Jewry. Our next meeting took place at his office in the city. There, he suggested that I take charge of certain religious and communal activities either at the DP camp or with the Jewish community in Berlin. I told Friedman that I wanted to gain some firsthand knowledge of Jewish life in Berlin before I made any plans for the future.

Several days later, I informed the rabbi of my decision: I felt that rather than stay in the West Berlin enclave, which was surrounded by Russian territory, my family and I would move into West Germany and settle there, at least for the time being. Rabbi Friedman got in touch with another American Jewish chaplain, Rabbi Joseph Miller, who was stationed in Frankfurt am Main, then considered the capital of the American zone. Shortly thereafter, I received an offer to move to Frankfurt and become the spiritual leader of the Jewish community there. I eagerly accepted this offer, for I realized that my position in Frankfurt would afford me both a spiritual challenge and a broad field of activity.

Of the once-great historic Jewish community of Frankfurt, only 1,500 Jews were left. Most of them were not Frankfurters at all but had come from other cities. They had been uprooted from their former homes, had lost their families, and now were faced with the task of starting life anew. They were badly in need of someone who would not only give them religious guidance but also organize them into a close-knit community.

And so in 1946, my wife, my son, and I left Schlachtensee and moved to Frankfurt.

---

3. Herbert A. Friedman (1918–2008) was an American Reform rabbi who played an important role in helping smuggle Jews and weapons from Displaced Persons camps to Palestine. Later in life, he became a prominent Jewish community leader and philanthropist.

# AFTERWORD

אני הגבר שראיתי בעני עמי
וגם זכיתי למדינת ישראל

*I am the man who witnessed the affliction of my people and was also privileged to see the creation of the State of Israel.*

—Epitaph for Leon Thorne

With this epitaph, our mother captured the tragic destruction of our father's entire prewar life and his concerns, struggles, and hopes for the future. In his book, our father records in unflinching terms the collapse of his world. The reader may rightfully wonder what kind of a life he lived afterward: what kind of person he was, what sustained him as he tried to create a "normal" life, what values guided him, and what he hoped to achieve.

Our father emerged from his coffin-like cellar believing that he and his cellar-mates were the last Jews alive. Indeed, his belief that all the other Jews had been slaughtered may explain why he chose to write his book in German, not in Yiddish, his first language and the language of the European Jewish world. After the liberation, survivors had to figure out how to walk again, to get clothes, find food, and put a roof over their heads. And this they did, as our father describes so evocatively in the book.

But what happened then?

Our parents, like the other survivors, were shattered people who now had to make their way in a strange new country—in their case, America—not knowing its language or customs. They had to earn a living and raise children, attend to the mundane demands and distractions of everyday life, all the while keeping their sorrows to themselves because the American public—even American Jews—had little wish to hear about what they had suffered.

Family, children, friends, and community—the scaffolding on which most of our lives are built—clearly helped sustain our father and mother and other survivors. We lived in a community of Orthodox Jews, nearly all of whom were survivors. We spent summers together with others from our small world in a "bungalow colony" in the Catskills where social life was intense and rich. Our father loved this. He was a delightful man who was a marvelous raconteur and master of the telling anecdote and parable. People urged us to record his stories. We wish we had. Our father loved to talk genealogy with friends and family—to know who had married so-and-so and who had given birth—and he remembered everything. We were continually flabbergasted that a man who knew and loved big ideas could be so completely absorbed in matters of family relations for hours at a time. Perhaps it was both the historian in him and the simple, precious joy of life being lived again that underlaid his pleasure in hearing family stories.

Although our father was frustrated by the limited opportunities available to him in a strange country, eventually he found a way to pursue his rabbinic work as a mohel, an occupation that gave him a steady income and was also an avenue for other rabbinic and scholarly activities.

He continued his Jewish scholarship all his life. We remember how he relished the study of Jewish texts, such as the Talmud and Maimonides's *Mishneh Torah*, which he studied weekly with his good friend Rabbi Benjamin Kreitman. At the same time, he read constantly in history and philosophy; one night we happened to observe that his bedside reading included a volume of Plato's dialogues, Montaigne's *Essays*, and a history by Mussolini's son-in-law, Count Ciano. Our father was a complicated man. We say this not with critical feelings but with deep appreciation and admiration. His religious friends saw him, a person bridging the religious and modern secular worlds, as a man full of strange contradictions. He defied their categories and would not be pigeonholed.

Here is a story recalled by Emanuel: "When I was in college, I was assigned to write a paper contrasting the depictions of Mars and Venus by several Renaissance painters. My father joined me at the Metropolitan Museum of Art in Manhattan. He checked his hat and coat but kept his large yarmulke, which he always wore. I remember that, when we entered the Renaissance room, I found myself baffled by all the painted scenes from the Christian Bible. I had never read this text and so did not know the stories. But my father, the rabbi, born a Hasid, had studied the Christian Bible and began explaining to me what was going on in the paintings. Soon a crowd gathered around us to listen to my father in his yarmulke—erudite, patient—illuminating the Christian stories portrayed in masterworks on the wall."

At Emanuel's bar mitzvah in 1959, our father addressed an audience of family and friends composed largely of survivors. To this crowd struggling with measureless loss, he chose to offer comfort and a hopeful vision of the future. After the destruction of the Second Temple, he told them, Rome broadcast its great victory over the Jews by minting new coins with the imprint *Judea Capta, Judea devicta*—Judea is defeated, Judea is conquered. Citing the ancient rabbis, he continued, we too have a coin, that of our Father Abraham. On one side is an old couple, and on the other side are a young boy and girl. To the gathered guests, he interpreted the coin: Yes, we are old and weak and broken, and it looks as though we are going entirely under. But we can become young again; we can regenerate and arise to a new life.

He closed his talk with a charge to the bar mitzvah boy and to everyone else there, including himself: "We who have witnessed the merciless murder of our people must ask of our children and of ourselves that we be builders of a Jewish future and a Jewish continuity."

Our father carried in his wallet an ethical will that had been composed by his grandfather's grandfather, Meilich Backenroth, who in the mid-1800s was one of the discoverers of oil in Austria-Hungary:

My precious children, grandchildren, and all the offspring who come from their loins. Hold dear our luminous treasure, our sacred Torah; always love your Jewish people and what the Jewish people represent; never be over-proud and arrogant; help the Jewish people with your money; and have the faith of the righteous.

We believe that what enabled our father to carry on was his family and the charge he inherited, his many friends, and his beloved Jewish community. He found meaning in his Jewish and secular learning, which continued until the end of his time. It must be remarked too that his rabbinic work of circumcising baby boys was, literally, the act of making new Jews, fostering the continuity of his people.

And finally, our father was sustained by the imperative to tell his story in this book.

May his name be remembered for a blessing.

Emanuel, Irving, Risa, and Ziva Thorne
Children of Leon Thorne

# ACKNOWLEDGMENTS

Seventy-three years ago, my father left his cellar in Galicia, Poland, with a tattered manuscript written during the fifty-three weeks he spent in hiding there. The manuscript, written in German, has since been translated into English and Yiddish.

Part I of the book, which was published in 1961, was edited by renowned author Harold Ribalow, of the famed Ribalow prize for fiction. A number of years later, my father overhauled the manuscript in consultation with novelist Louis Falstein, author of several books on Jewish life in World War II. I am grateful for the contributions these two writers have made to the book.

I would like to thank Professor Dan Magilow of the University of Tennessee for providing a scholarly foreword to the book and enriching it with footnotes that familiarize the reader with historical places, events, and personalities mentioned in the book but not widely known to all, deepening the reading experience. I am deeply grateful to Professor Magilow for these enormous contributions.

I would also like to thank Steve Feldman of the U.S. Holocaust Museum, who believed in the book and persevered to make the history it describes available to a wider audience. Steve was the matchmaker who introduced the manuscript to Elisabeth Maselli of Rutgers University Press. I am grateful to Elisabeth for appreciating the importance of my father's account, for her expansive vision of the book, and for shepherding the project to completion.

Finally, I would like to thank my wife, Julia Paradise, whose loving interest in my father's manuscript and profound devotion to this project never wavered. Her years-long conversation with me about the book, her insightful questions and observations, and her wise guidance contributed beyond measure to the realization of this published volume.

Emanuel David Thorne, PhD
Brooklyn College of the City University of New York
March 2018

# NOTES ON
# CONTRIBUTORS

RABBI LEON THORNE was born in Schodnica near Drohobycz, the area of Eastern Galicia he describes vividly in *It Will Yet Be Heard*. He was ordained a rabbi at the age of nineteen, continued his religious studies at the Jewish Theological Seminary of Breslau, and earned a PhD at Würzburg in philosophy and history. He survived the Holocaust and became a chaplain in the Polish Army upon liberation in 1944. Rabbi Thorne immigrated to the United States in 1948, and in 1961, he published the first part of his memoir as *Out of the Ashes*. Now newly introduced, expanded, and with a previously unpublished second half, *It Will Yet Be Heard* offers rare insight into the Holocaust and its aftermath in Poland.

DANIEL H. MAGILOW is an associate professor of German at the University of Tennessee, Knoxville. He has published four books, including *In Her Father's Eyes: A Childhood Extinguished by the Holocaust*, also published by Rutgers. In 2005–2006, he was the Pearl Resnick Postdoctoral Fellow at the U.S. Holocaust Memorial Museum.

ISAAC BASHEVIS SINGER was a Polish-born Jewish writer who was awarded the Nobel Prize in Literature in 1978. His review of *Out of the Ashes* appeared in 1961 and appears here in English for the first time.

MARC CAPLAN is a scholar of Yiddish literature and the author of *How Strange the Change: Language, Temporality, and Narrative Form in*

*Peripheral Modernisms,* a comparison of Yiddish literature with the African novel in English and French. He has also completed a forthcoming book on Yiddish literature and German-Jewish culture in Weimar-era Berlin.

EMANUEL THORNE, son of the author Leon Thorne, teaches economics at Brooklyn College. He has been a visiting scholar at Georgetown University's Kennedy Institute of Ethics and the Aspen Institute for Humanistic Studies. His articles have appeared in the *Yale Journal on Regulation,* the *Wall Street Journal,* and the *New York Times.*

# INDEX